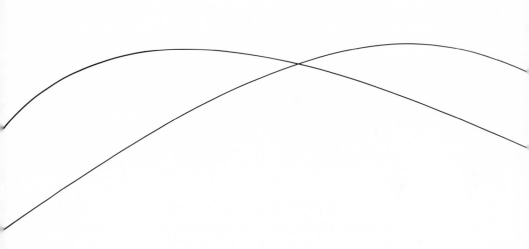

SOUTHERN ILLINOIS UNIVERSITY PRESS
CARBONDALE *and* EDWARDSVILLE
Feffer & Simons, Inc.
London and Amsterdam

Two Roads
to Ignorance

A Quasi Biography

BY ELISEO VIVAS

Copyright © 1979 by Southern Illinois University Press

Printed in the United States of America

Designed by Bob Nance

Library of Congress Cataloging in Publication Data

Vivas, Eliseo.
  Two roads to ignorance.

  Includes index.
  1. Vivas, Eliseo.   2. Philosophers—
United States—Biography.   I. Title
B945.V54A36   191   79-757
ISBN 0-8093-0916-5

To the memory of my parents

Eliseo Vivas Perez
and Maria Salas de Vivas Perez

Contents

Preface   ix

Acknowledgments   xiii

I   The Mixed-up Twenties   3

II   More Confusions   23

III   State at Midland City   41

IV   Teachers and "Teachers"   58

V   Alonzo As "Teacher"   75

VI   Borrowed Thoughts   88

VII   The Red Thirties   105

VIII   Objections to Marx   118

IX   The Blind Spots of Naturalism   132

X   Pragmatism and the Tragic Sense of Life   149

XI   Naturalism's Theory of Value   164

XII   The Question of Origins   180

XIII   From Protohominid to Homo Sapiens   193

XIV   Darwinians on Human Culture   204

XV   On Human Origins: Freud and Others   217

XVI   Alonzo Too Was Guilty   229

XVII   The Moral Life and the Ethical Life   238

XVIII   Politics or Idiocy?   253

XIX   Art and Knowledge   268

XX   Was the Quest a Failure?   290

Index   295

Preface

This book is an intellectual quasi biography of an intimate friend of mine called Alonzo Quijano. We were born in the same town the same year, and we have lived in intimacy all our lives. I know almost as much about him as a man can know about himself, and in some respects even more, since I can see him at times quite objectively. But among the numerous questions that I have never been able to get him to answer satisfactorily is why he spells his name with a *z* instead of an *s*, which is the proper Spanish way of spelling it, and more representative of his personality, since *Alonso* was the name of his spiritual ancestor about whom, under his *nom de guerre*, an immortal biography was written by the most famous writer of the period the Spaniards call the Golden Age.

I must declare before going any farther in this preface that the title of this book is not at all to my liking or to the liking of my best and most perspicuous critic, my wife. Were old-fashioned titles still acceptable I would have entitled the book *Alonzo Quijano's Squatting in Morningside Heights, His Trip to Moscow's City Limits, and His Safe Return Home*. The title I was finally forced to give it by default is, however, adequate, for the book tells the story of a man who started with a great deal of cocksure confidence about his knowledge of the ills of society and of the nature of the universe and ended up by having to recognize that he knew very little besides the fact that he did not know, because genuine knowledge about these matters does not exist.

I think of the book as a quasi biography because it is only concerned with the events of Alonzo's intellectual life. Personal details are included only when I thought them necessary for the reader to grasp the story of a mind's adventures. The events I have recorded are true, but not necessarily accurately presented. Much has been left out that is of a purely personal nature, of the kind that Malraux, in an interview, refused information on because it was, as he put it, *vie priveux*.

The book seemed to me worth writing because looked at as a whole Alonzo's intellectual career has been, until the last few years, representative of Alonzo's and my own generation. Whatever the value of the account, it does not reside in the fact that Alonzo was an original thinker, for he has never claimed or valued originality; he wrote more than once that he would have been worried about the truth of his opinions had anyone shown him that they were original. He once quoted Goldsmith, telling me that he had picked up the quotation at third or fourth hand. In a passage excised from the final version of *The Vicar of Wakefield*, Goldsmith had written that when he was a young man, being anxious to distinguish himself, he was perpetually starting new propositions, but he soon gave over, for he found that generally what was new was false. This does not quite apply to me, said Alonzo, since I have never sought to distinguish myself by starting new propositions. I always knew, somehow, that outside of science, what is new today is generally false—or trashy. If there is no discovery in science it is nothing but cookbook science. In questions of philosophy, however, today, for the men of our world, originality is suspect. There may be freshness in a thinker's thought but if there is, it is a matter of style, and of those idiosyncracies that are part of his temperament.

I agree with Alonzo on this point and warn the reader that if he finds originality in this account it is there by accident. But the reader will find what I think of as Alonzo's factitious little mysteries, that he likes to advance in obvious mock seriousness—a tendency on his part to create puzzles and even obfuscations for the fun of creating them and an obstinate and sometimes irritating refusal to explain them when he is pressed to come clean.

I had long been after Alonzo to write his autobiography but he persistently put me off by quoting Heine who said of Kant that no life history could be written of him, since he had neither life nor history. My reply was obvious. Alonzo might not have had any adventures to match Stanley's finding Livingston; but the development, such as it was, of his philosophical and political ideas, such as they were, from his freshman year up to a few years ago, his cooperation with the Communists during the Spanish civil war, his acceptance until the late thirties of the dominant philosophical orthodoxy, the naturalism that in one form or another thinking people then took and, less aggressively perhaps, still take, to be irrefutable truth, and his painful discovery that, however widely accepted, the varieties of naturalism current in our day contain fundamental errors that cannot be corrected and lacunae that account for naturalism's utterly shrunken picture of human life, and his desperate effort to find substitutes for doctrines that until then he had espoused with passion because he had found them sustaining—these episodes were genuine intellectual adventures and were interesting and even important because they were the beliefs of large numbers of men and women of his generation.

I finally confronted Alonzo with an ultimatum. If he did not write the story of his life, I would. Go ahead, he said, I can't prevent you. But if I do, will you help me? I pleaded. He thought about it for a minute or so and finally said he would if I agreed to three conditions. What were they? One is that you call the book *It All Came to Nothing*. I promised to think about that one. What was the second? You are going to be writing, he said, about a few people who are either locally or nationally well known. In the case of some of them, I want you to use the names I shall supply you with, although the real people will be easily identified by those who have known them. The other, implied in the second, was that he did not want me to aim at consistency. Some of the people will be called by their right names. Moreover, a few I am going to ask you not to give a true portrait of but to blend with their features characteristics of other people we have known. This is most important. The sketches, no doubt, will bear resemblances to the main sitters, but they should not be photographs, but rather caricatures made up with the attitude of a George Gross. Others will be pictures of people I have tried to forget. If you put them in your book by their right names you will be hurting their friends and will be opening unnecessarily old wounds that are best kept from bleeding again. The upshot, I hope, will be that the identifications that no doubt will be attempted by some readers will be false. But that is the way I want it. Just as you can recognize a picture of Karl Popper by the way his large ears are placed at a plane almost perpendicular to the planes of his face, and wrongly assume that a man almost five-five is Karl Popper when he is not. Readers of your book will wrongly assume that a number of people who figure in it are people they know. They will be wrong. And that, I say, is the way I want it.

I thought the condition was nonsensical and arbitrary, but I knew my man, I saw he was in earnest, and knew how obstinate he could be. If I was going to get his help I knew I would have to accept his conditions. The first condition I knew was negotiable. So I promised to follow instructions about the characters in the book. After all, I was not interested in writing a biography but a history of ideas in a biographical frame, a sort of fictionalized intellectual history of a large group of people of which Alonzo in a measure was representative. The fact that they were the ideas of a man that I knew was of little importance. What was important was that they had been espoused by a man who in a way was typical of his generation. So I promised to follow instructions about the characters in the book.

I knew he wanted to entitle the book *It All Came to Nothing* because in the past ten years, more or less, after a lifetime of earnest effort, he had arrived at the conclusion that the questions he had set out to seek answers for when he began thinking could not be answered, although they were, for him, as they must be for anyone seriously interested in philosophical questions, the most important that can be asked. He had set out with the unexamined belief that he could find true answers to first and last questions—to the questions of whence, and where, and why. After a number of false starts he had arrived at what he took to be a true conception of the world borrowed mostly from Dewey. In principle, answers to substantive questions are corrigible, but the chances that the theories he had borrowed were false, he thought, were very small. But he turned out to be wrong and discovered that his views were radically inadmissible. He started anew, and arrived at what he took to be a much better set of theories, although held in contempt by a large number of professional thinkers. But gradually, after thinking more carefully, he was led to see that he did not have the answers to the questions that had started him thinking, and that no one else did. The questions were meaningful, they were overwhelmingly important, on the answers we gave to them depended the true direction of life, they controlled human destiny, but they were unanswerable. The knowledge for which he had never ceased craving was beyond the reach of man—unless one was naïve enough to take *gato por liebre*, cat for hare, as he put it switching to Spanish, to take poetic myth, mere myth, for positive truth.

The reasons for his title were good, but neither his wife nor I cared for it. His wife finally came up with the title this quasi biography bears. His philosophical effort had come at long last to the Socratic answer. He knew that he did not know. As to his political opinions, they had little to do with truth, if we take the term seriously. That goes for all political convictions by whomever held. Political convictions must be relevant to circumstances and interests or they are silly, but circumstances and interests are partial and perpetually in flux. There may be self-evident political truths, but if there are they are the ground on which political programs are founded and never themselves the components of political programs. But fundamentally, his attitude toward political opinions and interests was elicited by their inherent and ineradicable partiality. He had read somewhere that "the history of politics since recorded times is a history of dark evil. *Homo homini lupus* has almost always been the prevailing rule in affairs of state." This is true and makes politics repugnant to him. It puts political opinions and interests at the opposite pole from the truth.

Acknowledgments

I could not name exhaustively the large number of persons who have given me valuable help in the writing of this book, but a few must be named or the lack of gratitude would be inexcusable. John T. McCarty, former assistant to the president of Rockford College, helped financially with the typing of some of the manuscript from a fund he controlled. Henry Regnery not only encouraged me but read the chapters as they were finished and saved me from several blunders. Professor Don Martindale graciously denies he helped, but his advice did. Thanks are also due to John F. Lulves, Jr., publisher, and David S. Collier, editor, of *Modern Age*, for permission to reprint a number of chapters that appeared in it in 1978. I have been fortunate in the number of persons who have been my students and from whom I have learned as much as they have from me. Two of these are today distinguished in their fields, the literary critic Murray Krieger and the philosopher William Earle. How much I owe them and the others I could not say briefly. Nor could I have done much without the help of my wife, Dorothy. It was priceless: Her forebearance of the irregular habits of work, her understanding of my difficulties, her continuous encouragement, and above all her critical acuity, were always generously given. The errors and defects of the book are all mine; whatever qualities it may have, such as they are, are not.

ELISEO VIVAS

August 1978   Wilmette, Illinois

Myself when young did eagerly frequent
Doctor and Saint, and heard great argument
About it and about: but ever more
Came out by the same door wherein I went.
     Edward Fitzgerald, *Rubáiyát of Omar Khayyam*

Que sais-je?

                      Michel de Montaigne

Truth marries no one.

                          Spanish proverb

I

The Mixed-up Twenties

1

ALONZO entered engineering school in the early twenties. His father, escaping from Gomez, the Venezuelan dictator, had moved the family from Willemstad, Curaçao, Dutch Antilles, to New York, in search of a good education for the children. Alonzo spent one year in public school and enrolled in a high school that was to prepare him for an engineering career. At the time he entered engineering school Alonzo was neither a self-conscious intellectual nor a liberal. But thinking about it later he realized that he had been both for a long time, unconsciously. It did not take him long, in his freshman English class, to discover that he had read considerably more than his classmates. He had written some verses in Spanish that fortunately have been lost. He was something of a thinker after the fashion of untrained minds; or, more exactly, he was opinionated, hating Yankee imperialism passionately, although he had not made a study of the problems. He had begun to read *The Nation* before entering engineering school because of the articles it had printed on United States Marines in Santo Domingo— or was it Nicaragua or where?—and he had totally broken with the Roman Catholic church into which he had been baptized. He did not need, therefore, the influence that soon came to be exerted on him by his freshman English teacher, Joseph Wood Krutch, in order to accept eagerly and in its incoherent totality, the liberal credo of the era that now took the place of his old faith. Almost overnight he became aware that he had been all along an intellectual and a liberal, and he took no small pride in the truth of the opinions which he now held. Later he would say, altogether in seriousness, that he had been born at the age of nineteen in Krutch's class. The moment of birth was a thrilling moment, for which he would be grateful the rest of his life.

Remember Plato and imagine what it would be like to live in a dim, dank cave for the first nineteen years of your life, groping in semiconsciousness, as if drugged, experiencing disturbing storms and entertaining inchoate beliefs that could not find clear articulation because they found no echo in others; imagine, further, that after all the gray long years of immurement you are taken out and after a brief period of adjustment you awake suddenly and fully to the crisp freshness of the morning, the coolness, the sparkle of the dew, the color, the dry rush of fresh air: If you have not known this experience you have missed some of the sweetness of living.

Not that Krutch made an effort to "convert" him. Krutch was not that kind of teacher. Witty, intellectual through and through, detached, amused perhaps at the antics and passion of this odd duck among the chickens, Krutch was friendly toward Alonzo, but he demanded neither loyalty nor adherence. Had he demanded it Alonzo would have reacted like a startled cobra, for personal partisanship he was not capable of feeling on demand. Loyalty Krutch could elicit without trying to, because he displayed virtues Alonzo found admirable, but discipleship he could not elicit, since he had no militant body of beliefs that called for acceptance. But loyalty and discipleship Alonzo felt, whether the older man was aware of it or not, in the sense that he recognized in his teacher an admirable person who set the norm for Alonzo.

There was nothing of the evangelist in Krutch. What was happening to Alonzo was that Krutch, discovering in the young man a range of reading and an interest in ideas that most of his other students did not have, invited him occasionally into his office on some excuse or other, but really in order to enter into conversation with him—a conversation in which the older man did most of the talking and the freshman most of the eager listening. As Alonzo got to know Krutch, he came more and more to admire him, admire his intelligence, his knowledge, his wit, his opinions, and the values of which his judgments were the expression. Krutch was a liberal and Alonzo discovered that he himself was, and had been all along, a liberal.

But Krutch was liberal as well as a liberal, and that Alonzo was not. For that reason I do not intend to suggest that Alonzo's incoherences were acquired from Krutch or that Krutch shared them. They were his own. He had been a reflective rebel all his life, as far back as he could remember; he had been a dreamer; an "idealistic," quixotic person, not too securely tied to the world of things and facts. What he was tied to was his passionate convictions. But no one had guided his thinking and it would be years before he would make the conscious effort to respond to the exigencies of intellectual discipline, coherence, and elementary clarity. What was happening to him in Krutch's office and classroom was that Alonzo's rebellion was given concrete and explicit expression for the first time. Krutch seemed to approve, tacitly, Alonzo's holding attitudes and opinions that until then others had disapproved. This was a new and exhilarating experience for Alonzo. Until then he had taken the disapproval of his opinions and attitudes as a more or less clear sign that he was wrong, but he could not repudiate them or eradicate them, as a sign that he was a black sheep, while suspecting that those who disapproved might not be altogether right. Now, for the first time, he came to see quite clearly that those who disapproved were wrong. And he thought he knew why.

2

Liberalism, the liberalism of the early twenties, for the fledglings of the day, was a fabric woven out of a number of attitudes and convictions among which one could not find, had one looked for them, many positive threads. What made all these attitudes and beliefs liberal was, chiefly, their negative character. Liberals were against the world in which they lived because they knew, they were certain they knew, its faults and its horrendous iniquities, and with equal certainty they knew it could be made better. Those who had directed the war that had ended only a couple of years before had been far from the front lines, far from the lice and the mud and the stench; they were totally discredited, whether they called themselves statesmen or generals. Their discredit took root and flourished luxuriantly in soil fertilized by millions of rotting corpses.

Long before Tenente Henry thought in his cadenced language his memorable repugnance of the hollowness of the rhetoric of the war, Alonzo and his young friends had felt, if not expressed as well, that they were "always embarrassed by the words sacred, glorious and sacrifice and the expression in vain . . . ." There were many other words that embarrassed the young liberals of Alonzo's generation. And these words became taboo unless pronounced in audible derision. No man could be a patriot, he could only be a jingoist. There were no statesmen, only politicians, and the word was a dirty word. Generals and admirals were butchers. Policemen were cossacks. The young liberals were against the rulers because they were incompetent and evil. Sellers of arms were merchants of death. Union leaders were heroic men guided by self-sacrificing love for the oppressed workers. Foreign policy was dollar diplomacy. The enemy was there, easily recognized.

All that was official was evil, anything in opposition was *ipso facto* good. The war and the peace that followed had turned Alonzo and his friends against nations, toward internationalism and pacifism. Of course they were against puritanism. They were for socialism in spite of the fact that they "did not believe in politics." They went to Bernard Shaw for their daily spiritual bread and to H. L. Mencken for guidance. That they were mistaken about Mencken, who was no liberal, they never suspected. They heard Scott Nearing in the Rand School every Saturday afternoon, and without a sense of incoherence they read Nietzsche in the subway on the way to and from the Rand School. Did they understand Nietzsche? Of course not. What they found in Nietzsche was for the most part what they wanted to find, and some of it was what they put into him. That Power involved the making of slaves and they were against slavery was no problem, since Power was to be used first against the enemy, and once the enemy was out of the way, against unhappiness and disease and for The Conquest of Nature: Not for the conquest of men, but for their liberation. Nietzsche had no such idea; he was against socialism, against humanitarianism, against the softening of the human type. But they could see no inconsistency in admiring Nietzsche and being socialistic. Since the inconsistency was glaring, why did they not see it?

Because Nietzsche believed in Life, and they also believed in Life. They would have dismissed with scorn anyone who pointed out to them that they reached their conclusion by a faulty syllogism—syllogisms were for professors, and the word *professor* was one of the words Mencken had taught them to consider dirty. What they found in Nietzsche was a general irreverence, an iconoclasm, a thumb-on-nose attitude that they took to sanction their own negativism. Nietzsche's passionate concern for the health of Western civilization they did not understand, since they believed that what was wrong with their world could easily be remedied by making a few political and economic changes, about the precise nature of which they were not clear. The core of the liberal faith of the young man of the early twenties was, in short, the repudiation of almost everything that was, because it was, and a hope in the future because it was not. Nietzsche, too, looked towards the future. So did all decent men, all those who, a few years later, were to be called men of goodwill.

These beliefs, or more precisely, these attitudes, made up the content of the liberal credo or, more precisely, the stance of the liberal young men of the early twenties. It would be preposterous to call these views "a philosophy," since they consisted of a number of attitudes shaped by a climate of opinion, borrowed without examination from here and there. Had Alonzo stopped to examine them he would have found that his opinions quarreled bitterly with one another. But how could he have stopped to examine them critically? His acceptance of them was sustained by faith, clutched to the heart, clutched with a desperation of which he was not aware. How could he and his friends examine their credo? They were young, impulsive, dogmatic, cocksure, egregiously ignorant, untrained, totally undisciplined morally, aesthetically, and intellectually, in desperate need of a faith, and committed to their faith without reservations and doubts. Their goal was the making of a better world, a world fit for human habitation—or so they claimed. But what was wrong with the world as it was now? The question did not deserve an answer. Anyone who asked it was congenitally blind in a moral sense, and an effort to make him see was hopeless. In short they meant well but they were hopelessly irresponsible. Their credo was a cage of fighting big cats. But let the enemy show in the distance and they united instantly against it. And the enemy, who was it? It was made up of anyone who accepted the world as it was.

The radical incongruity of the liberal stance was the contradiction between the claims that Alonzo and his friends made for themselves and reality. They thought of themselves as tolerant but they were intolerant; they thought of themselves as open-minded but their minds were closed; they thought of themselves as generous but they were no more generous than those they despised; they thought of themselves as good people but they were no better than anyone else. They were self-deceived and self-righteous. They thought of themselves as the salt of the earth and the hope of man, and they were ordinary human beings, as sinful and corrupt as men ordinarily are. Used to their corruption and in love with their faults, they had no suspicion of the truth about themselves.

Was there nothing to be said in favor of these young people? This must be said about their beliefs: They fulfilled an important requirement: They made up a convenient faith to live by. It divided the world clearly into two mutually exclusive sides: one good the other evil. It all was either black or white; there was no gray area in between. There are a number of advantages to faiths of this sort, radically Manichaean faiths, and preeminent among these advantages is the fact that they save those who espouse them the trouble of thinking. A liberal of those days knew where to place a person, an event, a plan, an activity, a goal, a social project. Hesitation was thus banished and the conscience and the judging mind worked in harmony, without strain and therefore without anxiety, without the dubieties that must arrest judgment when confronted with the baffling facts of human existence in their treacherously conflicting valances. That such simplifications had little to do with experience was no argument against them for young people insulated by their simplistic faith from reality.

It is hardly necessary to point out that there was nothing unique or original about the substance of the faith of these young people. For all their vaunted independence of mind and supercilious separation of themselves from the mob, they made up a mob of their own, smaller in numbers, more aggressive in temper, but as deeply imbued with its sense of being right as men have ever been. They thought alike, accepting what the manipulators of liberal thought told them to think, going where the bellwethers of the movement led them. A quick survey of *The Nation* or *The New Republic* during the twenties and early thirties will give the reader of today an accurate account of the faith passionately espoused by Alonzo and his friends.

An illustration of this fact was their response to the Sacco-Vanzetti trial. Neither Alonzo nor his friends ever took the trouble, when the trial was in the news, to ask about all the facts in the case, the facts on the other side as well as on theirs. All they knew about it was what was printed in *The Nation* or *The New Republic*. Liberals knew, they knew apodictically, that the two Italians were innocent victims of the system. In point of fact they did not know. And if anyone had tried to tell them that there was another side to the case, they would have turned against the man in hatred and contempt. Their ignorance was amply made up for by their passionate conviction.

What held together these incoherences without exploding? How could intelligent people, even if young, entertain seriously this mess of prejudice and faith and hope and free-floating, irresponsible, abstract goodwill? What informed their credo? As far as it was "in-formed" at all, it was passion that informed it, a passion that grew out of a general dissatisfaction and frustration and which they found expressed in the literature they read, the arts they had commerce with, and the "ideas" they devoured voraciously so long as they were "advanced ideas." Their faith and hope turned towards the world. But the world was clearly the world of the future, not the world in which they lived. The present and the past were things to be destroyed that the fair building of the future might be reared in their place. The present was not altogether evil. There were capitalists, industrialists, bankers, exploiters, imperialists, and their willing servants. These made up the cancerous tissue of the present. But there were also workers, the victims of exploitation, the victims of imperialism, and of course, Alonzo and his friends and their elders—liberals, the salt of the earth.

What in fact prevented them from noticing their incoherences? A strong drive to see the world not as it really was and is, not as what we can objectively find it to be, if we read history honestly and look around us, but as they chose to believe it was. But what did they take it to be? This is where their lack of knowledge, their need for a sustaining faith, and their lack of realism misled them. They knew the world to be evil. And in this they were not altogether wrong. But they were convinced that it could be remade, and remade in a short time, and remade according to their own blueprints of perfection. In short these young people were utopians, secular chiliasts, millenarians in reverse, for theirs was not a vision of The Kingdom of Heaven but The Kingdom of Here and As Soon As Possible. When they turned to the future, automatically and without their sensing it, built-in, rose-colored lenses fell before their eyes. When they turned to the past and present, black lenses took the place of the rose-colored ones. Hence the undesirability of the present, the horror of the past, and the promise of the future. History —and Alonzo had read a great deal of history before he entered engineering school—if it had taught them anything, taught what the past had been and the future should not be. Against this attitude no rational argument could be effective.

3

Alonzo's break with the religion in which he had been brought up was a long and difficult struggle, a protracted trauma, but once it was over it was complete, leaving neither remorse, nor regret, nor nostalgia. By the time he entered engineering school he took himself to be an atheist. His break had begun in high school. And as he remembers it, it began with the thought that if he had been born in a different society at a different historical epoch—in Greece, for instance, or in India, centuries past—he would have been no less convinced of the truth of the religion in which he would have been brought up than he was now of the truth of the religion in which he was actually reared because he was born a Venezuelan at the beginning of the century. It followed then that if a man came by his religion through the accident of his birth, his conviction of its truth had little to do with its actual truth or falsehood.

A believer was as capable of believing deeply and piously the absurdities of polytheistic animal worship, as Alonzo then took ancient Egyptian religion to be, as he was of believing monotheistic trinitarianism. That the doctrines of his own church were revealed while the others were not, was no argument, for other religions made exactly the same claim. That the true doctrine had been given the assent of thousands of great thinkers, holy men, martyrs, and that it had stood the test of time —he saw at first vaguely, and gradually more and more clearly, that these statements were no less valid for other religions than they were for the one he had until then believed in earnestly and was now beginning to doubt. Prophets, miracles, sacred scriptures containing divine revelations of the only true God or gods—were there any of the great religions that could not make the same claims?

In Caracas, it must have been when he was ten or eleven, he had heard a renowned Spanish monk preach a sermon he never forgot. The Church, said the reverend man, was the dyke against which the hammering waves of heresy and skepticism had beaten in vain for nearly two thousand years. It was the anvil that withstood the evil hammering of unbelievers. The Truth, said the holy man, had stood up. Alonzo now asked himself: Was it not the case that other religions had stood up as long or longer, against waves of equal force, if not stronger, against pounding as furious if not more so? If age, if the capacity to stand the hammerings of heresy and skepticism, were the criteria of truth, other religions were as true as his own—if not more true, for some of them were considerably older.

The depth and breadth of his religious trauma was the result of the fact that in his middle teens he had been deeply religious. He still remembers as if it had happened yesterday, how profoundly his cousin Carlos had shocked him in Curaçao, by Carlos's dismissal of the truth of Roman Catholicism and his scurrilous tales of the conduct of priests and nuns. Carlos was returning "from the North," where he had been wasting his time in a school, as Alonzo remembers, somewhere near Albany. Somehow while in the United States he had picked up a militant, atheistic anti-Catholicism. Alonzo was profoundly grieved for his cousin, because Carlos was risking the salvation of his soul, and he was shocked and hurt in his own deepest sensibility. Carlos went on to Mérida, his native city, and shortly after his arrival he was shot through the heart by a rival for the love of a woman.

To Alonzo the sad event was the sign of God's heavy punishment. But much later when he began to reflect on the truth of religion, he began to see that the belief that sin is punished by God on earth did not stand up to the facts. Nor did the belief that natural catastrophies were the punishment of God make any sense. Nor did the belief that evil men who inflict unspeakable tribulations on people are the punishing agents of God make sense either. Nor did the belief that God watched over his creatures make sense either. Gomez, the bloody tyrant who would have killed his father had not the carelessness of the police allowed him to slip out of their hands, was as much the creature of God as was any saintly man and everybody else. But it looked as if God watched over Gomez much more carefully than He did over Gomez's enemies, for Gomez prospered while they pined in jail or in exile. If God watched over His creatures why did He let this bloody tyrant destroy men who by comparison were decent men?

This fact could not be explained by the doctrine of Providence. If God used evil to punish the sinner, He indulged in a strange kind of justice: For His punishment fell with equal wrath on the sinful and on the less sinful. The sinking of the *Titanic* had carried many men to their death; but were we to believe that they were all equally evil? Shortly after the catastrophe happened he had heard that the sinking was the punishment of God, because the ship, before its launching, had been lettered with slogans that dared God to sink it. And God did sink it to punish its builders. Take the story at its face value, were the men who wrote the slogans the men who were drowned? And were not among the drowned a few, say three or four or even one, take one only who was a relatively decent, a relatively good man?

There were also the difficulties of the doctrine that gradually appeared as Alonzo thought of it: the virginity of Mary, the divinity of Jesus, His resurrection, the immortality of the soul. No, the central doctrines of his religion became less and less plausible the longer Alonzo thought of them.

Gradually disbelief took hold of his mind and he could not shake it off. As I said, his was not any easy, overnight shedding of belief, as it has been for others, but a slow, bitter fight every inch of the slippery way downward; it was a fight shot through with anxiety and fear and self-distrust. His efforts to talk his problems over with his father confessor were futile. All the reverend man could do was to dish out to him a number of clearly inadequate platitudes about God's providence, and urge the need for prayer to keep the faith. The father confessor was too glib and he did not understand what Alonzo was going through. Slowly his belief disintegrated.

Finally the time came when there was no scrap left of anything that he had been taught. Alonzo could not believe that the Son of God had been sent down by His Father to redeem mankind at a particular time in history and at a particular place. The doctrine was simply unbelievable. It was no less unbelievable that a man, however trained, and by whatever rites ordained could, by means of a few Latin words, change a piece of bread and a cup of wine into the body and blood of the Lord. If there had been a Lord, the literal transubstantiation was—what was it but unbelievable? But had there been a Lord? A prophet there had been, no doubt. Although Alonzo had no genuine knowledge of the difficult problem of the historicity of Jesus, he knew that there were learned men who held that the evidence was not satisfactory. But there must have been a prophet, a powerful religious leader who gave rise to the legend, whose teaching had, for reasons that he did not pretend to understand, altered the course of history. In him one could believe. But that the prophet was the Second Person of the Trinity, God Himself—that article of the doctrine became unbelievable for Alonzo.

These were not the exact words that Alonzo used at the time when he was wrestling with his beliefs, but something like these words, as he remembers, crossed his mind. The struggle to retain his belief, the effort to keep afloat, the agonizing lonely effort not to be drowned by disbelief, lasted between three and four traumatic years, and ended before he graduated from high school When it ended, let me repeat it, it ended for good. It was not any longer a question of keeping afloat or of drowning. The anguish was gone and he was filled with a sense of liberation. He felt free, free from false doctrines, free from a heavy incubus of superstition and a narrowing mythology. And in the process of freeing himself he had gained maturity and something else, the nature and power of which he was not to sense clearly until somewhat later.

The struggle taught him that one has to put everything one has on the line, if one is to fight through to truth. No reserves. No escape hatches. Nothing to fall back on. No half measures. It was years before the full import of this lesson would make its way clearly into his mind; but its effect became operative immediately. For Alonzo once said to me that since then he had never been able to feel anything but the deepest contempt for men who adapt their beliefs to their convenience. Trimmers, careerists, weathervanes among the intellectuals, sycophants that change their views with the political or social weather—these *canaille* are among the deepest dyed *bêtes noires* in his zoo. A man who had put everything on the line for the sake of truth—the salvation of his soul, the most precious treasure that until then he thought he possessed—would not be able ever to trim and adapt and adopt useful ideas and lie to others or to himself, whatever the price held out to him to lie.

Alonzo became an atheist. It was worth three or four painful years to be free for good, to be able to cut clean and without psychic suppuration. He observed at close quarters men who lost their religious or their political faith and could not break clean from doctrines they were no longer able to believe. Some never lost their nostalgia. Others replaced their lost beliefs by bitterness and antagonism to their lost faith. Alonzo may have been deceiving himself when, on several occasions, he told me that he had no bitterness or animus towards the Catholic church. As regards its doctrine his attitude is complex. Towards the truth of the doctrine he is as convinced as anyone can be that its claims have no validity whatever—whatever. But in the doctrines themselves he has great interest, and although quite ignorant of the history of dogma, I have heard him say that if he had another life to live he might consider preparing himself to be a historian of dogma, for he finds the orthodoxy that emerged slowly from the doctrinal struggles of the early church, he finds the heresies, the bloody and bitter fights among the Children of God, the shenanigans, the double-crossings, the street brawls and intrigues, the intellectual energy that went into the definition of the various credos, a superbly interesting expression of the human mind.

The historical role of the church is a much more difficult, more complex question, and one not to be settled with a simple judgment. Men who believe that the church in the Middle Ages subjugated the human being, are merely parroting clichés picked up from ignorant atheistic pulp publications. The claim is beyond contempt. The ignorance of which it gives evidence is typical of a certain kind of closed mind, a mind that has been subjugated by the illiterate and petrified misconceptions of the village atheist. On the other hand, those who argue that the Catholic church as an institution has always been on the side of civilization and who see in it solely a force for good are no less prejudiced or ignorant than the others. Alonzo knows enough history to know that as a political force the church has been on the side of evil as often as on the side of good—if in history, such simplistic dichotomies are possible.

But why are they simplistic? Because they fail to take into account the sincerity of the contending parties and the impossibility of deciding objectively at the time the quarrel is taking place the right and the wrong of the issues.

When Alonzo finally resolved his doubts he knew that many of the arguments that had led to his apostasy could have been answered by someone who was a better theologian than his father confessor; at least he knew that there was nothing original in his thoughts about religion and that there were standard answers to his standard doubts. But he also knew that the crucial problem of Roman Catholicism, of any form of genuine Christianity, indeed, arises from the relation of the prophet Jesus to the Second Member of the Trinity, the Son who is God Himself. The problem arises, in other words, from the claim to the divinity of Jesus, the claim for the literal validity of the Christian revelation. And it is this claim that he could not accept. This claim cannot be established by historical evidence. All the Gospels could tell us—if they tell us that—is that those who wrote them believed in the divinity of Jesus and his God-given mission. They cannot tell us that what they believed is true. Once he got this far, his faith was gone and gone for good.

I qualified above and wrote that for Alonzo the divinity of Jesus was the crucial problem for any Christianity that is serious, because he knew that there were a number of groups of people who call themselves Christians and who reject the cardinal tenets of orthodox Christian doctrine. Alonzo insisted that he was not a Christian because he could not accept these beliefs. One of these groups of *soit-disant* Christians reduces Christianity to social do-goodism, claiming that all of Christianity is to be found in The Sermon on the Mount, interpreting The Sermon entirely in secularistic terms, and ignoring that what The Sermon promises is The Kingdom of Heaven.

Some theologians of his acquaintance fall back on epistemic faith and speak of the *encounter*. This was one of their favorite words, presumably since Buber became popular among them. But encounter with whom, with what? That they encounter something Alonzo does not deny; that the encounter is immensely valuable he does not deny either. What he denies, or more precisely, what he questions, is the nature of that which one encounters. Until they show by some other means than their subjective asseverations that they encounter something other than themselves, until they show objectively that they encounter He Who Is, their epistemic faith with its certainty and self-evident quality, seems to add up to nothing more than the statement that they believe the truth of their doctrines—and this is quite different from the truth of their doctrines. What is sometimes called epistemic faith is therefore logically prior to the faith one has when one trusts someone. And it is this epistemic faith that for Alonzo constitutes the invalid foundations of their doctrines. What would be called for, before you can accept a proposition on faith, is a proof that a given belief in a given proposition discloses the truth of that proposition, as rationalists in the seventeenth century believed that a certain kind of intuition carried with it a sign of the truth of the proposition thus entertained. Today belief in intuition of this kind is no longer possible, although it seems to be held still by some followers of some forms of continental philosophies; by students of Husserl, for instance.

4

Before Alonzo entered engineering school he had acquired two attitudes that qualified him as a liberal: He had become a strong pacifist and for the first time in his life he had come across the phenomenon of anti-Semitism and had reacted strongly against it.

There was nothing in his family background or upbringing that could account for his strong feeling about war. His father, a Venezuelan politician, had fought in several "invasions" from Colombia into western Venezuela and had been wounded in combat against government forces. Although his father was a moderate man in most of his reactions, Alonzo never heard him or anyone in the family say a word against war. What then had turned Alonzo into a pacifist? What prepared his mind took place without his being aware of it, but what finally turned him against war—a sort of straw that broke the camel's back—was an event that he remembers vividly and that took place in only a few minutes. That the event I am about to recount could not have been the sole cause, that there must have been a long and preparatory series of experiences making the meaning he found in the event possible, is a safe guess. In any case this is what happened: The war against Germany was going on, and high school students were required to take military training at a New York City armory once a week. It was a nuisance that Alonzo did not care for, with student sergeants yelling at their squads, actual soldiers giving orders in an unnecessarily rough manner, a whole afternoon a week with no relieving features to it. As to the value of "military training," what was accomplished in the armory had very little value, for all it taught was how to form squads and how to march in step. Occasionally there would be pep talks, and these were invariably dull.

Alonzo does not remember who talked to his group and what they said, except on one occasion, when a soldier who had been in the trenches, gathered the group around him to talk about the need for discipline in combat. He ranted about the need to obey orders without making much of an impression on Alonzo, who was wool-gathering, when suddenly the man said that he would rather have at the firing line a small group of well trained, disciplined men, who could obey orders, than a whole company of undisciplined men. Disciplined men would hold their fire until told to shoot, and they would apply their fire where it counted. That was the kind of action that would stop the enemy. Efficiently trained men would kill where an undisciplined mob would waste their ammunition and would soon be dead themselves.

Suddenly Alonzo saw himself applying the fire where it counted. He saw a scattered group of advancing Germans and he saw himself shooting at them. He saw a man at whom he had shot fall. Something happened quickly, physical nausea and a psychic revulsion took hold of him. The vision was real, much more real than the soldier talking to the group, than the group itself, than the distant ceiling, the surrounding walls, the noise around him. The phrase, "applying the fire," cut through his mind, split his head like a hatchet, and made him reel. The throat-clutching insanity of the episode he had just lived through, the brutality, the monstrous disregard of human life, surged to his consciousness and left him fainting. Life and killing and combat and trenches and advancing Germans—he had never before reacted toward any of these things. Somehow he had been indifferent to them. They had not been able to scratch his consciousness. The madness of the war, the hatred, the stories, the five-minute ranting at the movies that interrupted the films, the hatred, the intense effort to whip up the population to a white heat of hatred, had so far left him annoyed, irritated, but in the privacy of his mind, untouched. And now all of a sudden the vivid experience he had undergone turned him against the war. He became consciously a pacifist in a few seconds.

For a few days he was not quite himself. He was not living in his familiar world. Externally nothing had changed. Yet everything had changed, completely, utterly. For all he could think about was the raucous, the odious phrase: Apply the fire where it counts. The phrase itself no longer meant what in a few seconds it had meant in the armory: It no longer evoked an image of a falling man, it no longer brought on nausea, revulsion. But the phrase echoed over and over, and while there was no violent, sharp pain, a dull, pervasive discomfort hung on. After a time—was it days or weeks?—his attitude towards the war became fully and clearly defined, as clear and obstinate and mordant as hatred can be. He now responded in exactly the opposite way from that which he was being urged to respond. He hated. But he hated not the Germans but war. His hatred was an active, a living, a strong passion. He had a positive need to save himself from the high flood of hatred on which he had before floated and which now he felt as a menace that was threatening to drown him.

What did pacifism mean to Alonzo? It meant of course hatred of war. It meant hatred of warmongering and all that he then took to be instrumental to warmongering: nationalism, the merchants of death, imperialism, national greed, dollar diplomacy—in short the whole goulash of liberal clichés, the main ingredient of which was pacifism and antinationalism that at the time among liberals passed for established, undebatable, self-evident truth. That the goulash had everything in it that liberals could throw into the pot but that the one thing liberals were short of was truth—that was something that Alonzo did not then know.

Pacifism meant something else, and this something deserves inspection. Pacifism meant, of course, that war was evil. From this statement it seemed to follow that it ought to be abolished. And from this statement in turn it seemed to follow that it could be abolished. In his saner moments Alonzo would allow that it could only be abolished if—if men could be brought to see the irrationality of war. That men could be brought to see this, Alonzo had no doubt. Active in his attitude was the willful failure to see that what ought to be is not always continuous with, or emergent from, what is.

The other attitude Alonzo brought from high school into engineering school was his dislike of anti-Semitism. It was not until he went to high school that he began to notice differences among his fellow students: Some were Irish, some Italians, some Jews. But he did not notice any significant difference between his fellow students because they were Irish or Italians or Jews. That among them these differences were felt keenly he gradually became aware, but their attitude toward one another did not communicate itself to him.

He learned what anti-Semitism was at a meeting of the Arista, a high school honorary society to which he had been elected. The election of new members was up for discussion and the name of Bill Greenstone was brought up. A member of the Arista, one of the leaders of the group, immediately got up and spoke against Bill on the ground that Bill was a Jew and no Jews were wanted in the organization. It was clear that Bill had the required qualifications—scholarship and activities. But he was a Jew. Alonzo could not see how the fact that Bill was a Jew disqualified him from membership in the honorary society. He spoke in Bill's favor and when the votes were counted Bill had been elected with sufficient votes to make Alonzo feel that his arguments had made the difference between keeping Bill out and getting him into the society.

This was the beginning of his friendship with Bill and of Alonzo's political activity at the school. This experience was followed by another which solidified his rejection of anti-Semitism. During the first week of his freshman year at engineering school Alonzo heard that the junior members of two fraternities that ran the school had called a secret meeting of a number of gentiles who had not been pledged to a fraternity and had asked them to vote for one gentile ticket while nominating two Jewish tickets. This was a gentile school and it was not right to allow Jews to control class offices. When he heard about the meeting Alonzo began organizing the independents and the Jews to form a solid front against the fraternities. It was too late to do anything about the freshman class. But it was not too soon to start organizing against the anti-Semitic fraternities for elections of sophomore offices. It took an endless amount of time and energy but he succeeded. And for the first time in the school the sophomore class was controlled entirely by a coalition of Jews and independents.

5

It is clear from the preceding that when Alonzo had the good fortune to be assigned to Krutch's freshman English class in engineering school he already had some of the most important components of the syndrome that is known among us as liberalism. What then did he get from Krutch? The question can be answered in one word: self-awareness. And this, he thought, is one of the most wonderful gifts that fortune can offer a man. There were other gifts Krutch could have conferred on Alonzo; tolerance, an irenic attitude towards the faults of others, and a suspension of his need to believe—these were virtues of which he was in urgent need that Krutch possessed in abundance. But he did not notice them in Krutch. Had he noticed them, he would not have known they were virtues. There were others. But surely awareness of oneself, Alonzo knew at the time he gained it, was a precious gift to receive from his teacher.

Until, by the merest chance, Alonzo met Krutch, he had been living the life of a drugged person. For until then he had been deceiving himself with the notion that he wanted to be an engineer. In a few days in Krutch's class he discovered the deception and knew with a conviction that brooked no doubt what he wanted to be. He had at first some difficulty formulating what that was. Finally he settled for *writer*. That was what he wanted to be—a writer. Ahead lay a bitter fight with his parents and the very difficult problem of earning a living. But these were minor problems compared with the discovery, the enormously important discovery, that he had found his—what had he found? Well, the word is a big one, but that is what he found—there is no better word for it—he found his destiny. The minor problems he faced without fear. What was important, what was cause for joy, was that by a sheer gift of fortune, he had stepped out of the cave in which he had been confined and out into the light of truthfulness to himself. Out into the crisp morning, into the light of the rising sun.

What actually happened is not a part of this account: How he finally won the battle with his parents, how he lived in Greenwich Village for a number of years and quite by accident heard of the Gale Scholarship at State University in Midland City. How before he came to Midland City he had had a few days in the Village in which, after his black coffee in the morning, he did not know where his lunch or dinner would be coming from; and finally, how he settled the problem of making a living with a compromise: the teaching of philosophy—these are stages in Alonzo's biography, but not relevant to the apologia I am trying to write.

What is part of that apologia is that it was not Krutch alone, of course, who led him out of the cave, but the books Krutch led him to, and on two of these I must touch because they were of immense importance in his early development. They were not "great books." Today they are unknown to anyone younger than Alonzo and even to well-read men of his own age. Nor would Alonzo assert that they do not deserve the oblivion into which they have fallen. They probably do. But to him, at the time he read them, they made an immense difference.

I must introduce my remarks on these two books with a very brief prefatory explanation. One of the earliest consequences of Alonzo's acquaintance with Krutch was his realization that he was altogether ignorant of contemporary literature. Krutch lived in a world to which Alonzo was a total stranger. Although Alonzo had read much more than the rest of his fellow freshmen, he had not read the books Krutch was interested in, the ones coming out at the time. To remedy this situation he got from Krutch a list of some ten or twelve novels. The list contained Dreiser, probably *Sister Carrie*, a novel of Hergesheimer, Joyce's *Portrait*, novels by Maugham, George Moore, and a number of authors who were being talked about among the intellectuals of New York at the time. One of the books was Floyd Dell's *Moon Calf*. Fifteen years later Alonzo tried to reread this book and the experience was so embarrassing that he could not get past the first few pages. But when it first fell into his hands he found it to be the cause of a profoundly valuable experience. For here was an account of a young man with whom Alonzo could identify himself, who began writing poetry in St. Louis, moved on to Chicago, and finally broke through as a writer.

What was of significance for Alonzo was that Floyd Dell showed by his hero's dedication to literature, by his uncompromising attitude towards the world of business, the real world, as Philistines call it, that Alonzo's discovery of his destiny (the big word again must be used) was something to be accepted with gladness of heart, whatever his parents and his parents' friends might think of his wrong-headedness. The writer's life was worth living. It meant accepting poverty, it meant cutting oneself off from one's family, it meant abandoning the possibility of being respectable, and in practical terms it meant taking an enormous chance, for there was no way of telling at the time whether he could succeed at all in what he proposed to do. But it was the life he wanted to live. *Moon Calf* was, or so he took it to be, a justification of the vocation of poetry. He was no poet and he had no intention of writing poetry. Somehow he had known that to write poetry one must learn the language at one's mother's knee, and he had yet to learn English before he could begin to write. But that was not important. What *Moon Calf* did was to show him that in turning as he did toward writing he was not, as his parents thought he was, utterly wrong.

From the novel he also somehow got the idea that it was wrong to compromise with the world in which his parents wanted him to live. His mother begged him to finish engineering school, and then, she said, he could do whatever he wanted to do. His parents tried to bribe him with the promise of a year in Europe to do whatever he wanted, after he got his engineering degree. But somehow he got from *Moon Calf* the clear warning that there could be no compromise. Or was it from this novel? In any case, he became aware that to compromise would mean to sign his unconditional surrender to the world he did not want to live in.

The second book that had a great impact on him was Ludwig Lewisohn's *Up Stream*. This book opened up many vistas to him; it revealed the prejudice that was to be encountered in the academic world, and which at the time of its publication was rampant and unashamed. It gave him a sense of his own lack of education. But what was of greatest importance for Alonzo was that the book established, whether Lewisohn intended it or not, the true dignity of the man of letters, the writer-scholar. Later on Alonzo was to meet a man who had been a friend of Lewisohn's at Columbia University during their graduate school years and Alonzo was to learn from him that *Up Stream* was not accurate. And when he himself met Lewisohn later he was to discover that in many ways the man could not sustain the respect and admiration that the book had elicited from him. But nothing he could find out about the man could relieve him of his heavy debt of gratitude for the writer of *Up Stream*.

II

More Confusions

1

UNDER Krutch's influence, Alonzo began to read voraciously, with a sense of desperation, as if he had to race against time. He read rapidly, without digesting properly what he read, out of an unappeasable hunger, out of a compulsive sense that the emptiness of his mind had to be filled and filled as soon as possible. And he read widely. He read philosophy, most of which was above his head, good literature—Shakespeare and Marlow, for instance—which he did not have the background to appreciate or the critical training to digest; history, which he did not absorb; psychology; quantities of criticism; some sociology and anthropology; quantities of novels, good and bad, just off the press, reviewed in the weeklies as the greatest books of the century; a great deal of poetry; and, of course, the liberal weeklies. There was something about Albert Jay Nock's *The Freeman* that made it superbly attractive; and of course *The Nation* was indispensable as a cornucopia of ultimate truth on anything it paid attention to.

Like many young people who have not been taught how to read, Alonzo read subjectively, picking from the page or chapter or book what interested him, not concerning himself with what the writer was trying to say. That a novel or play is an organized whole presenting a series of dramatic events, comprehensive as a whole, and often having several layers of dramatic comprehensibility and sometimes having philosophical or more precisely, theoretical overtones; that a philosophical book or essay is an organized whole, offering a thesis supported by arguments which lead to a conclusion; that a historian narrates events that he has organized into a whole, that he offers evidence for his grasp of a period—in short, that the content of a piece of writing, if it is worth spending time going over it, is worth taking full possession of—this was something that Alonzo at the time had no notion of.

While reading as if pursued, he began to write. He wrote essays, daily entries into journals, interminable letters to friends on any excuse and often without excuse, he wrote criticism, and he wrote stories and a few poems—all of which scribbling has fortunately been lost.

Besides Krutch several men stand out as formative of his mind. First, Bernard Shaw. He read everything he could get hold of by Shaw, and when he was done with what was in print he waited anxiously for the next book. About the time he saw the performance of *Saint Joan*, one of the worries of his life was that Shaw might die and he would be left without anything to read for the rest of his days. But Shaw became a bore or at least Alonzo became bored with him. From becoming bored with Shaw's ideas to seeing that many of them were muddled and many of them silly was a short step.

What did Alonzo get from G.B.S.? What Shaw did for him was to authorize his irreverence and flip radicalism. There are very few things that are sacred, in the primitive sense of the term—few that, if you touch them, would defile you. Irreverence was not an attitude he acquired from Shaw but that Shaw, with his wit and his talent for exposing mendacity and for turning middle-class values right side up (and this was precisely the point of Max Beerbohm's cartoon) authorized it.

The turning point of his Shavian addiction came when he began to perceive that the bourgeoisie enjoyed being stamped on, that it admired Shaw's brash effrontery, and that it respected his talent for self-advertising. These are all qualities that are placed high in its operative (as distinct from its pretended) scheme of values. Something else contributed to Shaw's success. Since his readers were deprived of the ministrations of confession and penance, they loved to be punished, and they loved it all the more since they were certain that while no doubt they themselves deserved a little punishment, their neighbors really deserved the full measure. Shaw performed an important redemptive job. Like the sermons of their ministers, they heard Shaw, admitted he was right, and went on being pretty much the same, being what they were. This is the reason they ate up what he dished out instead of resenting his insults. And this is the reason they rewarded him with fame and money.

When this fact finally got through to Alonzo's understanding it disclosed to him how the slapping and the enjoyment of the slapping were not quite the serious business he had taken them to be, how the whole foofaraw, effrontery, wit, and brashness and exposure were phony. When Alonzo finally understood the phenomenon, it was not difficult to become resigned to the fact that he would have to live the rest of his life without Shavian ministrations. But fortunately there was a substitute at hand. He found Rabelais. And the change from G. B. S. to the Master of Raucous Laughter was an immeasurable gain.

Next came Nietzsche, whom he read avidly and whom, of course, he did not understand. There is no need to go into minute details; all that needs be stated is that whether Nietzsche can or cannot be understood (and in a sense he cannot) Alonzo certainly did not understand him then. It was easy enough to take hold of phrases and thoughts picked up from this or that page or book. It was not difficult to get hold of a number of central ideas that one could not possibly miss. But these ideas can be understood superficially or at their full depth, and it was superficially, if at all, that Alonzo grasped them. The extent and depth of the German's thought was beyond him; nor can an uneducated youth in his early twenties be condemned for missing it. Educated and older men still miss it.

For instance, no young man with as exiguous an intellectual background as Alonzo's can fully grasp Nietzsche's repudiation of our modern world and its values. And it would take much more maturity than Alonzo had to perceive that Nietzsche's revulsion at European culture arose from a deep piety toward it. His anger arose from a deep love that was frustrated, by ideals that were implanted in him by his culture; ideals that he found absent from the world in which he lived. That some of the ideals were pure fantasy, that they had never been operative and by their nature could not have been, did not rob Nietzsche of his value as critic of the bourgeoise society of his day. The idea that Europe was dying is easy enough to grasp, whether one agrees with the notion or not. But the full meaning of the idea of the death of Europe and the realization, which is part of that meaning, that it was we, Europeans, or as we would say today, we, men of the West, who murdered Europe, that was not something that Alonzo in his early twenties could understand.

But then, how many could understand it? That God was dead was easy to understand. Alonzo had witnessed His death in his own soul. But that the death of God causes seismic commotions that affect us all, that it is not a trivial event which after a few years of teen-age agonizing one got over for good but that it was a major cataclysm, that God cannot be killed by a culture without endangering its life, that He cannot be killed without men rushing to put up loathsome idols in His place, and that this was understood by Nietzsche in his own crooked way— this was something that Alonzo could not and would not then understand. Had he been forced to listen to a statement pointing to the catastrophic consequences of the death of God, Alonzo would have answered flippantly that man is always better off with the truth than with fairy tales.

Alonzo was, of course, well acquainted with the famous passage in Nietzsche's *Joyful Wisdom*—possibly the best known of all pages that Nietzsche ever wrote—about the mad man who comes into the crowded market place, calling out unceasingly, "I seek God! I seek God!" and telling the crowd "We have killed him . . . ." But the depth of meaning these two pages contain cannot be gathered by a callow atheist who would not have been able to understand, had you tried to explain it to him, what the notion of God had meant in human history—whether there is any reality back of it or not.

But if Alonzo did not understand Nietzsche, how could the German become a formative force for him? Nietzsche did for Alonzo in a somewhat different sense what Shaw had done. He confirmed an "instinctual," a deep-rooted attitude of his, a sense he had that philosophizing is most serious activity. Just as he had risked the salvation of his soul when he began to think independently about religion so, when he began to read philosophy, what was involved was not a pleasant intellectual exercise but an activity in which the whole of himself was involved. If philosophy began in wonder, it was wonder about man and his destiny and whether his life could be made to have value or not, and how it could be made to have value. One did not have to read many pages of Nietzsche to grasp clearly the fact that for Nietzsche everything that could be thought to be valuable was at stake in the Europe of his day. About the time of which I am writing, Alonzo could not have proved this "instinctual" belief. When he began reading Nietzsche Alonzo did not know enough about the history of philosophy to have argued with success in favor of his hunch that the men whom one can call philosophers, the real philosophers, not the teachers of philosophy, were men who were totally involved, men who were risking their destiny, gambling for the meaning of their lives when in the loneliness of their studies they sought to solve their problems and clarify the puzzles that haunted them.

What Nietzsche did for Alonzo was to immunize him for life against the *niaiserie* that philosophy is an intellectual game. Such an attitude just did not go with his temperament. It was of great value to have been immersed in the Nietzschean universe long enough to have seen what was involved in philosophizing. Nietzsche was not playing a game. He was wrestling with a lot of feline demons, with a cage full of big, demonic cats, all of them snarling at him and ready to jump on him if he did not keep them at bay with the frail, weak, fragile chair of his thought. It was man, European man, Western man as we call him today, and his civilization that Nietzsche was defending against the big cats that were snarling at him.

What literally did Alonzo mean by Nietzsche's big cats? In answer to that question Alonzo was vague and selective because he did not line up with Nietzsche without qualification. Nietzsche hated pity, socialism, the religion of the slaves, decadence, hatred of life, the withering intellectualism that is glorified as respect for Truth but that shrinks a man into a zombi, contempt for man as expressed by Ivan Karamazov's Grand Inquisitor, the fact that the death of God leaves us with an empty universe and a life to which we must give value but to which we have not found the means of giving value, envy of superiority, and the contempt for excellence—these were the fiercest and most aggressive cats Nietzsche was trying to keep at bay. Nietzsche might have been wrong about any of them or even about all of them. That was not the point with Alonzo. The point was that Nietzsche was fighting for our civilization and that his prophetic eyes saw ahead to what is now happening and our purblind eyes cannot as yet see, although it is in front of our noses. What he saw is that "Europe," the West, was dying and that the slow death from which it was dying was brought on by us, men of the West. It was we who had murdered our culture.

This, then, was what philosophy was, this was what you devoted yourself to, when you took the vows. And it was vows you took if you were serious about philosophy: You swore to defend man against the ever-present danger of an encroaching chaos. There were those who dismissed Nietzsche because he did not think like the professors. But if Nietzsche's work was not philosophy, if the articulation of his fears and hopes for Europe, for Western culture, was something else, it certainly was worth spending one's life on it. It was issues and puzzles of this nature and of this weight that aroused Alonzo's interest.

As he studied the history of philosophy in the late twenties and began teaching it in 1930, he found that although the philosophers of Western Europe had not all been concerned with the questions that aroused Nietzsche's deep anxiety, they had all been concerned with questions of equal import. Take Hegel. The tale is told by D. D. Raphael (he got it, as he tells us, from F. L. Lucas) that Hegel used to greet the Sunday joint with the words, "Come, let's fulfill its destiny." It was more than a witticism by means of which to expose the High Priest of Reason. For when the vista of history and of the cosmos unrolled before Hegel's eyes he grasped, or thought he grasped, the formula of their procession, the key to their secret. In a dialectical hopscotch that might be funny to the irreverent but that revealed itself to its discoverers as the very heartbeat of the cosmos, Reason manifested itself in the ordered stages of the vast process.

Grasping the key to the mystery of the universe and of man involves the supreme thrill, the vertigo of the philosopher. It is for this moment of vision that he lives. It is his ecstasy. It brings with it joy, and for Hegel, who knows? it may have brought awe and terror. Let us assume the witticism true. The man who had had Hegel's experience had earned the right to laugh at himself by blessing with pointed levity his Sunday joint. Men capable of cosmic awe pray to their victims before they let fly the arrow that will bring them down. Having brought the cosmos and human history to their knees and wrenched from them the key to their mystery, it was not difficult to take from the joint its key—which, obviously, was to be carved by Hegel.

And much the same holds, quite obviously, for Spinoza. Nature or God elicited from him piety and reverence. The lens grinder of Amsterdam never ceased to be a pious Jew; expulsion from the congregation did not pluck from him his religiosity. What it did was to enable him to define clearly its proper object. And the proper object of reverence and piety was not a tribal deity that demanded that a father sacrifice to Him his son in order to test him, and whose heart was gladdened when the believer observed all sorts of prohibitions—that was the ceremonial order proper to a people at a given time in their history. The true object of reverence and piety was Nature, in its intricate and precise articulation, as thought revealed it to the free mind—the mind of

Spinoza. In the contemplation of that order was salvation, which he dubbed with a term that for us, men of the twentieth century, has a faint ring of irony—perhaps the only note of irony we can find in the works of this pious Jew—"the intellectual love of God."

And the same holds, quite obviously, for Kant. That frail, diminutive, sunken-chested wit of Königsberg was engaged in a vital fight. Hume had shocked him into awareness of the danger of a false empiricism. When Alonzo thought of Kant he was not thinking of the starry heavens above and the moral law within. He was thinking of the dramatic struggle in which he engaged with Hume, to put beyond Hume's corrosive reach the three great values Hume had threatened: God, freedom, and immortality.

To have acquired early in his career as a man of letters a sense of what philosophy is about was worth the price Alonzo paid for his acquisition: his confusion about Nietzsche's thought. When in the early twenties he read Nietzsche, he could not have passed an examination on Nietzsche of the kind that later he gave his own students in his course on Nietzsche. At the earlier period he did not understand Nietzsche at all. But the price, confusion, was worth it, for he clarified his "instinctual" sense that philosophy seeks answers to the desperate questions.

2

In the twenties Nietzsche did not engage Alonzo's interest for long. Shortly after meeting Krutch, Alonzo began to read contemporary Spanish literature, which then meant "the generation of ninety-eight," a group of writers who came to prominence after the defeat of the Spanish-American War. A towering figure among these men was Unamuno. Ortega y Gasset may come next or may even be a more important figure, but for Alonzo the most attractive of these men then was the polyglot of Salamanca, Don Miguel. Alonzo read *The Tragic Sentiment* before it appeared in English translation, he read a seven— or was it six, or eight, or nine?—volume edition of Unamuno's essays, his novels, and his poetry.

What captured him? The problem of immortality was not Alonzo's problem—at the time, Alonzo was a ranting atheist and philosophical materialist; he could not sympathize with a man who lived in agony because he wanted to believe but could not believe, in immortality.

Nor was Unamuno's claim convincing to Alonzo that one of the central themes of Western philosophy was the preoccupation with immortality. Nor was Alonzo interested in any immediate sense in a bundle of questions that made Unamuno famous in Spain and Spanish America, questions about the past and future of Spain. Nor could he have been attracted by Unamuno's philosophical technique, for Unamuno the philosopher was totally derivative, and his technique, if one could call it that, was a hodgepodge of argument, asseveration, rhetoric, and preachment, far distant from the illative argumentations and search for inferential relations of the true philosopher. A bit of pragmatism, chiefly from James's "Will to Believe," a tendency to reduce objective philosophical problems to questions of motivation, a wide range of knowledge, a syncretistic point of view, and a deeply religious sense that left a distinct heretical spoor behind it, Alonzo may have been very callow and ignorant at the time, but these traits of Don Miguel's did not escape his notice.

What then captured him? It might have been the problem of religion, that Alonzo thought he had settled once and for all before he entered engineering school but that might not have been as thoroughly settled in his mind as he thought or liked to think it was. Here was a man who was a heterodox believer (as Alonzo understood it) but who took the questions of religion seriously. But this could not have been a sufficiently strong magnet to keep Alonzo as firmly held by Don Miguel's books as he was for a time. What then did it? Alonzo was never clear about what attracted him to Unamuno, but what made Unamuno attractive was not his system or the substance of his thought; essentially what Alonzo found attractive in Unamuno was Unamuno himself, the man, the sense of whose strong personality came so clearly through the pages of his books. Here, through the pages, one could grasp a combination of profound passion, superb intelligence, and a gift of expression; a style, a vigorous, muscular prose, sparkling and lucid—however incoherent the thought might prove to be on analysis—that no other writer of his acquaintance could come close to, with the exception of Nietzsche. Here, then, was a man. And what a man. *Nada menos que todo un hombre*, in a phrase found in Unamuno himself, nothing less than a whole man. Unsystematic, incoherent— Alonzo would grant all that and more if it was called for. But what a man. What a deep reverberation of humanity one could catch in those impassioned utterances of Don Miguel. Those who could not see anything else than the unsystematic thinker who had swallowed more of William James than he was aware of, and who jeered at his anguish about immortality, had long lost, if they had ever possessed, a capacity to respond to the power of a human being; they were professors born, not bred; "professors" in the full supersaturated sense of contempt that Mencken could dissolve in the term. They looked for the illation of judgments and did not find it, looked at the conclusion and found not the consequence of a proof but the assertion of a passionate mind, they looked at the assumptions, the categorial equipment, the definitions, the transitions from one statement to the next, and found the whole business to be a mess of passion; since they were totally anaesthetic to that which gives some men their superior manhood, they rejected the mess, because it was not "philosophy." One such man Alonzo knew hated Unamuno, but the hatred could not be accounted for by the fact that Don Miguel could not think, which in the poor devil's sense of thinking the Spaniard certainly could not. But since for the poor devil nothing but what he called "philosophy" was thinking, Alonzo knew better than to point out the qualities in Don Miguel's work that made him admirable.

For Alonzo, the attraction of Unamuno deserves to be dwelt on because the failure to grasp it truly reveals a fundamental defect of a class of men who are influential and who pullulate in our academic world, men who all too often succeed in securing for their judgments an acceptance they do not deserve and in the not-too-long run lead to a detrimental misconception of the nature of a civilization worth the name.

In *The Tragic Sentiment* Unamuno had written, *"no me da la gana de morirme,"* and in seven words, all ordinary, he had revealed himself. The translator of *The Tragic Sentiment* had rendered the Spanish idiom in the tame "I do not wish to die." What else can the poor translator do? There is no other way in English to say what Unamuno had said through the idiomatic expression *"no me da la gana."* A man *a quien no l da la gana de morirse,* who does not wish to die (if that is how you must put it in English) is a colossal egoist who rejects the mud of which he is made, and somewhat dotty; no wonder that his patron saint was the Knight of the Sorrowful Countenance, on whom Unamuno had written one of his important books. But then, that's your Spaniard for you: a rank individualist, a man capable of deep passion, a man who asserts himself in the teeth of destruction, a linear descendant of Don Rodrigo Manrique who, as his son Jorge tells us in his famous *Coplas*, when death called on him with many lengthy arguments to quit this deceitful world and its flattery, replied somewhat impatiently; *conciento en mi morir*, which translates exactly, "I consent to my death."

3

Unamuno's hold on Alonzo did not last as long, perhaps, as Nietzsche's. Alonzo is not certain what caused him to turn away from the surcharged worlds of the German and the Spaniard but one important factor was his first meeting with Morris Cohen, professor of philosophy at The College of The City of New York, a teacher who was exercising a profound influence on some of Alonzo's friends. Paul Weiss, who at the time was president of the philosophy club at City College, knew of Alonzo's interest in Nietzsche and invited him to talk to the club on the German's philosophy. As incentive he promised to get Morris Cohen to attend the talk. Alonzo accepted the invitation.

Cohen was one of those teachers about whom legends circulate among the students. Feared for his ruthlessness toward fools, revered for his immense learning, his wit, his lightning mind, he had an enormous reputation, not only at the City College but in the profession, as a man of encyclopedic learning. In the middle of the twenties, when there was a widespread rumor that only five or six men in the United States understood Einstein's theory, Cohen was said to be one of the group. If the myth says nothing about American scientists, it says a great deal about the awed respect in which Cohen's learning was held by his students. He gave his students the impression that he had read everything. A story that circulated about him had it that some of his students, tired of never finding a hole in his learning, decided to lay a trap for the old boy. They read up in the *Britannica* on Chinese porcelain and, loaded for bear, asked their question. To which Cohen replied, "Well, that's what I used to think when I wrote the article for the Britannica on Chinese porcelain. But I have changed my mind since." And he proceeded to give the awed students an impromptu lecture on Chinese porcelain with dynasties and dates and technical details of firing and glazing.

The story was apocryphal, since it had been told by Gogarty about one of his teachers, who himself might have picked it up from an earlier worshiping student; but it was interesting because it was one of those tales by students about teachers who generate myths because the teacher is deeply respected, admired, and loved. Whether borrowed from Gogarty or made out of whole cloth, this story had a kind of truth to it that a well verified observation that drags its centipede body over the mire of mere fact lacks. It is one of those tales which Alonzo, not altogether in jest, said possesses a Higher Metaphysical Truth. For Cohen deserved, without question, to be called "An Abyss of Learning," as they used to call Master Rabelais when he graced the earth with his living laughter.

Around the table, the afternoon of the talk, there were some twelve students, with Paul Weiss sitting on one side of Alonzo, and after being introduced, Cohen on the other. When Alonzo finished Cohen said quietly but with a deep conviction that Nietzsche did not know much about power. A romantic, Nietzsche, when he thought of power, was obviously thinking of dominion over men, although he extended the notion as a principle of explanation to the cosmos. Nietzsche never realized that true power is knowledge.

The immediate impact of Cohen's statement was blunted for Alonzo by his callow irreverence. He discerned a small, slight man, an utterly vulnerable Jew. A friend of Justice Holmes, with whom Cohen corresponded because of their mutual interest in the philosophy of law, widely admired as a philosopher of science and a logician, Cohen physically could not have been more vulnerable than he was. Cohen had been the victim—how else can one explain it?—of the pestilential anti-Semitism that then flooded the campuses of the nation. It was rumored by students at the time that Cohen had never had an invitation to teach in a University out of New York. And if he had ever taught outside New York City—later he did—he had never had a permanent job offered him, although his reputation was solid and widespread. This vulnerable man, this slight secular rabbi, unquestionably an Abyss of Learning, pronounced with a quiet but deep conviction that only knowledge is power. And the sight of the ironic incongruity—for power Cohen had, of a kind, and power he utterly lacked, of another—saved Alonzo from the immediate impact of Cohen's statement.

But the momentary sight of Cohen as he saw him, so utterly vulnerable as to be a living refutation of his own faith, Alonzo soon came to realize, was but a futile bit of tactics used by himself in self-defense from the damaging effect of Cohen's remark. Cohen had not only refuted Nietzsche in a few words, but he had also winged Alonzo's Nietzscheism in its flight. And if Alonzo's views did not visibly plummet, in front of the members of the club, in a few days he found out that his opinions had been mortally wounded. Something in Cohen's superficially quiet but deeply fervid wisdom had torn into the surcharge of passion and unreason in which Alonzo had been indulging until then and from which he had been erroneously taking sustenance. Furthermore, what was true of Nietzsche was no less true, with appropriate alterations, of Unamuno. If the romantic figure of an armoured Polish knight charging at a gallop could be discerned back of the worship of power of the German, the kneeling figure of a mystic, with hands suppliant and eyes turned to Heaven—some dark figure of Zurbaran, perhaps—could be discerned back of Unamuno's brilliant, vigorous, pulsing prose. And Alonzo no more wanted to be, he could no more dream of being, a Medieval knight than he wanted to be or could dream of being a Zurbaran mystic.

Not that the passion was wrong or had no place in the work of a man who was dedicated to letters. This bit of dogma, universally held by so-called philosophers, Alonzo had no use for. Properly controlled, passion was right, it was an essential component of living thought. It was indeed passion that gave thought its life. Alonzo would never give up the conviction that it was essential for any enterprise of any significance whatever, in any field whatever. The tepid mathematician or physicist, the really cold-fish logician, was condemned to mediocrity, his work could not take flight. In philosophy, even Hume included, the great philosophers had been men of deep passion: Heraclitus, Plato, Saint Augustine, and if one had the sense to perceive it, Hobbes, Spinoza, and Berkeley in his youth, and Schopenhauer, who was an inveterate hater. Distilled water did not circulate in the intellectual arteries and veins of these men, but warm blood, rich in red cells. It was passion that gave them their thrust upward and kept them going. But something else was required, and that something had been lacking in Alonzo's diet during the years of his novitiate for gaining admission to the order of clerks. And somehow Cohen, though not directly, had conveyed in a few words what the missing component was. It was knowledge that was power, and there could be no knowledge without reason. Alonzo would never be seduced into worshiping at the altar of that eighteenth-century old bitch, Sovereign Reason. To be allowed to wear the habit of that branch of the order, after a novitiate in which the aspirant clerk is trained to see less and less of the world of men, a man has to emasculate himself, as the priests of Cybele did in ancient times. That of course was not for him. If to be a proper thinker one had to join the order of the castrati, he would not become a clerk. From that moment on he accepted his fate, which was, in Cohen's own memorable phrase about himself, to be "a dog without a kennel."

This is of course a simplified and abbreviated version of the process of thought that began with Cohen's quiet remark and ended sometime later in Alonzo's acquiring a copy of Santayana's *The Life of Reason*, an event that gave a new and fortunate turn, as he sees it in retrospect, to his development. Through Cohen's immediate agency, Santayana saved him from Nietzsche and Unamuno. The banner of unreason which, unwittingly, he had been flying, was to be hauled down. It had flapped in the wind too long. In its stead went up the colors of the life of reason. But Alonzo would never deny his early mentors, the German and the Spaniard and the man at whose feet he never sat, officially, who believed that only knowledge is power.

But this man, Cohen, for whom Alonzo had quickly developed immense admiration, respect, and gratitude, had a side to him that was not admirable. Cohen could on occasion be a merciless person who used wit, irony, sarcasm, and outright rudeness without mercy, to annihilate a student. Had Alonzo known when he accepted Weiss's invitation to talk to the philosophy club about this aspect of Cohen he would have turned down the invitation and the course of his life might have been considerably different. A short time after his talk Alonzo sneaked into Cohen's famous course on Santayana's *The Life of Reason* and was present at an incident that exhibited Cohen's ruthlessness. A student objected to something Santayana held.

"But Mr. Cohen," said the student, "that is not noble enough."
"So, how far up the hierarchy should it be, to be noble enough for you?" replied Cohen in a cutting voice. You could hear the Yiddish *nu*, behind the *so*, in the accent.
"Mr. Cohen," said the student firmly, "I did not mean noble in that sense, I meant it is not high enough."

"So," said Cohen, "how high above sea level should it be to satisfy you?"

"Mr. Cohen," returned the student trying to hold his ground in spite of the snickers of the class, who fully enjoyed the roughing up the poor fellow was getting, "you know I do not mean 'high' in that sense. You know what I mean."

"But if *you* know what you mean," returned Cohen enjoying his triumph, "why don't you say it?"

The class was by now in a state of total enjoyment. They came to Cohen's classes not only because Cohen was a superb teacher, endowed with a powerful mind, but also because they enjoyed the ruthless wit of the master. Very few dared get into the ring with him. And those who did once, were soon dragged out by arms and legs, and seldom climbed into it a second time. The ruthlessness was part of Cohen's teaching technique, and it could not have succeeded anywhere else than in City College at the time. For it was still a time when the majority of the students, Jews, brought from home a deep respect for knowledge and reverence toward thinking and learning.

4

Alonzo turned to Santayana as a man would who has been crawling in the desert for hours and unexpectedly comes upon a cool, clear stream. He drank copiously of the wisdom of his newly found master. Here was a philosopher who was systematic, whose thought was well-grounded on principles that could be stated clearly and could be defended, and one who, moreover, covered the whole range of human experience. *The Life of Reason* was made up of five volumes, the first of which, *Reason in Common Sense*, the foundation of the edifice, expounded a theory of knowledge, and above it in four tiers, were reared a theory of society, of religion, of art, and of science.

The Life of Reason was not only a persuasive discussion of the good life and how it could be achieved but it was also a philosophy of history that, or so Alonzo thought, withstood empirical examination. As moral theory it defined the good life as a harmonious organization of desires which, each by itself, was neither good nor bad. A desire could be said to be good or bad by the effect it had on the organization of desires. It was good if its satisfaction helped the satisfaction of the others, it was bad if it hindered it. As a philosophy of history, Santayana argued in what Alonzo took to be three masterly chapters that there had

been periods in which men had not yet achieved the life of reason, periods of prerational morality or of barbarism; and there had been others
in which men had tried the life of reason and found it wanting; these
were periods of postrational morality, of decadence. And there had
been one glorious period, which Santayana referred to under the name
of Hellas, in which reason had governed men. It was to bring about another such period that Santayana urged his reader to achieve harmony
within himself and within his city. This at least was what Alonzo found
in Santayana in the joyful flush of his discovery.

Santayana's philosophy had two essential requirements: It was a
materialism in which there was room for all the values of the spirit and
it was a philosophy that spoke in the idiom of the twentieth century.
Santayana himself was indeed very much a man of the twentieth century—a cosmopolitan who, since men must be born somewhere and
must have parents in order to come about, had met these requirements, but had soon left them behind, and was as much at home in
London or Oxford, in Paris or Rome, as he was in Spain. He had tried
to be but had never been at home at Harvard. Santayana could be admired as a man, and his work could be admired as more than philosophy. He had walked out of Harvard one day, the first man ever to
leave of his own volition this Heaven on Earth, this Jerusalem of all
academics born west of the Atlantic. And writing from Oxford, from
Paris, from Rome, he treated the provincialism and the barbarism of
his mother's country not with anger but with superbly condescending
irony. Here was a man whose contributions were welcomed by literary
magazines of the highest quality—*The Dial* for instance—as were his
technical papers by professional academic journals.

The whole range of human experience was organized in the five
books of *The Life of Reason* with a wit, an urbanity, a grace, and a lord-
ly authority that were as rare among philosophers as they were the essence of high quality. There was much that was attractive about his
thought, but chiefly, for Alonzo, after the disdainful dismissals of
Nietzsche and the concentration on a few themes of Unamuno, there
was Santayana's catholic mind—*catholic*, of course, with a small *c*.
Although an unbeliever, he treated religion with sympathy. Art he discussed with the authority of an insider, as the maker that he was and
not as a mere spectator. Alonzo, who had always valued good writing,
could value Santayana as much as he could value Nietzsche and Unamuno, for although his style was not to be compared to theirs, it was

in its own kind the attainment of perfection. The preciosity of Santayana's prose, the fundamental, the ineradicable obscurity of his
thought, and its many other defects, did not trouble Alonzo at the
moment. Here were wisdom and insight and wit and beauty fused into
one.

There was much to be valued in the thought of the author of *The
Life of Reason*. It was immensely relevant to Alonzo's need of the
hour. A full immersion in Santayana revealed to him how overcharged
had been the universe in which he had dwelt since his discovery of
Nietzsche and Unamuno, worlds from which, thanks to Cohen, he
had escaped. It was very pleasant, very invigorating, to breathe dry,
crisp, cool air, and that was what Alonzo now realized he had lacked
and now had in rich abundance.

But where had he picked up the notion that the schools that had
dominated the academic scene in the United States until only an hour
or two ago, as such things go, did not meet the needs of a free mind?
Wherever he had picked up this notion, he took it for revealed truth.
He knew nothing of Royce or Peirce, little of Bergson, and Santayana
had closed for him the thought of James—for *Character and Opinion
in the United States* was, of course, along with everything else that
Santayana published, part of the new revelation. As to Dewey, his war
record, which Alonzo understood to have been shameful, made him
unavailable. And the Germans? Well, the Germans had had their day.
Ditto for the British idealists. It was time to let the dead bury their
dead. One might as soon ask about the Chaldeans or the Etruscans.

The fertility of Santayana's philosophy had its source in the principle in which it took root, the insight that everything ideal had a natural
basis and much that was natural a possible ideal development. In this
principle was also to be found the secret of its strength for the modern
mind: You did not need to appeal to miracles or transcendent factors
or mysteries or authoritative revelations. If a human institution had
lasted and thus seemed indispensable in history, it had a solid natural
basis and that basis could be discovered by looking for the actual operative human needs it met. Because its central concern was the recognition of the extant needs of men, it was a generous and liberating philosophy. No arbitrary prohibitions that were beyond the examination of
reason, no parochial taboos imposed on the chafing soul and body under the arrogant claim that they were universally valid categorical imperatives. Santayana's authority rested on his lucidity and the attrac-

tiveness of his conception of the good life. The arrogance of Nietzsche was accounted for in *The Life of Reason* indirectly, and in *Egotism in German Philosophy* directly. The agonizing of Unamuno was also accounted for indirectly. It was the wringing of hands of a man who could not accept the nature of things. This was a peculiar form of post-rational morality. Here then, in Santayana, was a philosophy that encouraged a man to be what there was in him to become by permitting the expression of his virtues and powers under only one controlling rule: that any desire that sought satisfaction had to allow others, or as many of the others as possible, to find satisfaction.

But, perhaps above all, here was a philosophy that did not have the redolence and exclusive concern with technicalities, the tired dullness that Alonzo had already begun to notice was the distinguishing mark of academic philosophy. He could never think of the teachers of philosophy that even at that early date had already begun to pullulate in the universities without seeing men with dandruff on the back of their jackets and a high polish on the bottom of their blue serge trousers.

Alonzo soon found out that for the most part academic philosophers did not think highly of Santayana and when they condescended to notice him, their objections were academic in the worst sense of the term, or trivial or both. It was not difficult to see that one of the reasons for looking down on a man who had had the effrontery to leave Harvard to roam about where his fancy led him was the elegance of his prose. A man who could write as well as Santayana could not be a sound thinker. But reading about Santayana, Alonzo was soon to find out that there was one serious objection to *The Life of Reason* as a moral philosophy that Santayana could not dispose of. Santayana was a consistent materialist and an epiphenomenalist, which is to say that he believed that the propulsive force, the direction and control of both the universe and man, were the energies resident in the material world. But these energies were blind. Bursting with energy, as matter might be, or if you preferred it, being energy itself, matter was, nevertheless, blind. It was not something capable of the calculations, anticipations, and reckonings which reason had to undertake to lead man to happiness. Mind was there, and mind could carry on these calculations and anticipations if it decided to do so. But plans and calculations had nothing to do with the propulsion of matter, which went where it did irrespective of the plans that mind had carefully laid out for it. Mind, of course, there was; and if a materialistic philosopher or a psychologist argued that it was nothing more than the gurgling of a larynx, surely there was a difference between such a gurgling and the embarrassing rumblings of an overfed stomach. But for the epiphenomenalist, mind was only a noninterfering spectator, utterly incapable of wresting from the energies of matter the reins that would be needed to control the process.

Thus the life of reason was at worst a glaring inconsistency and at best an idle dream of impotent reason. In no case could there be a life of reason. This inconsistency was discovered by Santayana's critics early in the century, shortly after the publications of the five volumes of *The Life of Reason*. All one had to do was to come upon it to see it for what it was. When Alonzo came upon it he realized that he was more or less where he had started from. The pleasant dream that was to free him from the irrationalities of Unamuno and Nietzsche was only a dream. Having been awakened by Santayana's contradiction he had to acknowledge to himself that he was still in trouble.

III

State at Midland City

1

ON A COLD, drizzling morning Alonzo found himself listening to a welcoming address, given in the open air, by State University's new president, Mr. Pound, at Midland City. Midland was then a town of between fifty and sixty thousand inhabitants, charming, thoroughly civilized, and very proud of its culture. Of it an erudite poet, who soon became a good friend of Alonzo's, had written in a sonnet sequence.

> The shining City of my manhood grief
> Is girt by hills and lakes (the lakes are four).

Alonzo had just registered at State as a Gale scholar, a special scholarship for students who had given some evidence of literary talent. The evidence that Alonzo had given consisted of a few reviews for *The Nation* that had impressed Krutch and his friends.

At State Alonzo was given two and a half years of credit for his previous schooling. But he was under no illusions; he knew that his schooling was exiguous. He had begun to see more or less clearly that he had not developed methods of study and had not learned how to read and digest what he read; since he still read for what interested him, he was not able to give an adequate account of what the text contained. Worse, he lacked the tools for an education. Worse yet, while he was right not to respect the man who sought learning in order to exhibit it, Alonzo confused the scholar-peacock with the man who sought knowledge in order to slake his thirst for it. Knowledge he valued, but the knowledge he valued was prejudicially selected. For sound scholarship, lacking an understanding of it, he had no use.

Alonzo had found his way to State through the suggestion of friends in Greenwich Village, because he had begun to see clearly that he was up against a serious difficulty. He had to find some way of making a living that was compatible with his aim: leisure to read and write. He had tried all sorts of jobs and had found none that could give him what he needed. He tried writing for money but soon found that what he could write did not sell and what sold he did not want to and could not write. There was another factor aggravating his difficulty. During his years in Greenwich Village he has discovered that, however deep and genuine was his revolt against his family and their respectable bourgeois way of life, however much he wanted to live the life of a bohemian, he lacked the necessary psychological equipment of the true bohemian. To continue to live as he had been living in the Village in the last few years he had to be a true bohemian.

The Prince of Bohemians in Greenwich Village in the middle twenties and for quite some time afterward was Joe Gould. Alonzo often had Joe up for breakfast in his attic room in West Eighth Street. The better he got to know Joe, the clearer it became to Alonzo that he did not have the psychology that enabled Joe to live the kind of life he lived. Alonzo was too proud to be forever pursuing a handout from friends. And he could not get used to going about unwashed and in the dirty shirts and shabby, greasy clothes in which Joe lived and, apparently, slept. But more important, he could not stand the anxiety of not knowing where his next meal would be coming from. Without these qualifications a man could not plan to become a free lance.

Joe could and loved it. Those who did not see that Joe could do it with what was undeniably some dignity, were imperceptive or did not know the man well enough. Joe had decided, for God knows what reason, that he was a clowning dog and that the world was his hydrant. But if you had heard Joe read his essay on the sinking of the Titanic, as Alonzo had, you knew that back of the clowning and the bumming for half dollars (he would settle for less if you could not afford the four bits), back of the dirt and studied quips, back of the deliberately perverse humor, there was a man.

At State Alonzo met Antonio Solalinde, a distinguished hispanist who was married to a woman friend of Alonzo's family in New York. Solalinde urged Alonzo to stay at State and get a Ph.D. with the aim of teaching. But the idea of becoming a professor was not at all attractive. He did not want, nor was he ever wholeheartedly to want to be a professor. From Mencken he had acquired a radical distrust of the academic life, and it would take much living, some painful experiences, and a few pleasant ones, to get rid of the stereotype of the professor that he had picked up from Mencken and Ludwig Lewisohn. What he wanted was to live a life of the man of letters with philosophy as his central concern. But to live the life of a man of letters one had to eat and one needed leisure, and he had found no means of getting what he wanted.

After much hesitation he accepted the compromise that Solalinde had urged on him, with one important mental reservation: he would meet academic requirements as best he could; he would get a Ph.D.; but he would not forget, he would try never to forget, that he worshiped at an altar different from that of academics to the manor born. Early at State a young instructor in the Department of Philosophy had taken him aside and in friendship warned him that if he continued to write for *The Nation* he could not expect to get along in the university world. Alonzo thanked the friend for his kind interest but decided that if he could not make it on his own terms he would not make it at all.

But what was wrong with the university world? In 1926, when Alonzo was trying to make up his mind about an academic career, universities were redoubts of conservatism and puritanism: They stood for everything Alonzo stood against and against everything he stood for. They were the citadels of aggressive conservative values, and one of the reasons he hesitated to "take a chance on an academic career," when he decided to go into philosophy, was his knowledge that the philosophy and English departments of the land considered themselves the guardians of the Anglo-Saxon tradition and were not open to foreigners: not open to Catholics (among whom he might be reckoned) or Jews or people like himself with a Latin-American background.

After fighting it out with himself, Alonzo made up his mind: He would continue his graduate work toward a Ph.D. in philosophy. But he did not think of it as anything more than a choice of the least undesirable of several alternatives. What made the compromise possible was that the prospect of a job at a university met two basic, indispensable requirements: It offered him a modicum of leisure and a promise of security. This was before the crash. The promise of leisure was fully met. True, the university put in his way an obstacle in the form of "requirements" for the Ph.D. But these could be met somehow, seeking always the way that permitted a minimum of trouble. On the other hand the university made available to him a good library; and once he began teaching, it required of him that he read philosophy, which for the most part, he found superbly interesting. The university environment did not provide him with rebellious friends, people as interesting as the friends he was leaving behind in New York. But Sarah, his wife, had come to Midland City, Solalinde and William Ellery Leonard, in spite of their ranks, were genuine friends; and there were a number of young people at State, who although they did not have the fury of rebellion in their souls that burned in his, were stimulating individuals capable of looking at the academic world ironically. And thus the first seven or eight years at State were more or less happy years.

The compromise was also made viable by the discovery he made the first day he stood in front of a class. As a teacher he was a natural, and teaching was fun. He could hold the attention of the class, he could handle it without fear of running into problems of discipline; and as he was usually prepared, he could impart to his students ideas and information that most of them found interesting.

2

In his own teachers Alonzo was for the most part very fortunate. The first year at State he majored in Spanish literature and took all the philosophy he had room for in his schedule. Antonio Solalinde was a gifted teacher, a learned man, and a man who, although a philologist and a painstaking editor, could make his course on the Drama of the Golden Age a most exciting adventure. But Alonzo's heart was not in Spanish literature, and to get a Ph.D. in Spanish he would have had to plow through a vast amount of dull stuff written between the end of the Golden Age and the Generation of 1898. This was more than he could stomach. Alonzo had read Pérez Galdóz and knew Bécquer and a few writers previous to the Generation of 1898; but from the golden period until you came to Unamuno, Baroja, Azorín, Valle Inclán, and the other writers of ninety-eight he found Spanish literature extremely dull; Alonzo could very well do without it. As for Spanish-American literature, very little of it was of major value. After one year in the Spanish department he took a chance and transferred to the philosophy department.

The philosophy department received him cordially and gave him an assistantship before he had completed his requirements for the bachelor's degree. Because he had begun to appear in print a few years earlier, the department thought he was better trained in philosophy than he was. But he worked hard to make up for his ignorance and he enjoyed his work.

The philosophy department at State was small. It included two professors who were distinguished men, highly respected by the profession, E. B. McGilvary and F. C. Sharp. McGilvary was an outstanding teacher and a thinker of great acuity. When Alonzo first reached State, McGilvary was beginning to write once more—an activity that had been interrupted for a number of years by the shock of a personal loss. His son, a most promising young man, had joined the American Escadrille and fought in Italy under, or at any rate with, La Guardia. The murder of McGilvary's son upon return from the war had thrown McGilvary into a shock. But when Alonzo began his work under him, his classes had the freshness and the excitement that a class can have when the students are being treated to the spectacle of the birth of thought.

While a demanding teacher, McGilvary was, above all, scrupulously fair and both in the classroom and in his office he was unsparing of his time in his efforts to answer questions. He was patient; he was never too busy to enter into a discussion if you knocked at the door of his office; he was occasionally amused by Alonzo's unacademic approach to technical problems, but he never descended with him or any of his students to the level of personalities. Alonzo soon noticed an admirable quality of McGilvary the teacher. If a student's question was either foolish or made little sense, or was irrelevant, McGilvary had a way of listening patiently to it. When the student was through, McGilvary would reply with a variant of the following request, "I am not sure I understand you. If you will let me rephrase your question, to make sure that I have not misunderstood it, what you are asking is . . . ." As rephrased, the question became either intelligent, or relevant, or important, or all three at once; and it left the student with his self-respect. He never ridiculed a student; his was a totally different technique from Cohen's.

McGilvary was a thoroughly well-educated man, a man who had a wide range of knowledge, although it took time for one to discover it, for he was too serious a scholar to be animated by the desire to display it. His prose was elegant, although in his writing all he strove for was lucidity. He was as much a precisionist in oral discussion as in his writing; and he was a formidable opponent in argument. Alonzo never saw him lose his temper with a student in a discussion, however foolish the young person's questions might be. He listened seriously to objections and always met them head on, or indicated that this or that was the best that could be done, given the nature of the problem. The slick evasiveness of some teachers was not in harmony with his character. Unfailingly urbane, slightly formal although warm, McGilvary was a scholar-gentleman of the old style.

If McGilvary's training sharpened and disciplined the mind dialectically, Mr. Sharp trained the student in the way of scrupulous scholarship and alerted him to the complex problems of moral philosophy, particularly British ethical theory. F. C. Sharp did not have the graciousness and the charm of McGilvary, but he was a dedicated teacher, eager to help any student who sought him for help in his field, ethics, of which he was a master. For German philosophy he did not seem to have much sympathy but he knew the history of British ethics thoroughly. Mr. Sharp—or Professor Sharp, for none of his students would have dared address him, any more than he would have dared address Mr. McGilvary in any other way—was no less of a finished gentleman than McGilvary. But in the classroom he did not generate the intellectual excitement that McGilvary generated. Alonzo soon discovered, however, that Sharp was a thorough, exacting but fair teacher, conscientious, accurate, well-informed and utterly devoted to his subject, ethics. He put considerable time into the preparation of his seminars, as was evident from the notes he brought to class and the questions he asked. His seminars were not conducted as a free discussion session as were McGilvary's. He started at his right, and managed to ask a question of each student, in order. He stuck strictly to those topics necessary to cover the subject thoroughly. In Sharp's seminar one answered questions or asked them; one did not advance opinions; the questions students asked were invariably answered if they were relevant, politely dismissed if they were not. Consequently the student, knowing what he was in for, prepared with care. The two hours a week spent with Sharp in the classroom did not have the free-wheeling quality that gave McGilvary's seminars the excitement and educational value for the student of philosophy. With Sharp one stuck to the chapter and left it when Sharp was satisfied that it had been thoroughly covered. The upshot was that one knew what he was expected to know and knew it well—or didn't, and then Mr. Sharp knew that one did not know it. A clever student of philosophy can always bluff in a discussion, but Mr. Sharp could not be bluffed. He asked straight questions to which there were, and to which he expected, straight answers.

Alonzo purposely delayed taking his preliminaries for as long as the department would allow it. When he was finally forced to take them the one subject about which he was altogether free from anxiety was ethics. He did not know, as Mr. Sharp did, the differences between the several editions of Sidgwick's *Methods of Ethics*; but had it been required of him, he would have known them, for Sharp would have seen to it that he did. He knew the methods, however, and was quite ready to prove "the unity of the moral consciousness of the race," although he was never convinced by Sharp that the unity was to be found in universalistic utilitarianism.

Mr. Sharp was kind and generous in a much more obvious way than McGilvary, and while he was not as much of a *simpático* as McGilvary, he was more friendly to the student. He was less reserved. One found out his political and moral beliefs sooner and more clearly than one did McGilvary's. Nor would Alonzo or anyone else have dreamed of contradicting him. It took Alonzo no time to develop respect for the thoroughness of the scholarship and the conscientiousness of the teacher that Mr. Sharp so abundantly possessed; but while it took him some time to develop an affection for Sharp, when he did, it was without reservations.

3

Mr. Sharp's moral philosophy had been wrought with the care and the skill of a Swiss watchmaker, but it had the strength that a military engineer gives his defenses. Sharp had surveyed the problems and had found answers for all of them; there was little that escaped his scholarly attention. To achieve his ends he employed the empirical method with scrupulous care—a method that many of those American philosophers who consider themselves empiricists do not usually employ or pay any attention to. Of course, fashions in philosophy change rapidly, and Sharp's main contribution, a treatise he called *Ethics*, sounds today as "dated" as some treatises in metaphysics written by idealists in the nineteenth century. But what a sad comment on our notion of the value of the works of the mind, when we ignore the fruits of a life of dedicated labor of the highest integrity, spent cultivating a discipline whose name is the love of wisdom, as we ignore last year's products of the *haute couture*. In our scholarly world wisdom is seasonal and the truths of yesterday will be as invalid tomorrow as styles in dress. While claiming dedication to the pursuit of truth, scholars are as conscious of fashion as debutantes. Ours is not an age of the horse and buggy. Once in a while, a rare while, one runs into a reference to Sharp's *Ethics*. But contemporary ethicists have no knowledge of it, and no use for the method employed by him, although it was as empirical as one can employ on the subject matter of morality.

Alonzo valued highly the method employed by Sharp and in his own work on aesthetics he used it, but he could not accept the results so carefully arrived at by his teacher. Sharp was as conscientious in his thinking as he was in his teaching, as honest, as thorough, his views as meticulously defined, with a probity and a scrupulous attention to detail that were admirable. But utilitarianism, whether egoistic or universalistic, was not Alonzo's cup of tea.

The standard arguments against utilitarianism have long been known and Alonzo was not ignorant of them. Sharp knew them and answered them with ease. But his refutations did not convince Alonzo. There were two sets of reasons keeping Alonzo from accepting Mr. Sharp's system. The first was objective; the second, of course, subjective.

Since the utilitarian argues that the good is the pleasure of the greatest number, he will have to agree that the Roman Circus was, in its day, a good, since the greatest number of Romans derived great pleasure from it, and those that did not—their number is unknown—must have been small by comparison to those who did. But the Roman Circus could never have been right, since it not only gave expression to the brutal impulses of the Roman people, but by so doing, it increased and intensified those impulses. Only a radically committed cultural relativist can say that what the Romans found to be good was good for them. But can a cultural relativist who is a utilitarian say that the killing of the decrepit and the mentally crippled by the Nazis was a good? For the most part it was done painlessly. The nonsensical aim of improving the quality of the nation can be ignored. But it did indeed increase the pleasure of those who were not killed, the majority, since it increased the quantity of the food available to them and it relieved them of the pain, the burden, of caring for the crippled and the decrepit. In terms of pleasure, no doubt, in the long run and perhaps in the short, the effect would have been an increase of pleasure for the fit. The utilitarian, since he cannot have a concept of the sacredness of the personality, has no defensible ground for objecting to the killing of the unfit, for the temporary pain of those close to the victims could not compare with the increased pleasure of those who profited by the killing.

Because Alonzo was fully aware of Mr. Sharp's moral rectitude, he concocted a casuistic story designed to test Mr. Sharp's commitment to his theory. The story was about a man who was distributing dope to public and high school students in order to hook them. What he was doing was known, but somehow he had placed himself entirely beyond the reach of the law. Was it right for a man who could murder this criminal in such a way that it was not known it was a murder, to do it? The full story, in all its complexity, is not to the point here. It was intended to elicit an answer to the question while rigorously ignoring all such aspects of a complex act that could be said to imperil the principle of the greatest good of the greatest number. The story was not intended as a refutation of universalistic utilitarianism as such; it was an inquiry about how long Mr. Sharp was willing to stick by his theory. After a lengthy discussion it became clear to Alonzo that Mr. Sharp did not want to approve the murder. Mr. Sharp was no more consistent than the rest of us. Some of his conduct was ruled by maxims deeply ingrained in him that had nothing to do with his theory of universalistic utilitarianism.

One weakness of Mr. Sharp's utilitarianism was sufficiently radical to render it inadmissible. Hard as it was for Alonzo to believe, Mr. Sharp did not account for the sense of categorical obligation and did not seem to understand the meaning of the term, or rather the part it played in ethical theory and in moral experience. The ought, the voice of conscience, to which Bishop Butler had given such concentrated attention in an age of cynics and blatant egoists and which was one of the two fundamental notions in Kant's moral theory, did not seem to have any function whatever in Mr. Sharp's theory. The genesis of the phenomenon of obligation can be explained in several ways psychologically—none satisfactorily. But its validity, whatever its genesis, called for an account that was absent in Sharp's theory.

This led to Nietzsche's criticism of utilitarianism, the force of which Mr. Sharp simply did not feel. He dismissed Nietzsche's criticism of bourgeois values as he dismissed the whole of Nietzsche's philosophy, with a wave of the hand: it was not worthy of serious attention by a serious philosopher.

Alonzo was very much concerned with the problem that arose when a man or a people felt the need to disregard consequences. Mr. Sharp accounted for it by the observation that it was sometimes necessary to disregard immediate consequences for the sake of maintaining the principle of the greatest good, for in the long run the maintenance of the principle might affect a larger number of people. If a principle is disregarded the act would lay down a precedent that would lead to consequences as bad or worse in the future. But Alonzo took this solution of the problem to be a partial answer. He could think of many casuistic examples in which the principle that denied the relevance of practical consequences now or later, claimed absolute primacy. A dramatic instance was that of a person or a whole people who stood by a principle when so doing meant a total catastrophe. As far as the utilitarian could explain the fact of standing by a principle irrespective of consequences the explanation ignored the nobility of the act and the admiration it elicited from people who did not approve of the principle for which sacrifice was made. Instances of this phenomenon were common in war, when one side admires the conduct of the adversary and thus approves of it.

Thus viewed, what was wrong with utilitarianism was that it was blind to the need for the heroic dimension in human beings. Otherwise stated, the ought often transcends any reasonably conceived sense of what is or is not useful at the present or at a later time. Utilitarianism cannot account for certain kinds of heroism the consequences of which are not only disastrous to those who act heroically but benefit no one else. Grant for the sake of the argument, that the heroic self-sacrifice of an individual is often useful to a group, of what usefulness can we say is the sacrificial heroism of a whole group? Yet we often approve of it. Alonzo did not find it difficult to see that utilitarianism tends to push towards the rear certain virtues, to downgrade others, and to ignore or even dismiss others—virtues that are essential to certain forms of excellence.

The limitations of utilitarianism came out most clearly in Hume, whose moral theory has been greatly admired but that seemed to Alonzo to be narrow and parochially intolerant, for all the irenic decor with which it was adorned. In *An Enquiry Concerning the Principles of*

Morals the Stoics are dismissed with contempt and without any understanding of their vision of life and its relevance to the situation from which that vision emerged. We are told by Hume that the Stoics with their perpetual cant concerning virtue, their magnificent professions and scant performance—Seneca was not a morally admirable man—bred contempt in mankind. But not all Stoics had been Senecas, and Alonzo had learned—was it from Stokes's little book on Stoicism?—that Stoicism had made it possible for the Romans to carry the heavy burden of empire. But then there were many peculiar blind spots in the much admired Hume, as for instance, his dismissal of Thucydides because he recounts the trivial encounters of the small cities of Greece; as for instance, the fact that he has so little to say and what he says is so utterly inadequate, because it is ambivalent, about heroism and grandeur; and again, as for instance, his dismissal of the religious aspirations of men and the way in which men have expressed them—through celibacy, fasting, penance, mortification, self-denial, humility, silence, solitude, and other virtues of the kind, disposed of by Hume as "the whole train of monkish virtues" that, he tells us, are "rejected by men of sense." Who were men of sense? Of course, men like Hume and his kind.

Alonzo's difficulties with Sharp's philosophy could be resolved if one could trace them to a difference in temperament and nothing more. But no such way out was acceptable to Alonzo. That temperamental differences contributed to differences between thinkers and that they may—probably do—play a varying part in the choices men make of philosophies, it is not possible to deny. But if they played an exclusive or even a dominant role, the choice of a philosophy would tend to be more or less as arbitrary a matter as the preference for bourbon over scotch or rye. Such subjectivism did not make any sense whatever of what could be found by even a superficial perusal of the history of philosophy, particularly the persistent search for objective truth, the dramatic struggle against what philosophers took to be error. Of course they might have been mistaken and the subjectivist might have been right. But Alonzo could not dismiss the history of philosophy with such assurance and in such sweeping terms.

At the time Alonzo was struggling with Sharp's views, towards the end of the twenties and during the early thirties, he did not know how to account for Sharp's inability to convince him, although there was no question that his teacher had forged a formidable engine, protected by impenetrable armor and equipped with logical cannon of great range and penetrating power. In 1933 Alonzo came upon Vernon Lee's *Music and Its Lovers*, and this book brought about a crystallization in his mind of matter that had lain there in solution for some time. Nietzsche had written much about two types of art, the Apollonian and the Dionysian, and Alonzo was acquainted with psychologists and aestheticians who had investigated the different modes of response to art. He was acquainted, of course, with William James's *The Varieties of Religious Experience*. But somehow he had missed the import of these investigations. Vernon Lee's book now made him see that the full significance and difficulty of these problems was both methodological and substantive. Vernon Lee herself did not go beyond relativism; there were two general modes of response to music, the listener's, as she called it, and the hearer's. She did not see how one could choose one over the other. But this was, for Alonzo, an inadmissible conclusion. Sharp, a full-fledged, armchair anthropologist, had faced the problem of varieties of moral response. Fully reckoning with the varieties of moral response—the diversity and heterogeneity of value patterns and the cultural pluralism of mankind—Sharp had sought to go beyond this pluralism to what he called "the unity of the moral consciousness of the [human] race."

By the expression Sharp meant that back of all serious and responsible moral judgments, when uttered properly by competent judges, is the criterion of utility for the group affected by the judgment. This in turn meant that the moral judgment was made from the standpoint, not of private interests of single men, but from the standpoint of disinterested spectators who could judge fairly all needs by whomsoever concerned. That such judgments are actually uttered, Mr. Sharp could show with interesting empirical examples. What he never faced was the fact that the defect of his theory lay at its roots, in the elastic meaning of the term *utility*. This was, for Alonzo, the radical problem.

Alonzo was confident that the moment one tried to state what was meant by *useful* or by *utility*, it would turn out that it was so elastic a notion that it would be impossible to arrive at agreement about its meaning. Above the minimal biological level, a level at which no human community lived except perhaps in extreme situations of a calamitous nature, such as a number of men in a lifeboat at sea beyond the hope of rescue or a community hit by a natural disaster, the useful was determined by social factors: custom, availability of resources, the level of technological development a community has achieved, and other factors of the kind.

What is useful? Is it what is truly useful or what men take to be useful? If the former, how does one define human needs? Up to the eighteenth century philosophers had no trouble. Man was conceived of as exemplifying those needs in an ascending scale that ended with eighteenth-century European man at the top, at the very summit of this fortunate group, the upper classes, and crowning them, stood the English upper classes. The reason savages and *infima species* of humanity had no need of what the upper classes in Europe needed is that they had not developed sufficiently to need it. But such an attitude was not possible in the twentieth century, not because it was *passé* but because it had been liquidated by Darwin and Franz Boas—using both names eponymically. Until we could come up with a definition of man that stood up against the attacks of relativists it was idle to speak of what was truly useful for men.

Or is the useful what men take to be useful? If this is the case, in the very short run it turns out to be, above basic biological needs, what men are accustomed to. What is useful is a mere accommodation, mere habitual acceptance, of what is available, given social arrangements as well as "natural resources." The so-called natural resources were not natural materials there in the soil or above the ground, but what men in their ingenuity had found the means of turning to their use. The vast material resources of the United States—coal, iron, oil, and the rest—were there before the white arrived, but the aborigines had no awareness of their existence, although some tribes used shale; they simply had no knowledge of how to use them. In any case, what is useful to a Jivaro Indian is not what is useful to an educated, upper-middle-class American and vice versa. But there was more, for the harsh fact is that men can get used to, and manage to live more or less satisfactory lives—or lives they consider satisfactory—under almost any condition. If we do not accept this harsh fact we would have to say that the inhabitants of the Kalahari Desert, or those of the desert of Central Australia, or the inhabitants of the northern polar regions, or some Brazilian Indians, are men who live in conscious and complete unhappiness. This is not the case.

It turns out then that utilitarian ethics is based on an implicit relativism, which the search for the unity of the moral consciousness of the race, had it been successful, could not have done away with. Why

had this not been noticed? Alonzo did not know, really, whether it had
or not, and he did not think it important to find out whether the critics
of utilitarianism had made this objection against the doctrine. In any
case he did not have to answer the question, if it had not been found
out, why it had not been. He was under no obligation to give an account of other men's errors, if he was reasonably certain that they were
indeed errors. But he had a hunch that the reason it had not been
noticed was that the utilitarians, whether living in the eighteenth,
nineteenth, or twentieth century, were equipped with what he thought
of as pre-Boas minds; minds, that is, that take for granted often without
awareness of their assumption, that the needs of the British or American middle-class people are standard human needs. But Mr. Sharp did
not make this mistake. He was fully aware that the diversity of value
patterns force on the moral philosopher one of his basic and most difficult problems. And Sharp thought he had found the answer, but he
had not.

There is a well-known scene in *King Lear* in which Goneril and
Regan take away from their father the last of his knights.

> GONERIL: Hear me, my lord,
> What need you five-and-twenty, ten, five,
> To follow in a house where twice so many
> Have a command to tend you?
> REGAN: What need one?

To which Lear, in a fit of anger whose edge is dulled by his dawning
sense of the futility of the struggle replies:

> O, reason not the need! Our basest beggars
> Are in the poorest thing superfluous.
> Allow not nature more than nature needs,
> Man's life is cheap as beast's. Thou art a lady:
> If only to go warm were gorgeous,
> Why, nature needs not what thou gorgeous wear'st
> Which scarcely keeps thee warm.

If it is true, as indeed it is, that if we allow not more than nature
needs, man's life is cheap as beast's, the unity of the moral consciousness of the race could not solve Alonzo's problem. For by the time he
began to work under Mr. Sharp Alonzo had begun to see what for him
was the central problem of ethics. With increasing clarity Alonzo saw

that a moral philosophy that did not offer a general formula for the moral resolution of radical moral conflicts was a philosophy that had no answer to a might-makes-right theory.

When Alonzo finished stating his reasons for rejecting utilitarianism I said to him that I had been acquainted with them but that I thought that below them there were subjective reasons. Wasn't that the case? Yes, very much so, he replied, and I am not in the least inclined to conceal the fact. To assume that one's response to a philosophical theory, particularly a moral theory, is based only on rational grounds, is to believe that the sole connection between one's mind and one's body is biological, and that the rest of one's psyche is hermetically sealed off from one's "reason." That is something that my old pal Greenstone or Haten could believe. And it may be the case when the mind is employed on pure mathematical problems—I say *may be*, not *is*, since the aesthetic element enters into the acceptance or rejection of proofs; but it is clearly not the case when the mind accepts or rejects philosophical theories, particularly moral theories, which somehow bear directly on one's conception of one's life and destiny. Any philosopher who claims that he is after the kind of truth the mathematician is after is an ass, and he brays because he does not know himself. In fact, my attitude toward utilitarianism is much more than objective, although the objective grounds I have adduced are sufficient to make it wholly inadmissible. But my rejection goes much deeper. The theory is profoundly repugnant to me, and sometimes I feel toward it as one feels toward something that is physically nauseating. A wholly coherent utilitarian, could I actually encounter one, would be as revolting as a human being could be. I would feel toward him as I would toward a Nazi who was posted to Auschwitz or Dachau; I would feel about him as I would toward a rat swimming in an open cloaca, as I would feel toward something foul and unendurable. But of course, no such person can exist, and a man like F. C. Sharp was a moralist whose code of conduct—as I have already asserted—went way beyond utility.

But please do not forget that I have never been in doubt, since I became acquainted with Sharp's theory, about its high importance. That importance consisted, for me, of his heroic effort, as I would put it, to take account of the pluralism of value patterns that are constitutive of the diverse human cultures we know about. Pluralism is a fact that Sharp tried to go beyond. Sharp posed the problem and tried to solve it. He failed to solve it, but he saw it clearly and tried to solve it.

You know why I believe the importance of the subject cannot be exaggerated. Moral relativists—Herskovits, for instance—base their views on the heterogeneity or pluralism of value patterns exhibited by cultures throughout the world and throughout history. But relativism in value theory, it is not difficult to see, leads fairly straight to might-makes-right—than which, as you know, I find few worse abominations in human action and theory.

4

Alonzo learned a most interesting and valuable lesson from Sharp. When he registered for his first class with Sharp, the latter was clearly an opinionated conservative. He was a perfect example of what his friends at *The Nation* were fighting against in politics, in cultural matters, and in morality. A convinced conservative, Sharp had no use whatever for anything Alonzo valued. Knowing that Alonzo had contributed a few reviews to *The Nation*, he snatched at the first opportunity that presented itself to let Alonzo know that he had no use for what *The Nation* stood for. Although not a teetotaler on principle he was one in practice. With intensity Sharp once said in a seminar that he'd just as soon allow an intoxicated man—not a drunk, but an intoxicated or perhaps, he said, an inebriated man—at his table as he would allow an open garbage pail to be brought into the dining room.

Alonzo at that time believed that conservatism, which to him was a sign of senility anyway and in young people a sign of premature senility, was a condition that increases with the years. But towards the end of his life Sharp's attitudes changed considerably. He became a tolerant man, morally broader, politically less intense and more irenic, and much more of an agnostic on social questions than he had been in the late twenties or early thirties. He was not for Franklin D. Roosevelt—one could not expect him to be. He did not serve martinis in his living room or wine at his table. But he did not refuse them at Alonzo's home. He widened his interests in his last years and gave evidence of a capacity for generosity and genuine charity toward men of whom he had always disapproved, that he had not permitted himself to show at an earlier period of Alonzo's acquaintance with him. If conservatism was a trait that increased with the years, Sharp's brand did not follow the rule, for in general he had become much more liberal than many of Alonzo's *soit-disant* liberal friends.

Although Sharp became more liberal than he was when Alonzo first made his acquaintance, it was only a matter of degree, for a conservative he remained until his death. However Alonzo learned to respect him for his political views as he learned to respect McGilvary, for both were men of solid value. They had their defects, these older gentlemen, and some of their defects were not venial vices but serious, unpleasant faults—which is to say that while these men were the product of a process of refinement they were, nevertheless, human beings. But they were men who embodied values of decency, honor, formality, and independence of mind and conscience. They were the inventors of door knockers, to vulgarize for my purposes a phrase from *The Portrait of A Lady*. They had their silly vanities, their capacity for enmity, and their purblind prejudices. They were oligarchical in their deepest instincts. But they did not pretend to be other than they were; and in Alonzo's experience one could depend on their word, their decency, their generosity, and on the largeness of their spirit and their minds; a largeness, as Alonzo soon found out, that is more genuinely liberal than the stingy concerns of the academic liberal.

IV

Teachers and "Teachers"

1

AFTER a short period in Philadelphia, where he served as consul of Venezuela, Alonzo returned to State with an appointment as part-time instructor of philosophy, in order to work toward his doctor's degree. Although still exiguously prepared, he was slightly better equipped to teach philosophy than he had been when he left State, for he had taken a couple of graduate courses at the University of Pennsylvania, had attended Albert C. Barnes's lectures at his Foundation in Merion, Pennsylvania, and had also done considerable reading because his consular duties took only a few hours a month. He had also begun to study more systematically than when he first went to State, because he was beginning to learn how to read.

Barnes's lectures made him realize that while he had thought he knew how to look at paintings, there was much in a canvas that had escaped him. Barnes's lectures were not the last thing in how to look at paintings—no one man's can be. But they made a fundamental and permanent difference in his life. As is well known, the Barnes collection is fabulous; as is less well known, Barnes was an excellent teacher who could point out much in a painting that Alonzo had never noticed before. Together with a magnificent collection of modern paintings and a few old ones the foundation housed a large and equally fabulous collection of African art of the highest aesthetic quality; Alonzo, who had never before looked at African art, began to appreciate its non-Western qualities, its own kind of beauty, lyricism, delicacy, sense of form, its own kind of powerful expressiveness, no less than a quality that was hard to put into words and which was decidedly an expression of the barbarism of the superb carvers that had made these things.

Barnes had never been in good repute because he was a very difficult man. He enjoyed fighting and had money to satisfy his taste for litigation. His teaching was limited in its scope. He avoided formalism by adding to the formal values of a painting that he perceived what he called *human values*. But being no philosopher he did not see that the addition merely covered up a difficult and fundamental problem about the relationship of form to substance in painting—a problem that all critics of any art and not merely of painting have to face—but came nowhere near resolving it. However, if you took Barnes as he came, with his limitations as well as his positive virtues, his lectures were a broadening and deepening experience. You stood with a small group of students in front of a picture and Barnes pointed out some feature of it—the disposition of masses, the treatment of depth, use of line, color, and the rest—you moved to another picture in another room and he pointed out similarities and contrasts with the one just discussed, and you moved to a third picture, and a fourth. As you moved from one picture to another and looked at what Barnes was pointing to, you had to admit to yourself that until then you had been nearly blind.

Much has been said of Barnes, much of it in denigration, and much of the latter in truth. His quarrel with Bertrand Russell has given him in addition to the place he earned in the history of art collection and appreciation in the United States, a secure place in the biographical history of modern philosophy; less well known is the fact that he learned what philosophy he knew from Dewey to whom he imparted a deep and broad interest in painting. It has been said among other things that he did not write the books that bear his name. But if you heard him lecture before a picture you realized immediately how utterly factitious this piece of gossip was; his books were completely authentic, although no doubt the women who surrounded him, all of them intelligent and well trained by him, made their contributions along the lines he had introduced to them.

Alonzo registered for graduate work in the University of Pennsylvania and the courses he took there differed widely in value from one another and from the work he had done at State. One thing they had in common: All of them were dull. If you judged by the Department of Philosophy at Penn, you could with justice say that one of the requirements for a Ph.D in philosophy was the capacity to sit through interminable hours of sheer unadulterated and unmitigated boredom. A seminar in aesthetics was as soporific a course as Alonzo ever took:

He could only compare it in its capacity to put him to sleep to a course in solid geometry he had taken in the Evening Session at CCNY years before. The aesthetician had published a book that was well written and here and there sparkled with brilliant prose; but as a lecturer, he was utterly dull, and no effort on Alonzo's part enabled him to keep his attention alert upon the teacher's remarks. A graduate course in the history of philosophy was of genuine value, although also dull. The third course for which he registered he dropped soon after the semester began, because it was given by a man who was silly if not malicious. The teacher was a distinguished thinker who claimed to have expounded behaviorism before Watson and proved it by pointing to the title of a book written before Watson made a name with his revolutionary doctrine. The seminar consisted of the teacher reading from the manuscript of a book already in the publisher's hands. There was a copy of the manuscript in the departmental library that the students were supposed to read in advance of each session. The teacher took special delight in reading long quotations in Italian, Latin, French, and German. Turning to the students, he would say with a smile, "As graduate students you are, of course, prepared to study philosophy, you have the tools." A long passage in a foreign language would follow. That he had a right to expect his students to understand German or French could not be denied, unrealistic as it was; to expect them to follow Italian or Latin was silly if it was not malicious. The subject of the seminar was important; the teacher, again, a distinguished thinker; but Alonzo did not get much out of the few sessions he attended. Since Alonzo was not planning to get his Ph.D at Penn, he dropped the course. It gave him more time to read.

2

Upon his return to State Alonzo became the assistant of Professor Maximilian Klotz, one of the most popular teachers of the university. Klotz taught a course in logic which registered between one hundred and twenty-five and one hundred and fifty students and a course in the nature of man and his place in the universe which sometimes registered as many as five hundred students. Maximilian Klotz was one of the four senior professors of the Department of Philosophy at State, but in spite of his great reputation as a teacher among the undergraduates, he was not teacher at all but the most relentless and successful propagandist not only in the philosophy department but in the whole College of Arts and Sciences. He never liked Alonzo and their close contact in the large course to which Alonzo was an assistant did not improve matters: Gradually Klotz became a determined enemy of Alonzo under a surface of friendliness. Behind his back some of the graduate students called Klotz "Maxie Waxie."

Maxie Waxie was a man who presented quite different facets to the various persons who had dealings with him; he was one of the storm centers at State—chiefly in his own conceit. Once a street corner evangelist in blue, after a career of saving souls for Christ with a tambourine, he had gotten a Ph.D. in philosophy at State and had been "teaching" there ever since. Though fully bedoctored, he had never lost the urge to save souls. At State he did it by means of his theatrics instead of his hymns and tambourine. An outstanding ham, he now had much larger audiences than had congregated around his troop in blue in the large middle western city where he carried on his work for the Lord. A superb speaker, he employed superior rhetorical powers in dishing out the thin gruel that he took to be philosophic wisdom— relativism and atheism. He was at his best before large audiences, especially when the audience was not altogether with him: The voice became softer and deeper, the attitude more gentle, the manner more appealing, expressing a generous desire to lead his students to a better life than their conservative parents led, if they accepted his reasonable views. His appeal was to the unconventional and critical resentment of the students towards the *status quo.* He addressed the students in a humor they could not miss and in a quasi-poetical language that was as corny as it was middle-to-low-brow. He suggested to them, clearly but never explicitly, that he and they were victims of an irrational system, hedging them around with absolutes and false theology. The students loved him and his message.

The substance of Maxie Waxie's courses went a long way toward proving the falsehood of the medieval maxim that nature abhors a vacuum, for although his lectures were chock full of puns, corny humor, pseudopoetry, sentiment, and propaganda, their philosophical content was very low. If you were near Klotz several days a week, you had to be blind not to perceive that he knew very little logic, and hated it intensely. Alonzo—who at the beginning of his relationship with Klotz was as ignorant as Klotz—once came upon a reference to the two meanings of *all.* The writer assumed that a man reading philosophy knew what they were. He asked Maxie Waxie what they were, and the latter was furious: it was evident that he did not know that *all* means all taken together, or *collectively*, and each and every one, or *distributively*.

Klotz hated logic because it boxed him in, expelling him from the comfortable, ambiguous, fluid universe of thought in which he loved to dwell, which allowed him to change his mind as his interests fluctuated, irrespective of promises or commitments he had made. The disjunctive syllogism he hated as intensely as one can hate a malicious power, since it forced him to take only one of two or more mutually exclusive choices. His argument against exclusive choices was that neither in nature nor in human relations can the sort of "joints" be found of which Plato spoke, since evolution presupposed a continuous change, and a division between one sort and the next was artificial. There are therefore no either/or's, it's always a question of more or less. The remedy for his aversion was beyond him; it was simply to think through the relationship between logic and reality. Even if one makes the false assumption that there are no joints in nature or in human events, which means that the world is not "logical," for the sake of clear thought distinctions must be made or the world becomes a *cauchemar* of indiscriminate change in which nothing is what it is because it could just as well be something else.

Klotz's relativism was anything but relativistic. He was, one felt like saying, "a born partisan" who was incapable of seeing any point of view but his own; all those who failed to agree with him were in error when they were not perversely seeking their selfish interests. Hadn't he reasonably explained to them why he had arrived at the conclusion he favored or at the choice he had selected? He did not say that error has no rights, but if you lived in close relationship with him, as you had to if you were his assistant, you gradually came to see that it was on this maxim that he acted. A hater, being the supreme actor he was, he managed to give the impression to those he had need to keep on his side that he was mild in his reproof or rejection of that which he put away from himself. Overwhelmed by a sense of his very humble antecedents—his father, he let once slip, had been a drunkard who could not keep the manual jobs he sometimes was able to get—he hated social distinctions until, through his friendship with Bill Folley, the man who for a time controlled the state, he became one of the two or three most powerful men at State. But just as the genuinely socially elect of Midland City—the old families—never accepted him, he never accepted them.

From his relativism some of his students naturally inferred that the girls of State should come of age in the same way as those of Samoa and that they, the boys, were the ones to help the girls grow up. A co-ed once told Alonzo that when a girl resisted the advances of a young man she was advised to take a course with Klotz. "He'll rid you of your silly antiquated prudishness."

That students should interpret Maxie Waxie's teaching in this manner was, in one sense, very incongruous, for his relativism was never intended to reach Samoa or cannibalism. The man who had shed his blue uniform, his tambourine, and Christ, and had put William James and John Dewey in Christ's place, had not rid himself of sexual prudishness.

In another sense, the use to which students put Maxie Waxie's teaching was not at all incongruous, for Klotz told his students that "good" was relative to desire, and if there was one good some of them desired strongly it was to help their dates grow up as girls do in Samoa. Had Klotz known the use to which his students put his wisdom, he would have had an apoplectic fit. But he could hardly have objected to the practical implications they drew from it, for he constantly repeated that the truth was what worked, and how better to put their truth to work—than in the back of a car or in the bushes in Willow Drive?

Alonzo assisted Maxie Waxie for five years, more than ample time to get to know him pretty well. The better Alonzo knew him the more puzzling became the problem the man presented to him. How did this man manage to give the favorable impression he gave to his friends? Alonzo tried several answers to the question but neither one nor all the answers taken together proved satisfactory. That the man could pour a torrent of charm as he did, at will, was not enough to account for the high esteem in which his friends held him. Maxie Waxie was fully aware of his charm, and an explicitly stated policy of his was to accept all invitations to speak outside the university, no matter how humble a group requested his presence, in order, as he put it, to show his fellow citizens that he was no devil. That he had a facile intelligence and a popular, if corny, sense of humor, and that he was a superb actor, were undeniable; but these traits in no way explained the warm regard his admirers had for him.

Alonzo's colleagues were, by and large, poor psychologists. By the time Alonzo had begun to assist Maxie Waxie he had found out that academics, however perspicuous about their fields of competence, were myopic about human beings and prone to take human appearance for reality; this held for professional psychologists as well as for grammarians, historians, teachers of literature and of course of philosophy.

His friends knew that Maxie Waxie had power through his friendship with the head of a powerful political family in the state; this accounted no doubt for the deference with which he was treated even by those who disliked his views and had no respect for his mind. After the head of the political family managed to oust President Pound from State Maxie Waxie had been one of the principal men who helped to choose the new president. That his admirers were partisans no doubt also accounted to some extent for the high esteem they expressed in public for him. When Klotz was attacked, they were in the habit of presenting a solid front to the enemy, and they would not have considered it shameful to be convicted of practicing the doctrine of double truth: exoteric truth for the public and esoteric truth among themselves. Their doctrine of double truth became evident when, occasionally, some of them let slip remarks in private that indicated clearly that the high esteem they expressed publicly for Klotz was not as unqualified as their exoteric expressions would lead one to believe. Indeed, the dean, a very discreet politician who occasionally could be astonishingly indiscreet, told Alonzo once, in the process of reassuring him that there would be a place for him at State (there were no tenure rules at State then) that Klotz was no philosopher.

When Alonzo put together all the reasons he could think of for Maxie Waxie's prestige, they did not add up to the enormous power he had gained in the institution. How did he get that way, how did he achieve the position he achieved? The solution Alonzo finally arrived at with great reluctance was that his problem arose from false assumptions. Alonzo had supposed all along that a distinguished university was, in academic terms, an essentially honest world, where scholarly fakes, men who did not measure up to the high academic standard of serious scholarship and honest teaching—honest, not necessarily good —did not get by. He was wrong, although he had a hard time bringing himself to acknowledge that he had been wrong.

When you got to know Maxie Waxie personally you discovered that in addition to his lack of seriousness in philosophy and his confusion of preaching with teaching, he was a pretty shabby sort, possessing a constellation of morally odious traits fairly well hidden behind a moral front. A liberal who had to be opposed on principle to class or racial prejudice of any kind, Maxie Waxie was, before his assistants, outspokenly anti-Roman Catholic, and did not always succeed in concealing his anti-Semitism, although, of course, some of his best friends . . . as indeed they were.

Egocentric and ungenerous under the pretense of being a generous and considerate man, he was self-righteous and had a great capacity for judging everything from a moral angle, and of course his judgments were always right and the judgment of those who differed from his were wrong. No, men uttering such opinions were not wrong, they were depraved, or perverse, or malicious. A relativist on principle, it did not take Alonzo long to discover the reason for Klotz's position: He used his relativism as a weapon against orthodoxy; his relativism did not issue in charity, tolerance, understanding of the multiplicity of human motives and heterogeneity of desires. Maxie Waxie gave the impression, at first, of being a tolerant man; his charm covered a great deal that came out slowly in your day-to-day relationship with him. Being a sensitive person, it did not take Klotz long to know where you stood toward him.

The psychological myopia that was common among the academics at State was not shared by Klotz. His sensitivity and his sense of insecurity led him to perceive shades of response to himself. But when you got to know him well you found that he had never overcome his tambourine days. Until he began to rise in the academic social scale through power, his taste was distinctly pedestrian, and his point of view, which he passed off as democratic, was sentimental and unsophisticated. As he rose in power he gained friends who redirected his taste, a German teacher of art history gave him a list of pictures to look at at the Art Institute of Chicago on a trip to the big city. His wife, a scrawny *alte Vettel* about a foot taller than he, directed his literary cultivation by forcing him to read the novels proclaimed weekly the masterpieces of the century by New York and Chicago book reviewers. But for literature Klotz had fundamentally nothing but contempt— probably a vestigial remainder of his evangelical days. Under the vainglorious democratic stance and frequent boast of his lowly origins, never concealed from his "academic family," as he called his assistants, pulsed the deep resentment and distrust of anyone he considered superior.

Vain, his vanity flowed from self-distrust and a deep sense of insecurity that led him to demand from his assistants flattery for everything he did or said. But for Alonzo Klotz's two hardest traits to bear were, first, his mendacity, next his repugnance to stick with a decision once he had arrived at one in what appeared to be a consultation with his assistants. Alonzo discovered how to deal with this unpleasant trait. After a discussion he would write Maxie Waxie a letter saying that it was his understanding that this or that decision had been arrived at; he would greatly appreciate being corrected if he was wrong. Maxie Waxie got furious every time he received such letters, but there was nothing he could do about it except increase his resentment toward Alonzo.

3

Although Klotz's lectures were immensely popular, the better students soon found out that there was very little to them. When in England, in the early thirties, Alonzo met a graduate of State who had married a teacher at the London School of Economics where she had gone for graduate work. Alonzo saw one of Maxie Waxie's books on her shelves. "Yes, I took his large course," she said, "and loved it. I thought it was wonderful. But I have found out what philosophy is since I came to England."

This usually happened with the good students, unless they were not interested in philosophical questions or were mainly concerned with social reform. Among lower classmen the popularity of his lectures did not diminish during the time Alonzo assisted him. But the intellectually sophisticated students and the philosophy majors and graduates found out when they took other courses with the serious teachers of the department that Maxie Waxie had cheated them, that there was no nutritional value in his thin, inspirational gruel. For all of Klotz's popularity among the majority of the undergraduates, it was not until he became chairman of the department that undergraduate philosophy majors began taking "advanced" courses with him and that graduates began doing their dissertations under him. After he became chairman, philosophy majors and graduates in philosophy avoided Alonzo. In Alonzo's advanced course in aesthetics, which had a sufficient registration not to be open to criticism, Alonzo's students were for the most part nondepartmental advanced students. But Alonzo could not blame men intent on a career for knowing what side their bread was buttered on. One had to give Klotz credit, however, for attracting young people to philosophy who would not have taken any work in the department had they not taken their first course with him.

As Alonzo came to know Maxie Waxie better and as his own knowledge of philosophy increased, he became more fully aware of the man's vast ignorance of it and of his lack of interest in hard thinking. That he had once worked hard on Kant's *Critique of Pure Reason* Alonzo knew, because he had carefully examined the copy of it Maxie Waxie owned. Once upon a time he might have known sufficient philosophy to earn a Ph.D. from McGilvary and Sharp. But by the time Alonzo met him he had given up interest in serious philosophy and was only interested in the shallow preachments he took to be liberating truth. His lecture on Plato's theory of ideas was disgraceful, but it conveyed clearly his contempt for such nonsense. When Alonzo served under him, Maxie Waxie knew very little beyond James and Dewey; but of course he did not know either of them, since he did not know—or had long forgotten—the doctrines these two thinkers had fought against. Why trouble to acquire knowledge that had been shown to be in error?

The first open run-in that Alonzo had with Maxie Waxie was about the senior teacher's scholarship. Maxie Waxie used to teach a course in which he lectured against Kant's ethical absolutism and formalism and in which he showed that the doctrine of the categorical imperative was absurd. As is well known, the doctrine teaches that an action is moral only if one can turn its *maxim*—the abstract assumption that rules it —into a universal rule. Was it right for a starving man to steal a loaf of bread? Only if it could be shown that under similar circumstances men could do the same as he did.

But Maxie Waxie did not mention in his discussion of Kant the noble doctrine of The Kingdom of Ends, which is an essential part of Kant's ethics and teaches that one ought to treat others as ends in themselves and not as means. This doctrine, to which a liberal should respond with warmth, for some reason was repugnant to Klotz. In discussing Kant's ethics he did not criticize the doctrine, he simply ignored it. When Alonzo called Maxie Waxie's attention to his treatment of Kant, the older man was furious. He was constantly telling his assistants that he wanted them to cooperate with him and to criticize him honestly. But the "criticism" he got from them was what he craved for and loved, for their spinal columns had unlimited coefficients of elasticity and after becoming Klotz's assistants, they soon developed a strong yen for the taste of boots. Alonzo tried to develop both virtues by doing bending exercises after breakfast and tasting shoe-polish daily, but he never succeeded.

Maxie Waxie managed to convey to his students and his assistants that he suffered for his unpopular convictions, which he considered dangerous because they aroused the religious citizens against him. After publishing a number of sermons in which he preached atheism in so many words, he was certain he would lose his job and that his person was in physical danger. He asked Charles Holzkopf, the big, tall, and favorite lieutenant, to walk with him to and from the university. In fact his job was never in danger nor was his person in need of a bodyguard—except from his own self-generated fears. These came naturally to him, for in addition to being a physical coward his trembling need of reassurance required him to believe that he was shaking the foundations of society and men would not hesitate to beat him up or even take his life.

Like Stephan Trofimovitch Verhovensky, in Dostoevski's *The Possessed*, Maxie Waxie cherished the delusion that his doctrines were dynamite and that he was a marked man. It is true that he had been publicly attacked by the conservative press of the state; true also that the Roman Catholic chaplain serving the Catholic students of the university preached several sermons a year on Klotz's errors and in the spring ran a class in the basement of his church to refute Klotz's ideas. But on every occasion when Klotz had been under attack the department and the university administration had come to his defense. So little was his job in danger that towards the end of their careers McGilvary and Sharp earned fifteen hundred dollars less than Klotz's seventy-five hundred—a very large figure for those days in the Middle West—although both men had been Klotz's teachers and were men who enjoyed a professional reputation that Maxie Waxie could not lay claim to.

From the lecture platform, around the table in the seminar room, to his graduates and his undergraduates, with an air of superiority, Maxie Waxie disparaged the value of systematic, technical thought and interest in close reasoning carried on with careful attention to the demands of evidence and method. These concerns were in his opinion trivial games for which he had a deep-rooted contempt frequently expressed in irritation. What he urged his students to concern themselves with were actual human needs—from which, by his silence about the needs of the mind the latter were selectively excluded. When you got to know him you discovered that for him human needs were fully met by unquestioning loyalty to the program of the dominant political family that often ran the state. Verbally on the side of labor, the clashes between unions and owners troubled him only to the degree that they affected the success or failure of his "progressive" politics. International conflicts interested him only in so far as they threatened the peace that might force his son into the army. He once said to Alonzo with passion that he did not want his boy killed in the defense of corporations.

Alonzo countered Klotz's contempt for technical philosophy with the argument that the monkey chatterings of the armies of philosophers since Thales, throughout our Western history, the quarrels that had disturbed Athens, Alexandria, Rome, and later the Cordoba of the Caliphs, the shrill or raucous, endless *bouilleries* of the Moors and Jews of al-Andalus, the squabblings and bickerings of the wranglers and hair-splitters of Bologna, Paris, and Oxford—those mountains of words, often mere words, those vain quiddities were the heights on which stood the great thinkers of our world and from which they shaped our minds. The shrill or raucous monkey-chatterings were no doubt for the most part trivial, empty, often utterly silly and irritating. But without it the giants of philosophy—the truly practical men, if you had the vision to see it—would not have been able to dominate their day and the following ages. If Buridan's ass was the invention of a satirist bored with the verbiage of the schools, there was much else in the history of philosophy that was as silly but not the product of satirists.

The great ones were remembered and, after centuries, still exerted influence, because they had elaborated their doctrines with technical care. Insight the great thinkers always possessed and the professors not always did; but their insight would have had no power but for their superb technical abilities, which Klotz had contempt for. The year that Klotz had been elected president of the Western Division of the American Philosophical Association he read a presidential address calling for vision, in his usual sweet style. That same year Cohen had written a presidential address entitled "Vision and Technique in Philosophy." Both addresses had been read at the same meeting of the American Philosophical Association in New York. One could read Cohen's address as a devastating reply to Klotz's address. For Klotz philosophy was vision, not technique. Since Klotz had the vision—or thought he did—and since he could make no claim to having the technique, it was he who was the true philosopher and not men like Cohen, who built their speculative structures with care.

4

Another one of the four senior members of the department had only been at State a year when Alonzo arrived. He had been brought to State by President Pound to inaugurate an educational experiment. While Albert Littlemieck was not so obviously the propagandist that Klotz was, he also dispensed salvation, but by way of The Absolute, for he had once been a Kantian, and took it as indisputable that he had a corner on The Truth about man and society. Littlemieck became quite chummy with Klotz soon after his arrival at State. But their friendliness was superficial, for Klotz could not abide The Absolute and Mieck despised Maxie Waxie's relativism; in a superficially friendly way they were perennially disagreeing with each other. Two things, however, united them in spite of their radical differences: both were liberal and both were strongly united in their hatred of McGilvary and Sharp, who not only were conservative, but were endowed with a fundamental scholarly seriousness that went against the grain of these two great men.

Littlemieck's major trouble, as Alonzo found out in the second course he took with him, was that he was not interested in teaching that required preparation. He had a superlative skill for conducting a discussion, and that was all there was to his teaching. That he was no great shakes as a thinker, that the students engaged in great discussions without knowing what they were talking about, did not deter Littlemieck from putting on his brilliant act three times a week. The intellectual hamming Mieck engaged in could probably be explained by the fact that he obviously enjoyed immensely entertaining his audience in what they took to be high-level philosophical activity and the fact that long before he had come to State he had been engaged in administration, had long forgotten his Kant, and had lost whatever interest he probably started with in technical philosophy. Intellectually, he was sustained by books for general readers, mainly on social and political questions, popular among liberal intellectuals, and by *The Nation* and *The New Republic*. His taste in literature was middle-brow, as evinced by the high esteem he expressed for Charles Morgan's *The Fountain*.

Here was a puzzle similar to that presented by Klotz. A man who had a very high national reputation as an educator—a reputation Klotz never achieved—and who turned out to be a dud as a teacher. How was that possible?

The first course that Alonzo took with Mieck, as his students affectionately called him behind his back, was very exciting. It was a discussion group and there were a number of very intelligent students in it who carried on a serious and often exciting discussion not only during the three hours a week the course met but after hours, outside. Although not yet accepted as a graduate, on the strength of the first course, Alonzo got permission from Mieck to register for a seminar on *The Critique of Pure Reason* the second semester. But Alonzo was not prepared to read Kant. He had to spend the larger part of his study time on *The Critique* to the neglect of his other courses. And when during the seminar he brought up questions that arose from his failure to understand the text, his questions were seldom satisfactorily answered by Mieck. As Alonzo read into *The Critique*, a number of questions came up that demanded more and more insistently to be answered, but that Littlemieck had no answer for. Since these questions are technical, I can give only one instance, stating the problem as far as I can in nontechnical terms.

Kant holds that there is a world beyond the world of appearance, beyond the phenomenal world; this is the real world, the world in itself, from which messages come to our minds called "intuitions"; the mind elaborates these intuitions by means of its own innate equipment —the forms of intuition, time and space, and the categories of the understanding, such as cause and effect. The result is the phenomenal world, the world in which we live and know. We do not know, then, the real world, the world in itself, all we know is the mind's elaboration of messages that come from it. The question that suggested itself to Alonzo was this: if we cannot know anything whatever about the world in itself, on what grounds does Kant assume that we get messages from it? A little later, when Alonzo came to know more about the history of post-Kantian philosophy than he knew at the time, he found out that this is a question that was asked by readers of the first *Critique* immediately after it was published, and that led thinkers to throw away the world of things in themselves and assert boldly that the world is the product of the mind; this was idealism. But Alonzo did not know when he was reading *The Critique* for Mieck's seminar that the question had been asked and that it had led to the development of idealism in Germany after Kant.

Mieck's answer to Alonzo's question should have been a lesson on the history of post-Kantian philosophy involving either a concession that the question created an insurmountable difficulty for Kant or a demonstration of how the idealists could be answered in terms consistent with Kant's theory of knowledge. But Mieck did not face the question. And it was not because Alonzo failed to put it again and again and in different ways.

Alonzo finally came to the conclusion that Littlemieck's preparation for the seminar, when he was prepared at all, was inadequate. Mieck was doing in a graduate seminar on *The Critique of Pure Reason* exactly what he had done in the undergraduate course the previous semester. He wanted to carry on an exciting discussion. But it was not possible to carry on a discussion, whether exciting or dull, of the first *Critique*—as students familiarly refer to it—in the way in which Mieck had carried on in the first course a discussion of the merits or demerits of Socrates's resolve to drink the poison after having shown the injustice of his condemnation.

Littlemieck not only came poorly prepared to the seminar but on several occasions he did something that showed what little interest he had in the work his students were trying to do. The seminar met Thursday nights. One Thursday afternoon early in the semester, Littlemieck called Alonzo up and asked him to take over the discussion that night, because he, Littlemieck, had suddenly been called out of town. Alonzo was, of course, highly flattered. But when, a few weeks later, Alonzo got a similar call, while still flattered, he began to wonder why a man would allow himself to be driven away from his seminar for any reason whatever. The answer to this question was hard to accept: Littlemieck was not interested in teaching.

This conclusion was confirmed for Alonzo by Sharp who, because of the seminar on the first *Critique*, decided to offer a seminar on Kant's ethical theory the following semester. Sharp had no sympathy for Kant's doctrine, but it was not difficult to see that he worked hard at his preparation for the seminar. While his class was not as exciting as Littlemieck's, the students were learning something every week. The contrast soon became glaring.

How was it possible for a man to achieve a national reputation as a great teacher who was not a serious teacher? He did because he had been fired from a job as president of an eastern university and "public opinion"—meaning *The Nation* and *The New Republic*—had lined up solidly behind him. But as a teacher he had no claim any more than Klotz had. He had, however, in abundance, two qualities that gave him his reputation. He was brilliant and he had a commodity to sell—for this is the only way to put it—that is highly valued by men: a powerfully magnetic personality, radiating force and awakening those around him, making them alive and ready to display what energies they possessed. It was impossible to be passive or dull in his presence. If you did not like him, and many of his colleagues disliked him strongly, you could not ignore him; you burned inside, silently, but you were aware of him.

His power to vitalize people is shown by one incident of which Alonzo was a part. Charles Holzkopf had invited a number of friends for cocktails after a football game and when Alonzo arrived at the party there were already a few people in the living room, but the party was not moving; people tried to make conversation, they tried one subject and then another to no avail. It was dull, it was flat, it was embarrassingly dead. Suddenly Littlemieck and his wife entered the room and the party sprung instantly into life. It was like turning on the current on a child's electric train: Everything moved; conversation went back and forth without effort, interest was genuine, and Littlemieck was not doing all the talking; he was merely pouring out wave upon wave of magnetism.

But while the problem of Littlemieck's reputation is not puzzling since most men daily eat up the kind of superior magnetic charm that he exuded, the question remained. Was the university world, after all, different from the rest of the world? For personal magnetism should not have been as highly valued a commodity in a world dedicated to learning and teaching as it was. If one cannot avoid its influence—and in the case of Littlemieck it would have been generally difficult if not altogether impossible, to put oneself beyond its reach—one could at least make the serious and constant effort to value honest scholarship and genuine teaching above it. The academic world prided itself on its superior values, on the higher life its members lived, free from the taint

of commerce, free from the lies of the world of politics and the falsehoods of ordinary living. But a world in which a man could achieve a
local reputation who had nothing else to offer his students than the
inspirational, irresponsible, because muddy, liberal propaganda that
Klotz dished out, and another could achieve a national reputation as
a great teacher who had little more to offer than his magnetic personality—was the academic world much different from the outside world
in which snake-oil peddlers, whether in the world of high finance or
on street corners, made their way?

There might be no difference between the outside world and the
academic, but still the latter offered Alonzo what he most wanted:
leisure to read and write. Writing would have to be suspended for a
few years till he got his Ph.D., but the reading that was required was
sheer joy.

V

Alonzo As "Teacher"

1

ALONZO tried to make up for his ignorance in the years that followed with a measure of success since his capacity to work was above the ordinary and his enthusiasm was high. The courses he taught included the history of philosophy, ancient and modern, and the preparation for them added considerably to his scant knowledge.

Viewed from the outside, Alonzo's teaching was quite successful. Students crowded his courses and their reactions to his teaching were always strong: They were either wholeheartedly for him or against him; but enough of them liked him to take a second and a third course with him and to recommend his courses to their friends. For that reason in a short time Alonzo became known in the College of Arts and Sciences as one of its strong teachers.

But was he really a teacher at all? He was not teaching philosophy; he was carrying on a relentless job of propaganda for his views. He pretended to his students and to himself that he wanted them to examine his views objectively and to accept them or reject them on their merits. But this was mere pretense, and if it fooled him it did not fool some of his students. In fact he used all his powers of persuasion, of argument, rhetoric, and satire to pound his views into his students' heads and to discourage them from seriously considering the validity of those he rejected.

Being as ignorant as he was and as genuinely interested in philosophy, Alonzo himself was engaged in the exciting adventure of making vast discoveries. This was territory already explored, well charted, utterly familiar to mature scholars. But for him it was like the first trip of an American to Europe: Everything before him was new and nearly everything exciting and to be treated with loving reverence. It was supposed to be treated objectively, but Alonzo's commitments to liberalism and naturalism did not allow him to approach philosophical views opposed to his own in any but a partisan manner. There was much that he knew was not worth learning without looking at it; idealism, for instance, although Plato stood high in his esteem. But his response to Plato was arbitrary. In any case, with whatever objectivity he approached the philosophy he studied, he did not in fact permit his students to take the same stance.

Alonzo, who was perfectly well acquainted with the cant, often said in and out of class that knowledge was inquiry. But he did not stop to ask whether this belief jibed with what he was doing as a teacher. He was blocking inquiry with his indoctrinating. His students were being turned into various kinds of parrots, some more articulate than others, but all repeating the same ideas. He pretended that he wanted his students to think for themselves, but in fact he pushed his point of view, giving no quarter to objections which he disposed of seriously or flippantly, but thoroughly. It was not that he was obviously bigoted. Whether his dogmatism showed or not depended on the circumstances. Nor was it that he did not listen to objections, for sometimes he did. He was at fault, whatever his manner on any occasion, because gently or roughly, he rammed into his students' minds his own views.

But the matter is not quite so simple. Two other factors complicated it and may have extenuated to some extent his activity. One was that a teacher who loved his subject as much as Alonzo did and who had come to his insights, such as they might have been, by hard, honest work had to be allowed to present his views with warmth and to recommend them to his students with whatever powers of presentation he had, often not knowing that he was doing a hard job of selling. In any case, it would have been impossible for Alonzo to have been a dispassionate teacher. If he was to teach at all, he had to do it his own way. It was difficult to decide whether he was allowing his students sufficient freedom to choose or not. Even when he presented all sides of a problem, something liberal propagandists seldom did, however much they pretended to do it, he could not be expected to be a John Stuart Mill, of whom it has been said that he presented his opponents' views better than they did. To indict him for being a propagandist was a matter that called for fine discrimination. It was often difficult to decide, unless one knew him very well, and knew what specific act of propaganda he might be accused of, whether he was indeed in this particular case a propagandist or not and to what extent.

It was not easy to say, particularly in philosophy, a discipline in which a real stone and the idea of a stone cannot be as readily distinguished from each other as the egregious Grand Cham of eighteenth century "common sense," Samuel Johnson, thought it could be, "by striking his foot with mighty force against a great stone, till it rebounded from it." Difficult as it may be in philosophy to distinguish sense from nonsense, and more difficult still, to distinguish the hard sell from the soft—propaganda *à outrance* from an objective presentation in which the student was given sufficient leeway to use his mind —and more difficult still to build a student up so that he could use his powers of judgment, it was not altogether impossible to do these things. And because Alonzo and his friends put more effort into getting their own ideas accepted than they did into training students to judge for themselves, they could not be called teachers. They were catechizers.

The other factor that made it difficult to judge with confidence the quality of Alonzo's and his friend's teaching was that students usually came to college with minds stuffed with arrant nonsense. Throughout the thirties their views on moral, social, political, and theological questions were not merely naïve but often absurd. These views were usually fiercely defended behind impregnable ramparts. Their politics were dogmatic, their religious beliefs smugly fideistic. Surely it was the duty of a teacher to try to lead these young people to question their beliefs? Surely it was his duty to crack the nonsense of these ignoramuses? Surely he had to try to lead them to think, since all they did was parrot the nonsense they had learned at home? Surely no teacher could leave unaired the gross ignorance these young people exhibited? With equal confidence they not only asserted the millennial but nevertheless false religious beliefs but also the "smelly little orthodoxies" they cherished. They clung to both with passionate fervor. They hugged smugly their unexamined political prejudices, their dogmas on moral and social questions, their exclusive racial arrogance, their entrenched falsehoods. Surely the teacher had to air these cellars? Surely he had to bring some light into the impenetrable darkness?

But how far to crack the ignorance? Above all, how to crack it? It was much too easy for a teacher with his dialectical hammer to split open the student's mind and spill his beliefs on the ground, leaving him feeling total devastation, emptiness, acute and angry pain.

Furthermore, neither Alonzo nor his friends distinguished between the millennial, fragrant, respectable orthodoxies that had sustained the civilization they claimed to champion, and the smelly little ones. For Alonzo and his friends all orthodoxies except their own were little and smelly. Their own views, they complacently believed, were not an orthodoxy, mere opinion, they were The Truth. That their own views constituted an orthodoxy that had its antecedents in Protagoras and Pelagius, that it ran through one of the main intellectual cloacas of history from the classical age through the eighteenth century by way of Rousseau and the *philosophes*, that it ran red during The Terror, and down through the nineteenth century to their own day—that fact was beyond the range of their vision.

The work of these liberal teachers was sometimes cruel. Some of them enjoyed inflicting pain. The student was often made to feel culpably ignorant, as if the very fact of his being in college did not indicate that he was not a learned man. Why these physicians of the soul, these self-appointed makers of perfect men, enjoyed inflicting pain, sometimes they explained: It was good for the student to suffer. But why it was good, that they did not stop to explain.

Stripped roughly of the coverage of his beliefs, the student's personality underwent a shock from which sometimes he never successfully recovered. The upshot was that the smelly little orthodoxies that were discarded by students were replaced by devastating cynicism, and since the need to believe was not eradicated when the beliefs were shown up, the student was often ready to fall for the strong dogmatism that was at hand, Marxism. And many did.

But whatever complexities might obstruct arrival at the final judgment, the fact was that neither Alonzo nor his liberal friends were ever held off in their wrecking work by any scruples. What Alonzo and his friends were doing they did under the sincere belief that they were doing admirable work.

Alonzo's seniors were not ignorant of the activity in which he was engaged but they did not take it to be outrageous and indeed thought him an excellent teacher. He and his liberal friends objected passionately to Italian boys taken early from their parents, dressed in black shirts, and turned into operatic regiments of bullies-in-the-making. This practice Alonzo and his friends thought was outrageous. But why? It's never been the case with partisans that what is good for the goose is good for the gander. They objected, not because the *bam-*

binos were not being given the opportunity to develop their own nature, but because the wrong nature was being forced on them. Had they been shaped in the right way—which was of course the left way—would Alonzo and his liberator friends have objected?

Let us judge by what they were doing. No black shirts. But it was quite right to dress their students' minds in pink shirts, drilling them into intellectual bullies, into self-deceived intolerant preachers of toleration, into absolutistic relativists, into lovers of abstract mankind who were pumped full of hatred for "the enemy," into censorious, ungenerous souls guided by arthritic doctrines, into men incapable of giving expression in action to any of the virtues they pretended to embody and for the lack of which, or so they took it, they held those who disagreed with them in profound contempt.

True, they did not believe in *mare nostrum*, they did not humiliate their enemies with castor oil in the street, they were not dreaming of conquering medieval Ethiopians, they believed in freedom of thought, in democracy, in peace, in the full goldfish bowl of godly virtues, prominently placed up front, which constitutes the liberal aquarium. They themselves were decent; the others were not. But in fact they were doing to their students what Mussolini was trying to do to his black-shirted little cherubs. They undertook to shape the students according to a predesigned plan just as much as the theatrical Duce did, not a bit less.

It is hardly necessary to say that not all teachers at State engaged in the work of indoctrination to the same degree and with the same implacable intransigence as Alonzo and some of his liberal friends. But there were many teachers who assumed in a deeply implicit manner that any views they held were correct and those contradicting them were false and that was all there was to it. Particularly on political matters was this the case. Men otherwise mild and tolerant flared up when anyone had a mildly excusing word to say for "the enemy." They did not quite reach the apogee of bigotry and proclaim that error had no rights; on the contrary they constantly preached the value of tolerance; but they acted contrary to their maxim. Liberals were the most relentless indoctrinators. Men like McGilvary and Sharp sometimes presented their views in less than objective fashion; but they did not make blatant propaganda with intransigent persistency. The subject matter of their courses—theory of knowledge, ethics, metaphysics, whatever it was—was worth teaching. Theirs were courses in philosophy, not exercises in propaganda disguised as philosophy. And this held for other conservatives outside the Department of Philosophy with the exception of the social sciences, where there were no conservatives.

I hope, Alonzo turned to me in earnest, that I am not giving the wrong impression. Let me repeat that I am not saying that all liberal academics, wherever found, are relentless propagandists. Least of all am I saying that this is an exclusively liberal trait. I report my own experience. As far as State and the other universities with which I have been affiliated were concerned, propaganda was carried on chiefly by liberals and not by conservatives. But allowance must be made for the wide variety of human temperament and the intellectual ethos of a culture. The tendency to do propaganda is abundantly exhibited in Western history of all sorts of groups. For reasons that are not difficult to conjecture these traits seem universal—the Arapesh always excluded, of course.

2

Did anyone ever criticize Alonzo at the time for carrying on a vigorous campaign of indoctrination in place of genuine teaching? He was widely praised for his teaching, although, as stated, what he was doing was generally known by his elders, since students carried stories of what went on in his classroom to other teachers and since some students objected volubly to the way in which he battered down their convictions. Once Alonzo had a discussion with some older men about the objectives of education. The end of education, they argued, was to bring out whatever the student had in him as yet unborn. Alonzo had an easy answer to the objection. This notion of education, which in his *A Concise Etymological Dictionary of the English Language* Skeats says, is "allied to" the idea of educing or bringing out, assumes that before the process of education begins young people are endowed with a potential nature that can be brought to realization. This is clearly an Aristotelian notion. But haven't the social sciences proved that man is not endowed with a determinate nature?

Education does not actualize innate potentialities. Man is the product of his environment; and his virtues, skills, and talents are those that his culture implants in him or allows him to acquire after birth. Alonzo added that what he was doing for the student was not only for the student's own good but also for the good of society. For Alonzo was freeing the student from superstition and narrowness, he was teaching him to respect other cultures and the values of others, he was enlarging the student's horizon, uprooting his parochialism, and implanting in him the superior virtues of the liberal character.

He pointed out, further, that all organizations, all societies, all institutions, all religious and political bodies undertake to implant in their young members the virtues they espouse. Mussolini was not the only one. Each group justifies its action in terms of a view of human nature and a notion of man's destiny—even when they fall back on those purely materialistic theories that deny that man has a destiny and a nature. Christians emphasize one set of virtues while Fascists, Communists, Shintoists, and Muggletonians emphasize others. Alonzo argued that he was preparing his students to live in a modern, democratic society, and this meant, in a society in which truth had the primacy over traditional and now clearly mythical pieties, in which toleration and freedom from prejudice was essential, in which the belief in moral absolutes was an impediment to individual growth and social well-being.

Furthermore, Alonzo and his liberal friends added, the idea that the student would not be shaped by one agency or another, was utterly false. If the liberals did not shape the students the other side would— parents, ministers, the fraternity or sorority, the street gang: an ignorant pack of louts. It was better that the student be shaped by the liberals who were trying to prepare him to make his contribution to the progress of our modern, democratic society. This was the song and dance that justified in the eyes of Alonzo and his friends the outrages they perpetrated against the institutions that made possible their freedom to carry on their destructive work. If they had indeed taught tolerance, respect for truth, and open mindedness, it would have been outrageous enough since along with these traits they inculcated contempt for traditional values and what the parents of their students took to be rejection of the truth—their own traditional truths and values.

But they were not inculcating tolerance, open-mindedness, respect for truth. The students that went through their classes came out with a frozen conviction, completely unreasoning, that what their liberal teachers had favored was Truth and what their parents and their conservative teachers believed was error born of selfishness, superstition, and unwillingness to look at the facts. Respect for truth would have involved a diffident hesitation to arrive at conclusions on questions on which there was no evidence or on which evidence was not sufficient, a generous and objective examination of contradictory positions, a sense of the dubieties and perplexities of knowledge and human living. None of these attitudes the students showed. Often they were much more extreme than Alonzo and his fellow teachers. What Alonzo and his friends were doing was to substitute one encrusted dogmatism for another, one petrified intolerance for another, one set of unreasoning prejudices for another.

Philosophy majors, after they got through, carried with them a full kit of shibboleths and hardened prejudices that had a sacred don't-touch-me character to them. Alonzo remembers the reply of a student once to something he said in class when he had begun to doubt his views. This young woman was a very bright undergraduate philosophy major. "But Mr. Quijano," she exclaimed in visible and audible shock, "that's dualism!" The young lady's shock did not diminish when Alonzo replied that before they banished doctrines with bad names they should first look at their merits. By their opposition to dualism, their rejection of belief in values that had status in being in-dependently of man, by their uncritical acceptance of nominalism, their faith in the perfectability of man, by a large cargo of uncritical rejections and fideistic espousals, they made a formidable band of im-penetrable bigots. But they were liberals. Unfortunately the appeal of Alonzo and his friends to the majority of students, even the intelligent ones, was immensely successful.

How did they do it? Their sermons were not altogether false. They appealed to argument, to the truth, to science over mythological con-victions. Darwin had won the day and T. H. Huxley had made a mon-key out of Bishop Wilberforce in their famous encounter in Oxford on 30 June 1860. Those who did not agree with them were not looking at the evidence. But mixed with sound argument there was a great deal of rhetoric: appeal to "the spirit of the age," with which they claimed to be in harmony while their opponents were not, to enlightenment, on which by implication they had a corner.

These arguments were not solely appeals to allegedly objective truth, they were also exhortations to join the crusade. They were phony be-cause they were simplistic; they assumed that there was a spirit to an age, only one, and that the liberal party possessed an infallible means of recognizing it, and was its sole rightful guardian; they assumed that their opponents rejected the spirit of the age from mean motives, from lack of intelligence, from contempt of the truth, from a hard heart, from contempt for common decency. At best their arguments rested on a bad philosophy of history, since they assumed that the past was a sink of superstition, the present of which they were the advanced guard was an improvement on the past, and the future an unclouded and certain promise. At worst their arguments were circular, since they claimed that the liberals represented the spirit of the age because they possessed the truth and that they possessed the truth because they represented the spirit of the age. But whatever the quality of their arguments, they were not losing; they were immensely successful; they had the students on their side; they were shaping the future. That was what they were doing: They were shaping the future; they were not altogether lucid about it, but that was what they were doing; by winning the young, they were shaping the future.

If the liberals were shaping the future by winning the young, their opponents were losing it by default. They could not counter liberal propaganda with conservative propaganda, for that would have nullified their claim to scholarship. In this they were right. But they were not helpless although they behaved as if they were. First, they were not sufficiently alert to the meaning of what was going on, since they accepted as good teaching anything that attracted students to a course irrespective of what actually went on in the classroom. Of course, that way of thinking had its limits: When an instructor of freshman English brought his guitar to class the department put its foot down and the young man was soon looking for another job. But they did not object to the propaganda, which when complained about was defended by the liberals under the head of academic freedom. And finally they did not examine their views outside their fields with the same seriousness and objectivity that they brought to their specialties. Professionally they were critical. Outside their fields they were like the rest of men, prejudiced, opinionated fideists.

Where did the conservatives stand? The answer to this question would have been devastating had they heard it; it would have revealed to them that they were not as radically opposed to the liberals as they thought and therefore could not enter into combat with them. The differences between the conservative oligarchs and the liberals were important but not radical. The conservatives defended privilege and the *status quo* but they had no body of convictions with which to oppose liberal criticism and programs. They could not oppose social melioration without opening themselves to the charge of selfishness and cruelty, since they shared with the liberals belief in a purely secularistic concept of man. But if man is only an animal and if human existence had no metaphysical grounding, sooner or later pleasure of the most elementary type, requiring no effort, had to be acknowledged as the rational goal of behavior.

How can you tell a young man that he ought not to prefer the life of a happy pig to the life of an unhappy philosopher, if you first had convinced him, initially against his deepest sense, that there was no difference in kind between a grunting pig and a chattering philosopher? Conservatives also believed in progress, they were committed to the belief that all problems could be solved if only men had the will to solve them; they did not all know it, but they all believed in the perfectability of man. Although some of them thought of themselves as religious, almost unawares they had shifted the center of gravity of their faith from God to social melioration. They did not keep flowing in their hearts the springs of cosmic piety; they were not responsive to the ultimate mystery; they lacked the tragic sense.

What then were the differences between conservatives and liberals at State? Practically, most were relatively trivial: as to whether to install a municipal water-softening plant or who should be the next mayor of Midland City or the next governor of the state. When it came to theory the difference was enormous. Who did the conservatives have to put up against the heavyweight liberal thinker, John Dewey? A philosophical featherweight, an erudite rhetor who believed in the devil theory of history—sweetness and light before Jean Jacques and darkness and evil after him; a man who solved the problems of ethics as well as practical moral problems by pointing out that men are endowed with an inner check—Irving Babbitt. No one else? Oh, well, his friend More, a deeper man but no philosopher, and Eliot, *tres o cuatro gatos*, but no one of them capable of taking Dewey on.

Let me iterate with emphasis that Alonzo was not the only teacher at State who forced his views on his students. A large number did, including some who were thought by their colleagues and by the students to be the outstanding teachers of the College of Arts and Sciences. The departments of sociology, anthropology, economics, history, political science, and particularly English in the elementary courses, were manned by teachers who employed most of their time in the classroom and out indoctrinating their students. One of the earliest books on popular semantics, philosophically thoroughly irresponsible, shallow, and wrong headed—probably the reason it became one of the early classics in the pseudosubject—originated in an "experimental" freshman English course at State. There was nothing experimental about the controlling political assumptions and social orientation of the book. That some of its moralizing was such that no decent man, whatever his politics or attitudes, could quarrel with, did not make the book any less the instrument of propaganda that it was. That a book like that could make the impact it has made is unneeded proof of the low quality of the intellectual needs of the nation.

Soon after the anthropologist Linton arrived at State, Alonzo became a good friend of his, in spite of the chip Linton carried on his shoulder at the time against philosophy. In one of their early lunches, Linton said to Alonzo in a truculent manner that he could civilize his students more thoroughly and more quickly than Alonzo could. Alonzo agreed heartily. "Of course you can" he replied, "I have not lived among savages." But what was meant by civilizing the students? The assumption of course was that the values, convictions, beliefs, attitudes the student brought from home—unless, and in those days it happened rarely, the student already shared his teachers' outlook—were barbaric and the job of the teacher was to eradicate them as soon as possible, putting in their place the teachers'. Linton, so far as Alonzo knew, had never occupied a university post before he came to State; but he knew, as clearly as Alonzo and his friends did, what was the end of education: to "debarbarize" the students, as Linton once put it.

3

Were these propagandists liberal? At State both the administration and the faculty were extremely proud of the fact that they were in the forefront of the fight for academic freedom, understood as the freedom to search for truth wherever the search might lead. Without such freedom, it was generally agreed, the ends that the university was founded to serve would be subverted. At the entrance of Mocsab Hall, the central building of the Midland City Campus, there is a bronze plaque given to the university by the class of 1910, containing a quotation from a report of the Board of Regents of 1894, which reads, "Whatever may be the limitations which trammel inquiry elsewhere, we believe that this great State University should ever encourage that continual and fearless sifting and winnowing by which alone the truth can be found."

Noble words and true, that only a caitiff mind would deny. But how much reality was there behind these noble words in the actual day-to-day activity of the *soit disant* truth seekers at State? No one could doubt that in the science departments of the university much honest and fearless sifting and winnowing went on, to which activity State owed its eminence in science. Nor would Alonzo have denied that a great deal of sifting and winnowing went on in the social sciences and in the humanities and that some of it was honest sifting and winnowing for the truth such as it might be found to be. But was it always sifting and winnowing in a fearless way? Was it honest? Did it always sift and winnow chaff, which is error, from grain, which is truth? It was sifting and winnowing, no doubt, but of a very special kind, for it was not intended to let the blowing winds of inquiry separate all chaff from all grain, such as they might be. Properly speaking there was no inquiry, since what was truth and error was known in advance of the threshing. There was no genuine testing for truth. Why should there be, since the truth was already known or at least known in its main outlines? Whatever were the limitations that trammeled inquiry elsewhere, here at State, among liberals, there were strict limits which, if transcended, plunged a man from honesty and decency into dishonesty and erroneous evil. There was threshing, but it was like the threshing that goes on among Communist theoreticians and writers of apologetics in any field.

Free inquiry? Free inquiry, carried on honestly to be truly free, leads a man to question his categories, his assumptions, his definitions, and of course, his data. Nothing like that happened in these men's minds. The right of free inquiry was used by these men to advance ideas based on assumptions they would not consider questioning. These men were not inquirers: They were believers, men of faith, unquestioning partisans; they would no more question their beliefs to find out which of them fell by the weight of their truth and which were blown off by the wind of inquiry than any other kind of man of faith would.

Sometimes the intolerance was incomprehensible. When the forthcoming publication of Mead's *Mind, Self, and Society* was announced, Alonzo ordered the book with impatient eagerness. The reason was, as Alonzo knew, that in this book Mead had put forth a theory of the origin of the human mind that, Alonzo had heard it claimed, removed one of the most serious difficulties naturalism had to overcome. The day he heard that the book had arrived at the bookstore, Alonzo told Maxie Waxie that he could hardly wait to get the book. The older man did not ask the reason for Alonzo's eagerness. "What do you want to read Mead for?" Although he put his reaction in the form of a query, what he clearly expressed was his strong disapproval. Maxie Waxie did not approve of anyone reading Mead any more than he approved of anyone reading the greater number of contemporary philosophers. The canon consisted of Dewey, James, and Maxie Waxie's own weak emissions of instrumentalism and his unfocused love of abstract humanity.

But there was more to this special kind of threshing. It was never allowed that the error of conservatives arose in their minds honestly, that it consisted of a difference of opinion arrived at through the same kind of honest judgment that had led to one's own liberal convictions. The conservative was a man who put his private interests over and above the public good, he was selfish, hard, indifferent to human needs. His error was always the result of egoism. Thus the liberal, who considered himself the champion of tolerance, rejected his opponent out of hand, without charity, in anger, never making an effort to find out why animals who were in outward appearance human were inwardly so brutally inhumane. The result was that the possessor of truth was sustained by a self-righteousness and an ill-concealed arrogance that neither he nor his friends seemed to notice; they were all in possession of the truth.

VI

Borrowed Thoughts

1

WHEN ALONZO registered at State he was interested in literature as much as in philosophy; but when he began to study philosophy seriously, the subject aroused his passion and goaded by his ignorance he put every ounce of energy at his disposal into it. His interest in literature receded. Philosophy was an exciting, an absorbing, a jealous mistress; it left him little time for any other serious pursuit except that of playing—which he did as seriously and as hard as he worked. He had energy and could afford to divide it into work and play—or more precisely he could divide it into two different kinds of enjoyment.

During his first years as a graduate student Alonzo had been looking for a philosophy for himself. It was not a fully conscious search, but a vaguely felt but strong need, a semiconscious alertness for doctrines and ideas that he might make his own. Of course, he did not put it to himself in this manner; the need for a philosophy was not fully conscious, and he did not think he was looking for a satisfying philosophy, he thought he was looking for the truth. Santayana would no longer do. He kept his interest in Santayana, but Santayana's philosophy no longer rang true. It was not long before Santayana's cadenced prose, which Alonzo had admired, became an obstacle to Alonzo's capacity to grasp Santayana's thought.

What sort of truth was he looking for? He still understood philosophy to be concerned with fundamental, substantive questions of critical importance to men and peoples. In this respect, his increasing knowledge of the history of philosophy had confirmed earlier opinion. What it had contributed was the proof—if such it could be called—of the fact that philosophers, with their apparently useless wrangles, had played a most important role of a very practical nature, but in a mediate way, in the development of the civilizations in which they had flourished. Philosophy, as a purely intellectual scheme which adorned a man as a jewel might a woman, as a way of purely understanding the world, or as a solution of a number of purely intellectual puzzles to be solved purely for the fun of solving them—that kind of activity did no more interest him now that he had a little more knowledge of the history of philosophy than it had interested him earlier, when Unamuno and Nietzsche had entirely absorbed him. Alonzo realized that the way in which philosophy makes its impact on living is not the way in which physics does, as a set of formulas used to build bridges with. Its effect is mediate: It shapes attitudes, gives a man a stance toward his fellows, broadens and deepens his sense of the world, gives experience a density that the unthinking man's experience lacks.

The philosophy he was looking for had to include among its basic notions a number of tenets that Alonzo took to be beyond question, regarding the all-comprehensiveness of Nature, the nonexistence of God, and the definition of the meaning of human existence in worldly, secularistic, yet noble terms. It had to be a naturalism that went beyond Santayana's formula that every ideal development has a natural basis. He had once taken this principle as a liberating insight; but an empiricist had to show how each one of the ideal developments—life, the human mind, and the institutions of culture—had come about. Santayana's philosophy was not a genetic account of human institutions and could not answer, therefore, those who argued that naturalism was reductive. To answer them you had to do more than assert in general terms that man as he is today had come from lower forms of life. You had to have more than a mere extrapolation from biological evolution, which is to say, from the Darwinian hypothesis that showed successfully that the species had not come about all at once and had remained unchanged ever since their appearance on earth, but had changed, developed, evolved. Santayana had not shown how man's development had taken place. He had merely asserted it with superb eloquence, in a prose so elegant, polished, witty that it made academic philosophers (were there, at least today, any other kind?) suspect that he was not a fully accredited member of the guild. Envy? Of course not; lovers of wisdom do not descend to such human depths.

Dewey's philosophy was no more based on a worked-out theory of

the development of the animal into a full human being than Santayana's was. Along with all naturalists, he took for granted that the transition from brute to man had occurred. Neither philosophers nor anyone else saw the problem. We had to wait for old Freud to come up
with a theory—which, as Alonzo found out later, was as full of holes
as a theory could possibly carry and remain one theory and not a disintegrated sponge. Here we have another instance of the triumph of
faith over the need to know. Anyway, the hunt for the missing link
went on; it is still going on. Enough bones of pates of animals said to
be quasi-human had been dug up to satisfy the believers and perhaps,
who knows? to call for new wings in museums to house these reverend
bones. So-called Peking man had made a brief appearance on the stage
of science and the Sunday supplements and quickly departed. Piltdown man had his brief hour of glory and had been hooted off both
stages in disgrace. But no one had seen the need to dig the problem up
from under the bones and ask exactly how had the brute, sometime,
somewhere pulled off the feat and managed to turn himself—or more
precisely itself—into a human being.

While Dewey's philosophy did not still Alonzo's vague feeling—it
had not yet become a clearly formulated demand—that until the genetic transition was satisfactorily accounted for, naturalists could not
make the claim they made, to the effect that their philosophy was fully
grounded on science, instrumentalism had great advantages over Santayana's polished eloquence. Given Alonzo's circumstances, it was
natural that he should find, or that he should think he could find what
he was looking for in Dewey. Dewey was far from possessing the elegance of the Spanish Bostonian, the transparency of John Stuart Mill
or Russell, the infectiousness of Spinoza. No one could say that Dewey
was a gifted writer. Alonzo once tried to turn a few pages of *Experience
and Nature* into English; it was an almost impossible job, because it
was often impossible to make up one's mind exactly what the page or
the sentence was trying to say. But when you got past all these difficulties you ran into a thoroughness and solidity that was unequaled by
more superficially lucid writers, a relevance to the hour, as Alonzo felt
it, that other philosophers with whom Alonzo was acquainted, lacked.
In Dewey Alonzo thought he had found a complete account of the
world and society, of morality, religion, and later, art. Dewey had
closely analyzed the problem of knowledge, he was a liberal in poli-

tics, he was a humane man. He was, in short, the answer to Alonzo's prayer.

In 1932—or was it 1933?—Alonzo heard for the first time of the Vienna Circle. He became interested in it. But he was too seriously interested in art and in moral philosophy to be able to swallow positivism whole. There was much in Dewey that he could not assimilate, but there was much more in positivism that could not even be swallowed. As he became better acquainted with the doctrines of positivism he sought to integrate them with Dewey's philosophy. The job was not impossible because after *Experience and Nature* Dewey gave a prominent place to science in his philosophy. In disagreement with the positivists, Dewey assigned an essential role to intelligence (or knowledge) in the solution of moral perplexities and this gave instrumentalism a strength that positivism altogether lacked.

There is egregious moral crudeness, abysmal moral stupidity, in a mind that claims seriously that all the commandment, "Thou shall not kill" means is "I do not like killing, don't you like it either," or "I wish you wouldn't like it." Logical acuity did not make up for the lack of theoretical moral intelligence. Both Dewey and the positivists gave arbitrary primacy to knowledge but because Dewey understood knowledge in broader terms his vision of the world was not morally shabby. From the beginning Alonzo had felt that for all their superb subtlety of mind, their knowledge of science, their dazzling logic, their formidable methodology, their lucid proofs, for all the awe-inspiring panoply of argument, there was something intellectually crude about positivism. But in a sense its defect was much worse, for while positivists vaunted of their up-to-the-minute empiricism, they arrived at their moral philosophy by deduction from their narrow theory of knowledge. What positivism added up to in some respects was a crippling myopia toward institutions and modes of expression that for Alonzo were of the greatest concern: morality, art, the achievements of human experience outside science—although science was without doubt, at present perhaps man's greatest achievement—and his inscrutable destiny.

It was not that positivists as men were indifferent to justice, ignorant of art, deaf to music, or uninterested in literature; that they were on the side of oppression or indifferent to it, on the side of iniquity, indifferent to bad taste, inhumane, illiberal. As men, if you made the necessary allowances in this or that instance for certain deficiencies everybody gives evidence of, positivists were no worse than other men. The trouble with their theories had nothing to do with their persons and behavior. It was that their philosophy did not take full cognizance of their activities and interests and could not account for what in fact they were —fine, sensitive, humane, literate people, as complete as other men were. Alonzo did not know any of them who was a Jeremy Bentham, a crass Philistine; with one exception well known among them, Alonzo did not know any of them who was personally objectionable. But in their theory they left large areas of serious concern unaccounted, or poorly accounted, for.

Not that Dewey possessed what the positivists lacked. To some extent he did, but not fully. He offered a broader and more comprehensive account of human living than the positivists did. But he had defects of which Alonzo was more or less clearly aware. Alonzo somehow managed to keep his dissatisfactions from giving him serious trouble.

The satisfactions of understanding that Dewey so abundantly provided elicited Alonzo's assent and kept him faithful, in general terms, to the truth as Dewey saw it. But from the positivists he learned something of immense value: the need to challenge propositions that seemed to have factual validity but really floated on the thin air of more or less pure speculation; to challenge wild generalizations, facts that were inventions or the projections of wishes, historical assertions without proof, judgments based on views of man that were the sediment of prejudice and superstition. Politics is the field of human interest where this kind of irresponsibility flourishes most luxuriantly; in speculative philosophy the disregard of facts when they are available is systematic; but there is no aspect of human life which is not spoiled by judgments claiming a factual authority they altogether lack. Call it "pseudoitis" if you need a name for it, the prevalence of the disease and in some fields its virulence, cannot be denied.

Dewey's advantage over the positivists was that he held a broader and much more empirical notion of experience than they accepted. From Dewey's idealist days he had brought into instrumentalism the notion of the mind as playing a constitutive role in the activity of knowledge, thus developing a broader notion of experience than that developed by British empiricists, whose notion of the mind was initially, that of a *tabula rasa*. So far as its affirmations went, much of positivism was salutary, particularly its insistence that judgments should be tested; but its rotund denials led to a picture of the universe that could not harbor a rich life. The positivists Alonzo knew lived as rich a life as any man could live today, but they could not ground their lives on their philosophy.

2

What did he believe? There was nothing original in his thought except perhaps the manner in which he expressed his borrowings and the emphasis he placed on them. Alonzo called himself a naturalist and a whole-hearted empiricist. Naturalism is a body of beliefs—not a school of philosophy or a single system—that does not divide the universe into two different kinds of substances and that does not assume that the world has a cause beyond itself. With Spinoza, with the contemporary naturalists—men like Santayana, Woodbridge, Sellars and many others, but much more with Dewey—he held that there was only one Nature, and that all that has been, is, and ever will or can be, is to be found in it, springing from its womb and finding its explanation, if one can be found at all, in it. For Alonzo this was an article of faith. If you had asked him, How can you know so much? he would have replied that a philosophy was at best a hypothesis, and one that cannot be rigorously demonstrated or even proved in the way in which, say, a lawyer proves his case to the jury or a chemist his hypotheses. But he would have been anxious to make sure you understood him when he added that that did not make his naturalism arbitrary, for he held it on good grounds.

The grounds on which he held his belief, Alonzo argued, could be stated succinctly. Naturalism seemed to him to accord better than any other philosophy with the exigencies of scientific method, particularly with the principle of parsimony. This Alonzo took to be a fact beyond doubt. Fully modern in its spirit, nevertheless, naturalism was an old way of thinking. Greek materialism had been a speculative version of it and the early Stoics had been naturalists. It was therefore already an old philosophy when Copernicus erased the distinction between the celestial and the sublunary worlds. Since the seventeenth century naturalism had made steady and rapid advances. With Darwin it finally established itself firmly as the basic philosophy of science, the only adequate philosophy for a world in which science played the important part that it does in ours. Alonzo took naturalism to be a condition of scientific progress. On the other hand, he argued that he had not found any positive proof of any kind for the existence of a realm different from that of Nature. The contemporary arguments of spiritualists, idealists, and other such antiquated philosophers boil down, it seemed to Alonzo, to two negative propositions: that science is helpless before the problem of consciousness and before the problem of life.

Alonzo thought that naturalism answers these criticisms in the following manner: It is not the business of science and philosophy or any other human discipline to explain "the nature" of anything, nor is it at all clear what can be meant by the request. Physics does not try to explain the nature of matter; nor does biology the nature of life. What we can attempt to do, and what science has done since even before the seventeenth century with progressive success, is to describe, in formulas which are as exact and as objectively verifiable as possible, the behavior of selected isolates of the world in which we live. Now one of the things we are very much interested in is living processes, the conditions which make them possible, the forces at work in them, and the simpler elements or materials which make up living cells. If we must have the word *nature*, the nature of any thing is its how. What is the nature of life is a question that is answered by a detailed description of the process and the components that make it up. No small measure of knowledge is already available about the nature of life and our knowledge increases daily. Little or nothing seems as yet positively known about the historical conditions under which life began. And even if biologists should at some future time manage to manufacture living tissue from pure inorganic materials, nothing more than probable knowledge would then be available about the beginning of life. For the assumption that the conditions under which life began on earth were somewhat similar to those which obtain in the laboratory at the time of its successful creation of life in a test tube could not be tested. But we already know enough. De la Mettrie indeed knew enough well over two hundred years ago—*L'Homme Machine* was published in 1748—to know that "the problem of life" is a scientific problem, and not a metaphysical one.

Alonzo would emphasize that the philosopher is under no obligation to provide answers when the scientist lacks them. Until the biologist supplies the answer, he must make peace with his ignorance. It might be well therefore to remember Hume's words in this connection: "Nothing is more requisite for a true philosopher than to restrain the intemperate desire of searching into causes; and having established any doctrine upon a sufficient number of experiments, rest contented with that, when he sees a further examination would lead him into obscure and uncertain speculations. In that case his inquiry would be much better employed in examining the effects than the causes of his principles."

With appropriate changes, what holds for life holds also for "consciousness," but with this added qualification. There seems to be on hand more plausible hypotheses regarding the origin of consciousness than there are regarding the origin of life. But for some reason philosophers are less tolerant of a scientific approach to consciousness than they are of a scientific approach to life. This is their realm, they still feel. Ignorance seems to give them rights which they do not dare to claim where true knowledge is available. Nor is it possible to do much with them, as long as they retain the deeply ingrained habit of thinking that consciousness is a thing. That the problem of consciousness is far from solved Alonzo would readily grant. However, in the light of a theory of mind like that of Mead to say that it still eludes scientific analysis is irresponsible. Books like Mead's *Mind, Self and Society*, however, have to make their way, when they are published, against the same kind of prejudice which scientific inquiry encountered in the sixteenth and seventeenth centuries and later, even after 1859. Life and mind are the last redoubts of obscurantism, and we may expect that philosophers will defend them fiercely to the last man.

3

Since man is altogether a part of Nature his life must be lived here on earth, within the strictures imposed by the laws of nature, and without help from any source beyond Nature. Only within the conditions imposed by Nature, therefore, will human life find what meaning it can. This earth of ours, this life we are now living, they are all we can count on. Nor did he, when he had accepted this fact, feel depressed because he had to give up the thought of immortality. To the egocentric arrogance of the human animal who wants to clutter the universe with his puny self forever Alonzo opposed his piety towards the greatness and wonder of the whole of Nature of which we are a part. Why should we feel depressed because some day we shall no longer be? If we have lived well we shall be tired when our hour comes and shall be glad to return to the earth. And if we have not lived well, why should we wish to prolong in another world a life that in this one we have not succeeded in making worth living? Life for its own dumb protoplasmic sake he did not want. The activity of protoplasm may be wonderful, it is indeed, and it is basic to any higher activity. But by itself it does not seem especially desirable.

Although a naturalist, Alonzo added, he hoped he did not lack piety for Nature from which all springs. Nor did his faith in scientific method dry up his sense of wonder at the onrush of natural processes. Nor did his beliefs embody a naïve trust that Nature is ultimately intelligible. Such trust would be, in the light of our ignorance, as gratuitous as it would be dogmatic.

It has often been said that the belief in an intelligible universe is a condition of continued scientific effort. It may have been so in the past. But do we need it today? Would not our curiosity find it equally desirable to discover just how intelligible the universe is? It may not be intelligible through and through, and the invariant relations that science finds may be only superficial. But as long as science continues its successful advance, its results should increase our wonder rather than diminish it, and should intensify our admiration and our piety which, Alonzo believed, freed from darkness, would choose a worthy object for itself not compelled by fear but urged by love.

He added that it was not the naturalist in whom natural piety is weakened or extinguished. Those who separate from Nature that aspect of it which we may call its creative principle, and who personify it and worship it as omnipotent and all good, are the men in whom natural piety finds no fertile ground. But Alonzo would add that to deny a "creative principle" in Nature would be to fly in the face of facts, facts that are patent at the level of naïve experience. The rotation of the heavens, the wonder of growth and of reproduction, the movement of an insect's wings, the swell of the tides, the energy of the sun, the quick electric flank of a living animal, the subtle rush of morning —obvious facts no less than recondite, bear testimony to a creative principle in Nature and to its onward march.

The sophisticate may quarrel with the use of terms such as *force* and feel the need for a precise definition of them. Alonzo knew that once one has asserted one's belief in Nature's creative principle there remains a vast number of legitimate, if technical and abstruse, questions to be answered. Until we answer them we cannot deem our philosophy completely satisfactory. Nor could these be resolved until we have examined our conception of time and space, and inquired into the validity of extending beyond the range of verifiable phenomena the meaning of terms like *cause, effect, beginning, agent, substance, creation, power, force*. A conscientious investigation of these matters will show anyone, he would urge, that as knowledge becomes more precise and more adequate, animistic concepts like *force* are discarded and vague notions like that of a creative principle are useless to the scientist. It then becomes clear that our most cherished dogmas rest upon terms the meaning of which turn out on inquiry to be mere metaphors, more adequate perhaps for expressing our feelings than for denoting the precise and distinct notions required by exact thought. Nevertheless, Alonzo would point out, so long as the spectacle of Nature continues to move us at a naïve level of experience, we shall need terms of one kind or another to express the fact, half insight and half feeling, that we are aware of onrushing creative processes in Nature.

Men have usually called this creative principle *God*. Though a naturalist can offer no legitimate objection to those who call Nature's creative principle *God*, Alonzo objected to those who hold that it is (in fact as well as in logic) distinct from its creatures and transcends them. There simply were no grounds for this assumption that an empiricist could accept. He disagreed also with those who believed that the creative principle is omnipotent and conscious of ends as we human beings are; that it is all good and cares for man in preference to any other of its creatures.

There was no empirical evidence, Alonzo asserted, to sustain any of these propositions, and the deductive chains which one usually finds supporting them depend—hang from—sentimental ambiguities and infantile needs. *Omnipotent* means all powerful. What evidence, Alonzo asked, do we have to assume that Nature's creative principle can accomplish anything and everything at all? Even Leibniz would limit its power to a choice of the best. And today there is no need to assert more than that for which we have evidence; namely, that compared with man's own powers, Nature is wonderfully powerful.

That Nature's creative principle can do more than it has been observed to do at any one time is clear from the fact that our knowledge of its power is increasing. But how much more? We do not know and by the very essence of the subject can never know. For that reason Santayana preferred the word *omnificent* to the word *omnipotent*.

4

These few articles formed the groundwork of Alonzo's beliefs. He was wont to sum them up in a formula: Faith in naturalism arises from the empirical use of human intelligence. But he would point out that a realistic faith in man's intelligence should not be optimistic. Alonzo's faith in intelligence did not commit him to the belief that man will inevitably end by achieving the knowledge he needs in order to arrive at a satisfactory life. Nor to the belief that life is at present satisfactory. For a few it is, but for most men the world over it is hardly any better than the life of brutes, and he believed that no one can live the good life at its best as long as this condition of affairs exists. For in order to be able to live a truly good life, a measure of sensitivity is necessary. And to be sensitive in a world like ours means not only to be open to a great amount of pain over the undeserved fate of millions of our fellows, but it also means to be prey to fear over the necessarily precarious quality of our own accidental good fortune—it means to be stalked by the fear of war and economic insecurity, and by the threat that the victims of exploitation shall rise and expropriate us.

However, Alonzo still had to face the following question: Although it is not possible to live an adequately good life today, to the degree that it might be possible what would it consist of, how would it be lived? This was not a question to which Alonzo could return an answer in the terms in which it is usually asked. For the naturalist, Alonzo would observe, must hold that in some sense or other values are created by man and change as historical conditions and as personal circumstances change. And he would conclude that no one can tell someone else what his values should be. All such answers, he believed, are arrogant and dogmatic, and should be distrusted profoundly, for the motives from which they take rise are not always generous and noble.

But if a person holding Alonzo's views ought not to offer advice to others about how to live their lives, there are two things, Alonzo thought, that he can do. He can, first, state quite candidly in concrete terms what he considers the good life to be for himself; and he can strive to make explicit the formal conditions he believes any man's life must fulfill in order to achieve that end.

The life Alonzo wanted to live was the student's life. Practical activity Alonzo had no desire to engage in. He found in ideas the excitement and drama others find in politics, business, or adventure.

Alonzo had learned that this desideratum needs not only to be defended from attack, but protected from an overstatement of its value. Those who prefer the intellectual life are wont to exalt it above all other forms of activity and to call it by many noble and high-sounding names. Alonzo did not believe it was necessary to refer to it in mouth-filling terms. For those who crave it, it has satisfactions above all others, and for them it is the best manner of life. But he knew that there are other ways of living grounded on different needs, and each of these offers those who choose it out of an inner urge its own satisfactions, and each performs, in the social scheme, its own necessary functions. The student's life is one, only one, of the modes of the good life; but it should not be forgotten that it is possible only in societies which, having achieved a measure of ease and control of their environment, enjoy a margin of abundance to take care of those not engaged in material production. However, Alonzo was keenly concerned with pointing out that the student's life is today possible only at the cost of the exploitation and degradation of millions of men. This he took to be a hard truth; but one which cannot be left out of a proper estimate of the value of the student's life.

Alonzo would continue. Frequently, as if to redress the wrong of overvaluation, the intellectual life today is held up to scorn by a great many practical men as being useless and irrelevant. That it is remote from practical activity is, no one would deny, obvious. That it is relevant is not always easy to see, for its relevance depends on one's interests. But useless to society, Alonzo held, it is not. There are, of course, perversions of it. The term *academic*, when used in its pejorative sense, is not always misplaced; some academic work is worthless, some has little value. But one of the functions of the scholar is to keep alive the traditions of human culture and to make them available to his contemporaries. And one of the functions of the thinker is to give men a sense of the meaning of their activities against a larger whole than they are able to perceive, by analyzing the more distant implications of their current beliefs. In furnishing men with a background against which they can place their lives, the thinker—poet, philosopher, or myth-maker—gives content to men's lives. Only then is a man able fully to live in a culture; only then does life gain in interest, in intensity; only then does life gain its greatest possible density. Only then, Alonzo was sure, can life become truly civilized. This was a sustaining conviction of his: The student's activities are not useless activities, and human societies, for all their blind worship of brute force, have usually recognized, in their wasteful and halfhearted way, the intrinsic value of scholarship.

But what of the arguments, Alonzo asked himself, of those who scorn a manner of life which is not addressed centrally to political activity and social reform? The student answers these arguments with the observation that his job, if it is going to be well done, is a full-time job, just as a political job is. His own work, he would point out, was exacting and his time and energies were limited.

However, he thought, our world is so poorly organized and the opportunities for unavoidable conflict occur so often, that the student cannot be merely a student, the scientist merely a scientist. The values by which they live, Alonzo was keenly aware, may be threatened, and if the scholar is serious he will defend them. Again, the activities of the scholar have social consequences. The scholar must beware lest his activities be turned to use by the barbarians. The student ought to be alert, and not only for altruistic reasons but also for very selfish ones, lest his values be betrayed.

5

But not all men desire to live the student's life. There are an almost infinite number of tasks to be undertaken in a civilized society, and men are impelled by a bewildering number of aspirations and diversity of goals. Alonzo asked himself whether an account could be given of the good life that would apply to all men and at all times. Such an account would have to be abstract, but no less useful both practically and theoretically for that reason. The difficulty of the question cannot be underestimated, in view of the notorious disagreements among moralists and the mutually conflicting purposes of men. Partiality could not be avoided; again, an inevitable amount of subjectivity was bound to creep into such an account.

But the formal conditions of the good life could be laid down, nevertheless, and thus with a generous application of ideas from Santayana and Dewey, Alonzo was ready to tackle the problem. However, he was aware of an essential prior condition that a generalized notion of the good life had to meet. For the naturalist, a conception of the good life cannot claim a priori normative validity. Its obligatory nature derives from the actual existence of operative desires or drives in the individual, such as he is, functioning in a social world. Human beings not only dwell in culture but culture dwells in them. When Robinson Crusoe was wrecked he not only brought to his island a few tools and utensils, but the culture that dwelt in him. No person can live totally outside a social organization. Maroon a person young enough (before the culture into which he was born is well established in him) or for long enough, and you destroy him as a human being. That the social organization proves to be a greater influence on the person in the vast majority of cases than the person on it, tends to confirm this view. A totally isolate man, a human monad, may be conceivable but he is in fact not possible. Even Leibniz's monads reflected the universe.

The essential component of the good life is the possession of an operative masterful interest. A man is to be pitied who has no master drive, no dominant urge, no controlling passion, no exclusive and jealous purpose to which his energies are addressed, that save him from scattering his hours like a spoonful of mercury falling from a few feet onto a polished floor. A man for whom all things are equally good is a man for whom all things are equally boring or meaningless; such a man cannot live a good life. Unless a man discovers a masterful interest—which is to say, an interest that masters him—he joins the crowd of pitiful seekers after happiness, or pleasure, or sensation; he dies without ever having lived. To live it is necessary to choose, but to choose is to eschew.

The dominant interest that is the condition of the good life must possess a number of indispensable characteristics, Alonzo thought. One of these is that the interest must be such that it grows or at least is not extinguished for good but reappears periodically after its satisfaction. For to the extent that it ceases to be operative it leaves a man empty and purposeless. The satisfaction of our physical hungers soon surfeits us; if our activity is addressed exclusively to them we live only intermittently. But Alonzo knew that there were objects which, when achieved, strengthen rather than kill altogether the interest that initiated the pursuit. Art does this. Science does it, too. Many other activities, even the satisfaction of a drive to power in those cases, probably rare, in which the pursuit of dominion over others does not lead to arrogance and indifference to their interests. And friendship, when grounded not merely on mutual material interest but on native sympathy and a community of ideal ends. So does the practical activity of social melioration, when it does not kill the worker's moral fiber through the compromises it forces on him. So do the pursuit of useful activities recognized by major civilizations.

The master interest must also be such that in pursuing its ends, it does not starve out other strong needs, one of which must be the social interest. A narrow egoism, a clannish selfishness, a social indifference which belies our human sympathy, may intensify experience, but it also narrows it to the point of starving it. Frustrating the native needs of our social nature, egoism chokes sources of profound satisfactions. We count the contributions of the Stoics a gain in the history of thought, because in breaking the narrow clannishness of the Greek mind (a break made possible, let us not forget, through the material exigencies of Macedonian and Roman imperialism) it expanded the possibility of experience and enriched European living. This also was the contribution of Christianity, with its central emphasis on the brotherhood of man. On the other hand we ought to object to the brutalization of most of mankind which is demanded by our economic system because it narrows our experience, makes us insensitive, and gives our lives a quality of insecurity which pervades all our social relationships.

Another characteristic that often enhances the goodness of life is present when the dominant interest is satisfied by activity that allows a man to use his creative powers. But this condition can only be met in cultures that have achieved a high civilization. Nor must we restrict creativity to the arts and the sciences. Creativity manifests itself, or can manifest itself, in all modes of human activity, however humble. In a stable culture it may not be at a premium, but the initial creation of any culture, however low, is the product of the creative power of man. A primitive, however, can live the good life, although he is not able to live the life some of us live—a life which allows for the appearance and exercise of powers the primitive knows nothing of.

Alonzo took the possession of a masterful interest as qualified to be the condition of the good life. But he did not mean that life could not be lived well by those who had never heard of his formulation. He knew that men can live well, and have done so, without philosophy, especially in a society that is well ordered and which has, therefore, reared adequate institutions to satisfy the needs that man acquires as he grows to maturity. Nor did Alonzo claim for his concept that if faithfully followed it would inevitably produce a good life. For throughout the world there were, unquestionably, other valid factors of which he

knew nothing. Nor can life in the end be a matter of rules or principles. Even in the most petrified society life always involves some risk,
some chance, a modicum of novelty—it never altogether lacks the
quality of adventure. And it is well that this be the case, for surprise
tones the organism and novelty primes interest, risk adds zest to living,
and a measure of insecurity of possession shocks us into prizing that
which we value.

If we shift the subject of discourse from the good life to the moral
life, we must acknowledge that living involves qualities other than the
use of intelligence that one of Dewey's disciples has overemphasized,
while neglecting or slighting others. Besides sheer good luck it involves
qualities that we must call by the old fashioned term of *virtue*. These
cannot be acquired by the use of intelligence or reasoning, nor can
they be inculcated in schools, colleges, and universities. They do not
arise from ratiocination or knowledge. *Reasoning*, or *knowledge*—for
this purpose the terms can be used interchangeably—enables a man to
get what he wants and all too often to rationalize his actions on the
grounds that what he wants is good for others as well as for himself. It
is a faculty that enables politicians, Levantine rug peddlers in disguise
with which our world is supersaturated, and men on the make—the
kind of men who flourish like weeds in a world in which success is the
goal—a success, alas, all too often conceived in narrowly selfish terms.
But success, or what the world calls success, and moral living are not
always identical.

In a dynamic society such as ours, intelligence is indispensable in
order to avoid failure in any sense; but such qualities as goodwill, ami-
ability, decency, charity, honesty, reliability, loyalty, the capacity to
sympathize with the pain and frustration of others—these and other
virtues must interrelate with knowledge, or reasoning, to bring about
a life we can call moral. As G. G. Coulton puts it, these virtues do
not have their source in scientific observation or rigid logic, or as he
puts it elsewhere, in the naked intellect, but in character, which, says
Coulton, is sometimes more important than knowledge. Alonzo would
amend Coulton's statement and say that these virtues are not only
sometimes more important than knowledge, but they are at least as
essential for the conduct of the moral life as knowledge. To the virtues
mentioned Alonzo would add a virtue to which he gave pride of place,
a virtue that is not in abundance in our society: integrity. Without a
resolute integrity, Alonzo was convinced, men become either victims

of their own ambition or, and not against their wishes, the tools of those driven by the lust for power. In whatever sphere of life men find themselves, they will always find other men to enslave, whether materially or spiritually. The slave demands our pity; the enslaver, our contempt.

Alonzo was confident that he had sketched an abstract picture of the good life. But he did not forget that life is often uncertain, hard, cruel, and unmitigatedly ugly and painful. He had known a number of people who had committed suicide. We are often the victims of sheer arbitrary cruelty and arrogance. We are also the victims of natural conditions over which we have no control. More often than not the cruelty and arrogance of which we are victims are unconscious, and exact as high a price of the victimizer as they do of the victim. But not infrequently are they the expression of self-conscious malice. When men's treachery and hypocrisy and beastly malice—which we ourselves are usually as often guilty of as others—sting us, then the eyes go blind, the throat pulls, and the empty choke inside the chest beats up a chaos of hatred and pain. It is then that our resources of reason and courage are strained, and it is then that we need remember that without integrity and self-respect one cannot live the freeman's life.

The darkness, however, does not drag on forever; even in the midst of a long, drawn-out catastrophe the body reasserts itself and the mind gains a measure of equanimity. For no reason and from nowhere a liquid stream of joy runs in and floods us, lifting the anguish. The darkness breaks, is forgotten, and the day comes when life seems intensely worth living. All the more so if by understanding the source of evil we see the possibility of turning our impotent hatred into the creative task of eradicating its cause. This is what the good life is, a life that on cool reflection is judged to be worth living.

VII
The Red Thirties

1

HOW DID Alonzo come to slide from the blurred stereotypes of his liberalism to a more extreme, if no less stereotyped, Marxism? The answer to this question, were it possible to give it in detail, would furnish us the key, or at least one of the principal keys, to the insensate drift of a large number of members of Alonzo's generation towards the Left. But a complete account of the drift cannot be attempted here because Alonzo does not recall, or perhaps more exactly, does not want to make the effort to recall, the nature and the exactly felt quality of the pressures, the real and self-induced fears, threats, and tensions of the early thirties, that pushed him more or less consciously to the Left; pushed him to the Left, but not far enough to make him take the step that at one time he feared he would be invited to take, to join "The Party."

Until the middle thirties, as is obvious from the preceding chapter, Alonzo's social philosophy had been instinct with a generalized goodwill toward man—in the abstract. By *man* Alonzo and his friends usually meant *oppressed, exploited, victimized* man, the *worker*—a Platonic idea whose human embodiment neither his friends nor he had encountered in reality. Alonzo and his friends were the sons and daughters of white-collar parents, and their conception of the worker was an idealized embodiment of all the qualities and virtues that heroes and saints possess. Had you pointed out to them that they were indulging in fantasy, that oppression and exploitation did not always ennoble people but often made them coarse and brutish, they would have dismissed you as a prejudiced person, a reactionary and enslaver who wanted to keep men in chains. Because the worker was perfect and enslaved it was urgent to help him break the shackles that the enemy had riveted on him. It was imperative to cooperate with him in the building of heaven on earth.

How kind or decent Alonzo and his friends themselves were toward actual individuals, how much concerned for the dignity or self-respect of those with whom they had concrete relations, it is not pertinent to record in detail here. Enough to say that his memory of the years until the end of the thirties in Midland City makes him blush, although he was no worse than any of his friends. They treated their friends and colleagues without charity, they enjoyed carrying tales and spreading malicious gossip even about their own friends, when their backs were turned. They professed virtues that were not at all practiced and practiced vices they were not aware of. In short, they were ordinary people, whose only extraordinary trait was that they thought very well of themselves.

One of the first inklings Alonzo had of what a bitchy lot he and his friends were toward one another took place in New York one evening at a gathering at a literary critic's home in West 116th Street near Riverside Drive. There were a number of well-known writers in the living room and the conversation, as usual, was about recent books, current events, the danger of Germany and the probability of the United States' entering the war, about which a number of them were not very happy. All was going very well when one of the guests got up to leave. The moment the door was closed on him, the whole lot tore him to pieces. Some of the things they had against him were true, some grossly exaggerated, and some seemed to be of dubious truth or relevance. But there was not a word said in his defense. Soon after, someone else had to leave and the pack now turned to the new victim. And a third and a fourth. It soon became clear to Alonzo that some of them were delaying the moment of departure. Since Alonzo had to go relatively early he knew there would be enough dogs in the pack to lacerate him. And there was no difference between the men and the women: the pack was fierce and showed no mercy. These were the men and women who were going to create a better world.

Alonzo knew some of the things they would say about him. A hick from the Middle West. He once had heard Haten say of a brilliant professor of philosophy who taught in a middle western university that he was not good enough to teach in New York, although some of Haten's own departmental colleagues weren't good enough to teach where the brilliant middle westerner taught. That they would have at Alonzo the moment he left didn't matter. What mattered was the sudden realization of the abysmally bitchy nature of these men and women—all highly talented, all accomplished, but all mutually envious, each and every one, of the rest. Thus were the self-elected keepers of the intellectual and moral health of the nation. Their political opinions, in spite of slight differences, constituted a solid orthodoxy that could not be questioned, although all of them being avowed empiricists, they should have known that their views were corrigible.

2

But the world's social and political climate was changing rapidly: The threats that had hung over civilization since the beginning of the century and that had brought about the monstrous catastrophe of the war of 1914 were again getting ominous, the fears were getting more intense, the louring clouds more foreboding. Or at least so it seemed, and not only to Alonzo but to a large number of men and women of his age and older and even to no small number of younger people. These men and women, shocked by the threat that gradually became more ominous, were turning towards the side that was promising to build a better world.

It was a question whether the threats, fears, and the advancing darkness of which Alonzo and his friends were all so keenly aware were not to some extent imagined or self-induced. Some self-delusion no doubt there was; but the Wall Street gamblers who woke up on Tuesday 29 October 1929 loaded with money and went to bed stripped of every penny they owned in paper profits; the Kansas City broker who shot himself; or the broker in Santiago, Chile; or the man whose body was pulled out of the Hudson River; or the women who fainted in brokerage offices—these people were not deluded. Their paper profits may have been a delusion, but the gains of those who sold in time (Alonzo knew one who did) and their feeling of triumph, and the sense of catastrophe of those who did not, were real, all too real. The letter Alonzo got every spring renewing his appointment was not an unpleasant dream. There it was, in type, signed by the chairman of the department: The appointment, the letter said, had been renewed for the following year, but the renewal did not commit the department to renewal in the future. Renewal would depend on the budget. The cut in

salary was no bad dream either. Nor was the knowledge that if the
appointment was not to be renewed, there would be no academic jobs
to be had at all, anywhere, and the alternative would be a job with the
WPA Writers' Project. These were realities.

In June 1930 Alonzo took off a year from his job at State to go to
Germany to study the language. A valuable year, the experience was
not altogether pleasant, for the presence of the Nazis could not be
avoided either in Munich or in Frankfort on the Main, where he finally settled. It was especially unpleasant in Munich, where in order to
reach the center of town, Alonzo had to pass Nazi headquarters. Two
rigid sentinels at the door with their trench shovels at shoulder arms—
there was nothing imaginary about the threat these people posed. Nor
was the experience of being caught in a riot at night while returning to
his boarding house a pleasant experience. Alonzo had not realized that
he was entering a riot zone. Enormous police buses came on suddenly,
sirens screaming, and began disgorging police who swept the street
with their nightsticks. Fortunately Alonzo was at the opposite end of
the street from where the buses entered and had time to get away from
the charge. But the experience was no delusion. In Frankfort the Nazis
and the Communists arranged for a nightly fight in a certain square in
order to break the back of civic morale; and although he never saw the
actual fights Karl Heinrich, the self-avowed Communist with whom
he was very friendly and who gave Alonzo the information, was clearly
not lying.

These experiences were not illusions. Neither was another experience he had back in Midland City a short time before Roosevelt's election. Alonzo was talking with one of his brothers-in-law, Sasha, one
afternoon in the living room of their ground-floor flat when the bell
rang. A man at the door asked whether he could cut the lawn, and the
following conversation took place:

"No," said Alonzo, "there are two able-bodied men in the apart-
ment and we do it."

"Is there no other job I can do?" asked the man with a faint touch of
pleading in his voice. He would gladly do anything and for very little.

"No," said Alonzo, beginning to take notice, "we do all the jobs that
need doing." But he added, "Can't you get a job?"

"No," said the man, "I've been trying to for two or three days and
can't find a thing to do."

Alonzo came to, and with some hesitation asked, "Have you had lunch?"

"Lunch?" said the man. "I wish I'd had breakfast." He needed a job to get a meal. And he would do anything and for only the price of a meal.

"Would you accept lunch?" asked Alonzo.

"Yes," said the man almost breaking down, "Yes, if it is not too much trouble, I sure would."

"No, it won't be too much trouble," said Alonzo, leading him to the kitchen.

Four eggs were quickly scrambled and some bacon fried. Sasha put a loaf of bread and some butter in front of the man, a glass of milk, and asked him to start while the eggs were cooking. They heated coffee and set it before the man, with the cream and sugar. The eggs and bacon followed and were quickly finished. A package of cigarettes was pushed to him when he was through.

The man said that now that he had eaten he would hitchhike to Milwaukee, where he thought the chances of a job might be better. Alonzo offered him a half dollar. There was not much conversation and the fellow had a hard time thanking them.

An experience of this sort was not a delusion. Alonzo had never before come across real hunger face to face. He could not get the memory of the incident out of his mind for days; and the more he thought about it the more anxious, angry, and frightened he became. Frightened of what? Of nothing specific for himself, for he had a job for next year and the first stirrings of a breeze of promise were in the air. Just frightened. But what emerged in the long run was anger, barely conscious but steady, gnawing, bitter anger. The thought of the man came back unexpectedly for days afterward, for weeks and months, and it brought bitterness with it, it brought inward emptiness and a dry pull at the throat that was an acute physical pain.

This was the kind of experience from which the Communists were shaping with great skill an intense propaganda program which was to lead in a few years to a collective hysteria, a mass panic among a large number of intellectuals. The stage was set: the crash and depression in the United States and in the world at large was to lead to the triumph of Hitler. A few weeks after Hitler came to power Alonzo got a letter from Karl Heinrich posted in London. Alonzo, who had liked and thought highly of Karl and his wife, had kept a desultory correspondence with his Communist friend since his own return from Germany. Karl wrote that he had escaped from a concentration camp near Berlin and asked Alonzo whether something might be found for him to do in the United States, preferably a teaching job, but anything. Alonzo spoke to Perlman, the professor of labor economics at State, who obtained a fellowship for Karl. A few weeks later Karl and his wife found themselves in Midland City, where both made at first a good impression.

Time went by fast. Suddenly, although not unexpected by Alonzo and his friends, the curtain rose. The Spanish civil war began. The situation in Spain had been touch and go for some time. But they believed that the republic would be able to survive—a belief founded on nothing but hope. One morning in New York, where Alonzo was staying for a few days with friends, he picked up the *New York Times*. The army had risen in Spain. Two generals were leading Fascist columns toward Madrid. The one leading the army of Africa was named Franco. The pacifism to which Alonzo had passionately subscribed since his teens fell suddenly from him and broke in pieces on the floor. Had he decided suddenly—or was this the outburst of a gradual accumulation of forces leading toward what seemed a sudden break? Alonzo did not stop to think. No decent man could, at the moment, under the circumstances. One had to bet what one had, immediately, all one had, all of it, whatever the odds, without reservations. There was only one side, the side of the republic. That meant one was on the side of those who helped the republic. This included the Stalinists. For him this was the unconscious beginning of an attitude that ruled his conduct for the next few years: no enemies to the left.

3

On his return to Midland City the September after the beginning of the Spanish civil war Alonzo became active in the Teachers Union and when shortly after the beginning of the fall semester the Spanish Committee was formed to aid the Spanish republic, Alonzo became one of its most vociferous members.

The Teachers Union and the Spanish Committee demonstrated once and for all that Leibniz's principle of the identity of the indis-

cernibles does not hold in politics. According to the principle, if two
things have identical traits in every respect they are not two but one.
Here were two different organizations that had identical membership
and operative purposes—although this was not openly admitted—and
were indeed two, not one. They were one as to over-all aims, direc-
torate, hope, faith, and above all the unreasoning passion of its members. They were two, in the sense that with an identical group control-
ing both organizations, they were a double-barreled means of raising
hell.

Alonzo had joined the Teachers Union before the beginning of the
Spanish civil war, at the invitation of Phil Brickmaster. Phil was a man
considerably older than the average graduate student, with a colorful
IWW past, who had somehow found his way to State, had after a pro-
bationary period been admitted into the Graduate School, and was
working toward a Ph.D. in labor economics under Perlman. Alonzo
remembers vividly the day Phil asked him to join the Union. It was in
the cafeteria of the Student's Union. At Phil's invitation Alonzo replied that he saw no point in a college or university teachers union.
For such a union would never go on strike. And a union that was
known to avoid strikes had surrendered its demands before it made
them. In principle, Alonzo acknowledged, it could go on strike. But
Alonzo did not believe that sheep would ever turn against the wolves
that came at the flock or would resist the men that corralled them to
shear them and turn them into chops.

Phil replied that the union would be a school where college teachers
would learn the need for the strike if necessary. But Alonzo replied he
knew his colleagues too well to believe them capable of any such heroics. "You have to begin somewhere," said Phil. "Yes, but you also had
to begin with something, you could not begin with nothing," retorted
Alonzo, "and that was precisely what academic careerists and academic castrati—and the expressions were synonymous—could bring,
nothing." "Isn't that an exaggeration?" asked Phil earnestly. "Yes, I
beg your pardon, it is an exaggeration. I am wrong," said Alonzo, in
mock seriousness. "There are two great virtues that the academic possesses in almost unlimited quantity: the virtue of seeing all sides of a
question all at once, particularly the administration's side; and the
virtue of doing something about their grievances by bitching among
themselves, like Tibetan monks whirling their prayer wheels until,

sodden with somnolence, they slide off into a sour dream." He paused dramatically. "Perhaps you can use these virtues in a union?" Alonzo asked Phil triumphantly.

Phil would not give up. The union would discipline and teach those who could be taught and there were more of them than Alonzo was willing to concede, although he admitted that he had not been around professors as long as Alonzo. The discussion was coming to a standstill when Phil said—as a sort of afterthought—that there was something else the union could do, an important job, too. It could lend prestige to the public and high school locals and they certainly needed it. Alonzo replied, "You know enough about union theory to know that altruism is no part of a union's business. A union is an association of men brought together by a common interest, ready to fight for that interest." He added that the theory has nothing whatever to say about altruism. One fought for the material interest of a group because in the not-too-long run it is one's own. If you wanted to join a group in order to help others, you should join the boy scouts and help little old ladies cross the street. "That," replied Phil, "is to conceive of interests in too narrow a way."

Alonzo saw the point; he backtracked and went at the point that had been dropped a few moments earlier. "A union that does not strike, what sort of a thing is that?" he asked. "The strike is the point of purchase and the bar." "Bad physics?" said Phil. "Perhaps. This is the point: You push for your demands with the threat of a strike, and if the damned employer insists on sitting on his elbow, you hit him with the bar, you strike." "Finally," replied Phil, "the logic of the strike leads to the general strike." "Right, and the general strike is one step short of revolution. To the barricades, Phil." "The barricades? That's nineteenth-century stuff. Today you first infiltrate the army and then you take the radio station, the telephone exchange, the power plant, the railroad station, and the post office," said Phil. "But can you see Professor Castrado leading the charge on the radio station or manning the barricades? If you can, you must also hear mamma, as he departs for battle, telling him to keep his feet dry."

Phil probably enjoyed Alonzo's rhetorical tirades as much as Alonzo enjoyed sparring with Phil, who knew that one way to keep Alonzo going was to raise objections. But it was past one o'clock. Alonzo finally stopped and Phil asked, "When do we start?" "Start where?" "To the radio station, of course," said Phil smiling. "After you sign me up," said Alonzo sheepishly. "By the way," he asked, "what's the totem of our union, a sheep or an ox?" But Phil was serious about working men, unions, and strikes, for he was to the slums born, and as a wobbly he had had his brushes with the cops in the Northwest; whereas Alonzo, for all his identification with the worker, couldn't take seriously the theory or the practice of a teachers union and joined chiefly to please Phil. He paid his fees and never went to a meeting—until he returned from New York after the start of the Spanish civil war.

But now there was no more kidding about strikes and professors with wet feet and their totems. Soon after his return the Spanish Committee was formed. Both groups, committee and union, entered the fight and it was serious business. Controlled by Stalinists, the union became the tool of agitation for domestic causes while the committee collected money and made propaganda in favor of the Spanish republicans. With both objectives he was heartily in agreement. But if he was, why did he not join the Communist party particularly at a time when indiscriminate recruiting was going and people were being admitted to membership without any tests? He was asked to join a number of times but he had the sense to refuse. First, he knew he could cooperate with them from outside the party as well as from inside; and then he did not like the way the members were regimented, led, pushed around, losing their own individuality and yielding entirely to their superiors.

Take this experience: The Teachers Union carried on agitation for any cause that it could get hold of for the purposes of publicity against university, state, and federal authorities. The theory was simple and therefore effective. First you got a cause, an evil, or injustice, preferably real, but if not real, blown-up or even invented. Since institutions are always full of injustices, the job consisted for the most part in magnifying troubles. When you had your injustice, you drew up a petition addressed to the administration and you gave it to student sympathizers to circulate among the teachers for their signatures. The students who brought the petition for signing soon got to know who would sign without reading, solely on the student's statement of the content of the petition, who would read it carefully, and who would not sign at all. The latter were approached anyhow, chiefly to annoy them—which, apparently, was the only effect petitions had on the administration and the conservative members of the staff. That was what carrying the fight at the home front meant.

The expectation on the part of the comrades manipulating the

Teachers Union and the Spanish Committee was that all party members would sign the petitions. Party members, under party discipline, would not dream of not signing. But they had no means of forcing their sympathizers to sign. This fact led to Alonzo's first brush with the comrades. A petition about the housing situation was brought to him to sign. The grievance, a real one this time, arose from the fact that there were not enough university dormitories for girls at State. Girls were housed in private houses run by "house mothers" who were under the supervision of the dean of women. But a large number of house mothers did not accept Jewish girls and as a result a large number of girls coming from well-to-do families in New York, Chicago, and elsewhere, were forced to room in undesirable houses. The university did not want to get into a fight about the situation. And this was just made to order for the Teachers Union. A "Fair Housing Committee" was formed, fronted by a number of students, and the usual petition was drawn up. But it asked for more than fair housing for girls. It asked that fraternities and sororities should be forced to take in anyone who knocked at the door.

Alonzo already knew about the petition, and when a student came around with it, Alonzo refused to sign it. Fraternities and sororities were private organizations, he told the student, and therefore had a perfect right to select their members any way they liked, however arbitrary or prejudiced the criterion by which they made their selection might be. Rooming houses were a different matter. But if a group recognized by the university did not like to associate with Bostonians or Roman Catholics or Jews or Shintoists or Duk Duks, that was their business. On the petition's principle, he added, every time Alonzo gave a party he would have to be sure there were representatives of the population present, and that involved inviting Orthodox Jews and Chinese, members of the WTCU and bus drivers, Italians from the Bush, and a few Negroes. This was the only way he could conform to the principle for which the petition was being circulated: prejudices should be regulated out of existence. But he, Alonzo, did have prejudices, and they were strong, and he had not the least intention of giving them up. He'd be damned if he was going to invite Spanish Nationalists or Orthodox Jews or WTCU members to his parties. Nationalists and WTCU he would not invite for obvious reasons. As to the Orthodox Jews, some of his best friends . . .—but he'd be damned if he was going to get himself a second set of dishes or give up serving ham and oysters at his parties to go along with some of his friends' silly taboos. And he'd be damned if he was going to take it if anyone came around telling him whom he could or could not invite to his parties.

Friendship is a form of prejudice, and if the "Fair Housing Committee" wanted to abolish all prejudice, it should make its aims explicit and state how it proposed to do it. As far as he, Alonzo, was concerned, he would sign a petition asking for the closing of fraternities and sororities. There were good reasons for abolishing them. Alonzo had fought them in engineering school years back and he knew what a crummy lot of living anachronisms they were, with their odious anti-Semitism and their fancied superiority. They subverted the aims that Alonzo was hired to serve as a teacher. But so long as they were allowed to exist, they had the right to choose their members in any way they liked and to exclude anyone or any group they did not like, whether they excluded saints, angels, redheads, people with warts on their noses, people with six toes, or with or without foreskins.

It did not take long before the comrades heard about Alonzo's "insubordination," as one of them put it to him. And the attempt was made to treat him as they treated their own members. They called them on the carpet and ranted at them—and, of course, threatened expulsion. Alonzo was not exactly called on the carpet, but two members were sent to argue with him. He made it clear to them that he did not admit their right to dictate what he should sign or how he should think, but he did not mind answering their arguments. These were the cut and dried arguments about prejudice and the injustice of fraternities and sororities with their racial prejudices. Alonzo had a good time telling them off.

In retrospect the experience was unpleasant but immensely revealing. These liberators assumed the right to control the private lives, feelings, judgments, not only of their members but of their fellow travelers; these liberators were for the liberty of their friends so long as they toed the line. They could not understand that a person had the right to choose his friends on any ground whatever, however stupid or arbitrary it might be; and least of all could they understand the corollary of this right, the right to exclude anyone they did not want to mix with. The idea of forcing on a person a roommate or a tablemate he did not want to associate with was, as far as Alonzo was concerned, utterly inadmissible; it violated the right of the individual to be what he was. And that right, alas, included the right to be wrong from Alonzo's point of view.

Soldiers, galley slaves, Jesuits—men who are dead because they give up their bodies to the society—could not choose their companions, if their superiors decided they could not. But the "greeks" could, Alonzo held, so long as fraternities and sororities were a legitimate form of association on campus. The comrades could not or would not accept the assumption. To smash the fraternities and sororities by any means was good enough, even if their effort to smash them violated the right of a person to be himself. These people had, morally speaking, a considerably stronger stomach than Alonzo had.

Although after this experience the comrades were a little more circumspect in their treatment of Alonzo, there were a few other small incidents that taught Alonzo clearly that these heroes of liberty were not happy unless they had their members and friends goose-stepping and singing the marching songs they called. No dissent was allowed. For Alonzo, the point of the lesson was that a man who valued his independence, who, if you like, was a bit of an anarchist, could not join their party. He had known this in theory; now he knew it in actuality. He wouldn't have lasted many days after joining and the consequences for him would have been catastrophic.

Why? Because when you were thrown out of the party the comrades were not satisfied with letting you go, they undertook to destroy you; they did it systematically and as thoroughly as possible. They did not know it, but they worked on Bismarck's principle that it was wrong not to destroy your enemy if you had him in your hands. In the United States, as a rule, they did not go in for killing those they expelled or those who defected unless they had been in the underground. But they assassinated your character and made it as unpleasant for you as they could, and since it was a systematic job carried on by an organized group, the consequences could be very unpleasant.

4

Alonzo's drift to the Left had not been a sudden event, the result of a new sensibility that came suddenly into being with Franco's invasion of Spain. Nor was it solely the result of extending to the Left social and political ideas absorbed from Dewey or from his long association with liberals. Nor was it the result of his reading *The Nation* since 1917 and *The New Republic* since the early twenties. His liberal beliefs and attitudes were the result of a sensibility he had held since childhood. For

Alonzo's concern with justice had been manifested in Caracas and had been with him all along, dormant now and then, but occasionally aroused by circumstance. Unconsciously he had been a Quijote. Although quite capable of cruelty and injustice in his behavior toward others, there were some acts of cruelty or injustice that, when committed by others, he could not stomach.

The world was sodden with injustice, with the cruel, arbitrary abuse of power. It took no great acuity to see these qualities in the past and present. There was injustice at the level of personal relations, social injustice, international injustice—injustice and cruelty wherever you turned—even, alas, when you occasionally turned inwards, in recollection, and had glimpses in yourself of the traits you hated in others.

It was this sense of the permanent and ubiquitous presence of injustice and cruelty in the past and in contemporary experience that was the chief reason he could not share the optimism that was the mendacious component of the *Weltgeist* before 1914, which in spite of the war still endured. Even now, when he was cooperating with the Communists, this sense kept him from becoming a chiliast, a real, thoroughgoing believer in Kingdom-come-to-earth-tomorrow. And it was undoubtedly one of the factors that kept him from joining "The Party." He could cooperate with the Communists to fight injustice, but he could never quite bring himself to believe—although he tried hard enough—that utopia could be created in this world. Nor could he share another article of faith that was fundamental to the secular chiliast: the belief that the human nature one saw in action in the past and today was solely the result of "the system."

VIII

Objections to Marx

1

ALTHOUGH Alonzo could not be a chiliast, his sense of justice made him now veer Left. In a world in which hungry men cannot find work one had to do something, anything. But his stance was not merely a thoughtless, passionate response to the outrage of injustice and unnecessary suffering. In the late twenties and early thirties he had begun to read Marx and Lenin. As a minor for his doctor's degree he had chosen history of political theory. His feelings, had they not been informed by his reading and his discussions with like-minded friends, would have remained inchoate and sterile; the theory that gave them some shape, tempered them, and generated activity, was at hand—Marxism. There was no other political theory available for him at the time, since Dewey, for all his emphasis on practice, had no practical program worth considering. Dewey believed in education, as he conceived it; but education, conceived in any way whatever, was not going to feed the hungry. As a tool of social reform Alonzo could not take education seriously. It might be, indeed it was one of the indispensable elements in the reform of society, but education alone was not enough, and the liberal program was, thus, a failure. In any case, Alonzo had a strong, although vague, distrust of the instrumentalist theory of education. He could not have stated his feeling clearly, but it was there, deeply rooted, and it could not be done away with.

But what of Marxist theory did Alonzo accept? He was no student of Marx, in the sense that some of his friends were. He had read Marx and had learned from discussions with his Marxist friends, but there was a great deal of Marx he had not read, and whole components of Marxist theory, as he understood it, that were to him totally unacceptable—as he understood it, for he would not conceal the limitations of his knowledge of it. Marxism was a complete philosophy: a philosophy of nature, of culture, as well as a philosophy of action. As developed by Lenin it was an ethic, or rather a denial of morality, since the revolutionary morality of which Lenin and Trotsky wrote and spoke was, like the alleged honor among thieves, a program that allowed the revolutionist to behave as he chose toward his opponents. The whole edifice was based on Hegel's hopscotch of the dialectic—the skips from thesis to antithesis to synthesis in a never-ending upward swing of fuller realization and ever closer reaching to perfection, till it arrived at the Prussian State with Hegel on his chair in Berlin.

The notion of the dialectic had been advanced long before Hegel, but he had given it its final formulation by organizing in terms of it the process of the whole universe, including human history. If one went by the seriousness with which Marxists took the hopscotch, he had to come to the conclusion that for them it was uncontroversially true, as nothing else could be, since all knowledge depended on it; so true, indeed, that even some enlightened minds, minds not ignorant of the history of philosophy and of science, accepted it. It was claimed that the hopscotch of the dialectic was a universal law of change, a law that governed all change in the whole of the universe, physical and human. It was a law having a sort of absolute authority, a law of laws, to which all lesser laws conformed, and probably because of its supreme dignity, it did not have to be born as lesser laws are, in the travail of the mind working in the laboratory. It had come forth all at once, fully formed, from the brains of idealistic philosophers.

If you asked an ordinary non-Marxist scientist for evidence of a hypothesis he advanced, he gave you a complicated argument that consisted of hypotheses accepted in the past and new observations that forced a correction of the old hypotheses, which in turn gave rise to new observations; the scientist was now in possession of new data which led to a new hypothesis and further observations. The whole activity was grounded on empirical data. And it was corrigible through and through. Or at least, this was the official version of the theory; in actuality, of course, matters were somewhat different, but not so different that they made this sketch false. Nothing like that had given rise to the notion of the universal hopscotch of the dialectic. If you asked a Marxist for the proof of the theory of dialectical materialism what he gave you were illustrations of it, which after a while turned out to be frightfully boring because they were utterly simplistic and hackneyed, like the old chestnut about steam turning to water and water to ice. Only the Hegelian mind could take that kind of "law" seriously. Apparently Marx, on turning Hegel right side up, had failed to shake him, and the nonsense in his pockets had not fallen out.

The dialectic was the basis of Marxist truth. But Alonzo had read Hegel's lectures on the history of philosophy and remembered how supercilious the Great German was towards the physical sciences because, claimed the Great Thinker, the knowledge they offered was, as compared to philosophic knowledge, trivial. What is important is to have a philosophy of nature—a *Naturphilosophie*—a "discipline" toward which Alonzo had long had what might be loosely called an "instinctive" distrust. But to grasp Hegel's contempt for empirical science as compared with his respect for *Naturphilosophie* one must have read his students' notes on his lectures on the history of philosophy (not his philosophy of history), a book apparently as little read as it is hard to find. In order to develop a *Naturphilosophie*, the philosopher keeps as far from the laboratory as he can, he sits as close to the stove as comfortable, and by sheer ideation, never "putting nature to the question," he legislates for it. The ideation produces a "deeper" truth than empirical truth, and has at least two advantages over the quest for empirical knowledge: It allows the thinker to remain with his rump close to the stove and to keep his hands clean. Alonzo's two years of engineering and his more or less serious flirtation with positivism had inoculated him permanently against contempt for science, even when that contempt was expressed by a Great Philosopher standing on his head in a lecture room in Berlin.

Whether Hegelian or Marxist, the dialectic is pure speculation, although it is a scheme useful to organize experience and sometimes seems to lead to a true picture, for there was indeed a break between ice and water and between water and steam. But there is a radical difference between a scheme that organizes experience and a scientific explanation of empirical events. Religious myth organizes experience. However, the dialectic affords one great value for the historian: It leads him to include in his organization of human events a factor which until Marx had almost been altogether neglected: the economic factor. But the organization the dialectic achieves is selective and reductive as all organizations that lead to understanding necessarily are. That it leads to a better understanding of historical events says as much about history as it says about the dialectic: It calls attention to the fact that history is not like the natural sciences.

Marx did not have the contempt for science that Hegel and the idealists from whom Marx defected were afflicted with. When he heard of Darwin he immediately accepted the evolutionary hypothesis, as shown by the incident of the dedication of *Capital*. But did he accept the Darwinian hypothesis after careful consideration of the evidence or did he accept it because it strengthened his materialism? There is all the difference in the world between accepting a theory on its merits and accepting it on partisan grounds. Alonzo was confident that had Marx heard that Darwin had somehow confirmed Genesis, he would have rejected Darwin as readily as he had actually accepted him, with no effort at critical examination of the argument. This is the way in which partisan men generally accept or reject opinions that confirm or validate their cherished views.

In any case, Alonzo put no trust whatever in "laws" promulgated by philosophers or historians. He found it hard enough to take seriously the "scientific" works of social scientists and psychologists; but the universal generalizations based on facts that were seldom genuine, promulgated by men who did not seem to know the difference between ersatz and the real McCoy, even before he heard of Carnap and the boys—he had always found these generalizations impossible to abide. Philosophical treatises were full of such "laws." One or two instances which could at best support a tentative observation of a general nature was declared to express the broad sweep of events. Historians and philosophers had an endless supply of universal verities; one of the universal verities that the conservatives among them were very fond of was Santayana's beautifully turned epigram to the effect that those who ignore history are condemned to repeat it. Very pretty epigram, very pretty indeed, but nonsense all the same since history does not repeat itself and since what history seems to teach was that no one has ever learned or could ever learn much of value from it for the present or the future. It did seem to teach another truth; although Alonzo did not know much history in spite of the vast amounts of it he had read, he seemed to have learned from it that the only historical law there is is that the events that historians are concerned with are a record of men's capacity for murder. Of course there have been saints, but a good many saints seemed to have been pretty hard cookies.

When Alonzo heard a scientist advance a law—Avogadro's law, or

Boyle's or whoever's—he knew that back of it there stood a number of initial intuitions that had been formulated in a way that made them susceptible to testing, that it was the product of the application of complex, not well defined, but well practiced, procedures that have developed as they guided scientific inquiry from its beginnings. When Alonzo heard a philosopher or a historian pronounce a law, he instantly reared, for he had long known that as legislators, philosophers and historians are the brethren of Moses and Solon, not of Copernicus and Galileo. This kind of pussy cat could be skinned in several soul-fulfilling ways. A well-known and deservedly highly esteemed historian of Trotsky wrote about "laws of historical logic"—whatever that could mean; and on a critical occasion in the development of his account of the Russian revolution he wrote about "the ruthless logic of the revolution," as if the revolution had been some sort of impersonal earthquake over which neither Lenin nor Trotsky had control, or a flow of lava that buried farmsteads and the sorry animals that could not get out of its way—events which in principle at least could be understood as natural events can be understood.

2

While it is necessary to deny scientific status (in the narrow Anglo-American sense) to a dialectical organization of human history, it is equally necessary to emphasize that it is science in the broad Continental sense. History is the shaping of events into an ordered whole, and such a shaping is better knowledge than the shaping given to human experience by myth or by "poetry." Without it the past remains mere chaos, utterly unintelligible. Historians employ the notions of cause and effect; it is clear, however, that these notions do not have the same meaning as they have when used in the positive sciences. The dialectic enabled Marx to organize the past in order, as he thought, to prove that it was marching toward communism. It was a moot question among those who were conversant with Holy Writ whether or not he had taken the march to be inevitable. In any case, it was a means of writing history that made it relevant to the nineteenth and twentieth centuries. This was the difference between Marxist history and non-Marxist: Marxist history claimed predictive power, but Alonzo could not take that claim seriously. For crystal balls, dialectical or any other kind, Alonzo had no use whatever. Future events cannot be predicted.

If you drained its dogmatism from Marxist theory and took it as one way among many of organizing the facts of the past, if you took it as a philosophy of history, Marxism seemed to be more plausible than as a philosophy of nature; but when you stopped to look at it critically, the former was no more acceptable than the latter. A second look at Marxist philosophy of history disclosed its inadmissibility. According to Marxists, history has proceeded in a series of jumps, caused by violent challenges from below, which were forced on the challengers because the owners of the means of production exploited the workers beyond sufferance. Thus feudalism had given way to the world of the bourgeoisie, which had given way in Russia and would give way in the rest of the world come the revolution, to the dictatorship of the proletariat —whose advanced leader was "The Party."

The acceptability of this theory arose from the fact that it did seem to account for the transition from the feudal world to the bourgeois. And in view of the state of the world in the thirties, its prediction of the coming revolution seemed probable. The acceptability of the theory, or so it was claimed, depended on its "scientific" nature; but the claim made by Communists accepted no challenge, and in this the Communists showed that their theory was not scientific; it was dogmatic faith. In the Continental sense of the term *science*, Marxism was science, since it was a cognitive statement that purported to be true and for which evidence seemed to be offered. But in the American and English sense, "scientific" it was not. Whether the claim took advantage of the two meanings of the word *science* or not was of no significance. What was significant was that the acceptability of the dialectic derived in part from the generous feelings of those who reacted against conditions of the day; it derived from hope for, and faith in, a better world. If in order to make a better world one had to wreck the existing one, drown it in blood, consume it with fire—well, those conditions were not imposed on the makers of the new world by themselves but by those who resisted all change. There was always the "law" about omelets and broken eggs.

Apparently the Communists' notion of the relationship between theory and practice and their view of class science made anything true that was thought to be useful for their practical ends. One of Alonzo's Communist friends, Allen Spears, was a classicist at State. He was trying to "class angle" Socrates' death. One day Alonzo met him in the street and noticed that Allen was unusually happy. "What makes you so happy, Al?" asked Alonzo. Allen replied that he had just found in Diogenes Laërtius the proof of his thesis. The motive back of Socrates' enemies was a class motive. Alonzo suggested that no doubt one of the motives was a political one—this is clear enough from Plato's *Apology*. But was there only one motive and was it a political one? "In any case," Alonzo added, "if you are going to prefer Diogenes to the sources usually given primacy by the scholars, you will have to show why he is preferable, won't you?" "Yes, I guess I'll have to," said Allen, but it was obvious that he was not happy with the objection. If Allen had been looking for the truth, and had not been intent merely on extending the application of a hypothesis taken to be true to a field to which it had not been applied before—or applied as thoroughly as Allen was trying to apply it—he should have acknowledged that here, indeed, there was a problem that had to be given careful consideration.

When Alonzo surveyed the little history he knew it seemed to him that Marxism as a philosophy of history was a bold generalization that was made plausible by the disregard of historical detail. No one, today, questioned the existence throughout history of class struggles, and general acceptance of this fundamental insight we owe to Marx. Contrast, say, Gibbon, with a contemporary historian, say Rostovtzeff, and you cannot miss the difference between a pre-Marx and a post-Marx historian. The importance of the economic factor had been forcefully made clear by Marx and Engels. Class struggles were important components of the dynamics of history. But the minds of those Marxists whom Alonzo knew well were given to a few, major, total disjunctions, and these disjunctions led to a total disregard of other operative factors in history. It was possible to choose one of these factors as basic for the purposes of organizing historical data in a certain manner; while for other purposes other factors would be more suitable. But Marxist theory was not methodologically relativistic. The class struggle was the sole basic factor, and to it all other factors must be traced. The operative words were *sole basic*. As Alonzo saw it there were many other factors, and allowing that we can use the category of cause in history as we can in physics—as noted, a very large concession to make— he could see the purpose of the organization dictating the selection of what, for that purpose, was taken to be basic.

That the economic factor was important no one wished to deny— not today. But there were other factors and they could not be reduced to the economic without residue. This meant that the organization of historical facts was controlled by the interests of the historian. What factors? Altruism, for instance, was an important one. The Marxists that Alonzo knew, either in Midland City or New York, had no use for altruism as a motive leading men to seek amelioration of intolerable social situations in which they themselves were not at all concerned. But neither Marx's nor Engels' outrage was caused by being themselves exploited—although Engels was by Marx. They were altruists. And yet altruism was denied by their theory although it had been a powerful factor in shaping the labor movement and the history of the world since their day. Nor did the powerful rhetoric of the *Communist Manifesto* have its source in the calculations of surplus value. The power of the indictment derived from the outraged sense of justice of the writers of the *Manifesto*—a document that, in one respect, could have been written by a Hebrew prophet.

If the Marxists were contemptuous of altruism, Marx and Engels were the best refutation of their contempt. But they were not the only refutation. The history of the struggle of the hundred years before the revolution against the czar was a history of utterly selfless, dedicated fanatics, young people who were utter idealists, completely altruistic. although many of them possessed thoroughly thwarted minds. But few of them were people who had in their own persons suffered the mutilations of the system they dedicated, and in some cases gave their lives, to destroy. For instance Lenin's older brother. The Russians had been altruists; men and women dedicated themselves to the overthrow of czarism because they were outraged by its stupid, its utterly insane oppression. Idealism was something the Marxist hated. But idealism, in one of the many overlapping meanings of the term, was something that most clearly moved the Marxists.

3

As a philosophy of culture Marxism seemed to Alonzo to be quite inadequate. According to Marx, the superstructures that made up the institutions of society, such as art and religion, were determined by the economic arrangements of that society. This was the materialist side of dialectical materialism. Interpreted naïvely, as it sometimes was, the notion of economic determinism could be carried to absurd extremes. But even when interpreted by the better minds among his friends, it seemed to Alonzo to be inadequate to the facts. The death of Socrates might have been motivated by class factors; indeed it might have been solely motivated by them. One might go as far as to align the Sophists with a rising class and Socrates' search for unchanging forms and his belief in immortality with his conservatism.

But if the alignment denied, as it did, that Socrates was genuinely devoted to the search for truth, and asserted that all he was interested in was doing a job of apologetics, however unaware he might be of what he was about, the thesis ran into two difficulties, only one of which was enough to invalidate it in Alonzo's eyes. The first was that Socrates seemed to be motivated by a genuine desire to know the truth. The proof for this? It was to be found in the spirit, the pervasive effulgence, of the early Platonic dialogues, which we may take to report his quest; it was also found in the testimony rendered by his contemporaries about him. The other objection was that if we turn Socrates' speculations into propaganda, we must go further and argue that all speculation is propaganda; but if this is the case, this bit of speculation is also propaganda, and we land in Epimenides' trap: If Epimenides asserts that all Cretans are liars and Epimenides is a Cretan . . . . Of course this was not to deny that there may be varying degrees of self-interest and class loyalty mixed up, probably, with almost all speculation.

In the final analysis, the most serious objection that Alonzo had to the theory of the relation between superstructures and the economic structure that was supposed to determine them was Alonzo's sense— hunch if you like, or strong feeling, but one that could not be ignored —that the social process was much more complex than economic determinism allowed for, and that the interaction of "causes" prohibited the selection of any one of them without qualification as basic —as solely basic—to the rest. As a naturalist, Alonzo was forced to believe that values and the institutions that anchored them sprang from natural sources—from needs or drives that derived ultimately from biologic factors which were somehow transformed into the complex and often apparently irrational institutions one found giving form and direction to human groups.

No doubt economic factors were important in shaping the forms of institutions. But it would seem also as if other institutions were important in shaping the forms of the economic factors. The economic determinism of the Marxist seemed to Alonzo to overlook the kind of relative or limited autonomy and the profound inertia of institutions and groups as well as the heterogeneity of powerful drives displayed by men. Anthropology seemed to show that all thriving societies, however technologically unprovided, offered men forms for the expression of drives that transcended the economic need and in transcending it transformed it in such a fashion that to call it economic in a simplistic way was to misunderstand it. It all finally came down to the fact—for it seemed to be a fact—that men did not live by bread alone.

4

There were other objections to Marxism. The inevitability of the revolution was very doubtful. And what the classless state would be like when the dictatorship of the proletariat had withered away was left unsketched. Alonzo was told that to each would be given according to his need and from each would be taken according to his ability. The formula was patently utopian. There was, moreover, the problem of the end of life under communism. What would one do with one's leisure? What would one live for?

One day Alonzo had a battle with Karl Heinrich on these points. In *The State and Revolution*, Lenin had left the matter of the quality and objectives of living in the classless society in a completely vague, undefined condition. Lenin referred to it towards the end of the book but he said nothing that would give the reader a clear idea of what he thought daily life would be under communism. The argument between Karl and him got heated and Alonzo brought forth the book and asked Karl to point out what Lenin had said. Karl took the book and questioned the edition. A cheap trick that got him nowhere, because the book was brought out by unimpeachable Stalinist publishers.

In spite of the defects Alonzo noticed in their doctrines, he was able to cooperate with them in their practical objectives in the Teachers Union and the Spanish Committee. They were out to construct a world that was free of oppression, injustice, exploitation, war. What if their theories did not hold water when examined as philosophical doctrines? They were in the main practically acceptable, and that was enough. But he began to see that the Communists themselves displayed traits that were not admirable and that made them difficult to get along with. A few of the members of the Teachers Union–Spanish Committee were people he genuinely liked; others he was neutral toward. But sooner or later even those he liked showed ugly personality traits. The most difficult of their traits was the inflexible doctrinaire attitude and the arrogance with which they looked upon those who disagreed with them. The Stalinists with whom he cooperated considered themselves in thought and action better than their opponents, so that there were three classes of people: the large majority, ignorant and to be used when the time came; their opponents; and themselves. Their opponents were utterly beyond contempt, but among them there were those whom they hated with burning, implacable hatred: the Trotskyites. As to themselves, they were morally and intellectually superior: superior indeed because of the superior human stuff out of which they were made, it would seem. They took honest questions as criticism and immediately went on the defense. Apparently what was printed in Marx, Engels, Lenin, and Stalin was beyond correction: If you did not agree with it, it was simply because you did not understand it—or you were a reactionary, or worse, a Trotskyite.

Karl, with whom he had a number of discussions in Germany about Marxist doctrine, engaged Alonzo frequently in discussion upon his arrival at Midland City. When pushed to the wall, Karl appealed to a gimmick that seemed to Alonzo as intellectually dishonest as it was unconvincing: He appealed to the unity of theory and practice in Marx and Lenin. By this Karl meant that non-Communists could not appreciate Marxist theory—and at times Karl argued that they could not appreciate it at all—since its truth was demonstrated in action. This turned Marxism into a self-certifying theory; and had the added advantage of giving Karl *ab initio* an intellectual superiority over those outside the party with whom he disagreed: Since they were not party activists they lacked the equipment for understanding Marxist theory.

But while action demonstrated the truth of the theory, action could not disprove it; for Karl and other Communists always had some *ad hoc* argument by which they could show that Marx and Stalin were right and their critics wrong. No matter what happened in the world, in Russia or elsewhere, the men at the head of the party were right; they could never be wrong. To Alonzo the gimmick of the unity of theory and practice was not only irritating, because it was used for such intellectually dishonest purposes, but frustrating, since the attitude kept him from learning. Apparently the Communists wanted you to accept on their authority whatever they happened to believe. But of course Alonzo could not accept hypotheses that he could not understand or the truth of which was not shown to him objectively.

Finally he came to see through his friends of the Spanish Committee and the Teachers Union. They had no integrity because they were tools of the party; they had no respect for others because others were legitimately to be turned into tools of communism, to be used for communism's end. They had no honesty, no loyalty, no regard for other human beings. They had no hesitation whatever to let human beings suffer hunger, on the principle that the more suffering there was the quicker the system would break down. Alonzo had a Communist friend who was a social worker and who knew a family that actually had nothing to eat. He went to one of the leaders of the party to suggest that a collection should be taken to help the family. Let them starve, replied the man; the more they go hungry the sooner the breakdown will come. It was not merely the brutality expressed in the reply but the pleasure with which it was expressed. The machine was impersonal—or so it seemed on the surface. In fact it was ruled by a group of power-maniacs in Midland City, which in turn was ruled by a group of power-maniacs in New York, which in turn was ruled by a group of power-maniacs in Moscow. Thus to his old skepticism about building a good world was added the ripening insight that these people were not the men to whom the job of making a good world could be entrusted. Finally he saw more or less clearly that Communists were no better than anyone else and in some respects they were worse. Since he could not believe that the revolution could succeed with such poor human means, he lost what faith he had had in it.

5

Alonzo was not yet prepared to say, *tout court*, that the Communists were worse than the rest of mankind. Nor was he yet ready to look upon his political convictions as he would much later and as he was now almost ready to look on his philosophical convictions. His liberalism was, therefore, to stand untouched for quite some time yet. Of his Communist friends he began to expect less and less. So much less did he expect from them that when the Russo-German Nonaggression Pact was signed he was not shocked, as his liberal friends and some Communists were. Their acceptance of the pact merely proved what he already had personal proof of: their loyalty to Stalin. Of course Alonzo had no more expected the pact than anyone else; but he was not at all surprised when news of it came.

He could not take the final step, nevertheless, of breaking with his former friends. Why? Why did he continue to cooperate with them until June of 1939, when he left Midland City for a year's stay in New York? He was not innocent. He knew that he had been cooperating with Communists in the Teachers Union and the Spanish Committee even though at times he balked at specific plans. Isaac Rosenfeld and Isaac's Trotskyist friends at Midland City, with whom Alonzo was on very friendly terms in spite of his cooperation with Stalinists, had warned him clearly about Communist policy in Spain. He was not ignorant of the fact that the Communists had liquidated the opposition. Isaac had argued warmly that the money Alonzo was helping collect for the Spanish republic was used by the Stalinists in New York for their own local purposes. Why then did he continue to cooperate with them?

To this question Alonzo would not have been able at the time to give a fully satisfactory reply. He had many experiences with them that brought before his eyes—eyes that did not want to see—their unreliability, radical dishonesty, their utter incapacity for personal loyalty, their mendacity, the worthlessness of their word. The realization had begun early.

Before Alonzo got Karl the fellowship with Perlman, Karl had solemnly promised Alonzo in writing that during his stay at State he would not undertake any political activity, for Perlman had been worried about bringing a Communist into the economics department. But a few weeks after Karl's arrival Alonzo heard that his friend had started a Marxist study group.

There were many small experiences, and some not so small, with several of his Communist friends, all pointing towards the same conclusion. Why then did Alonzo refuse almost consciously to draw the conclusion that from these people nothing was to be expected but absolute partisanship to their ends and that all their other ends and commitments, pledges, promises, assurances were clearly subordinated to their loyalty to Stalin; not to communism, not to the workers, not to Russia, but to Stalin, who defined what communism was, defined the interest of the workers, and what was good for Russia—why had he not seen this? The answer, simplifying it in order not to sink into a psychological quicksand that Dostoevski would have had difficulty handling, was that he, more or less consciously, did not want to see it; or put differently, that he did not see it while he saw it, that he did not want to put it into the center of his consciousness and look at it for what it was.

Back of this refusal to see what was in front of his nose was something else: He was afflicted with the anti-Fascist fever. The Spanish war had crystallized the threat of fascism and had put a greater pressure on him and his friends to save themselves and their world from Hitler and Mussolini than they had undergone before. They were in a condition of high moral-political fever, certain of the imminent catastrophe. They had to ally themselves with the Communists because by themselves they were impotent.

It was unwise, therefore, to examine their morals too closely. If one was seriously concerned with the state of the world during this period one had to do something about it; that was what serious concern meant, action. But if one was to do something about it there was no one else with whom one could work than these people. The others were futile. He knew a group of New York socialists and when he visited New York he usually saw them. They were nice people, but politically they were a futile lot who, apparently, spent most of their time feuding among themselves. He was sympathetic with some Trotskyists, but these men, too, lacked organization and seemed to have only one end: They put their energies into sabotaging all Stalinist activity. He had met some Lovestonites, but here was another small splinter group that seemed to be going nowhere. It seemed then that if he was going to do something he had perforce to do it with the Stalinists, little as he came to like their dogmatic doctrines and many of their personal traits.

IX

The Blind Spots of Naturalism

1

I N JUNE 1939 Alonzo left Midland City for New York on a Guggenheim fellowship. He had decided not to risk a trip to Europe because of the seriously deteriorating health of his wife and because it was clear that the phony war on the Western Front could not last long.

His experiences with the Communists in Midland City had led Alonzo to ask himself a few basic questions. He arrived at the conclusion that it was not possible to create a better world by completely destroying the old one and building an entirely new one from the foundations up, as Marxist revolutionists thought that it could be done. First, it is impossible to destroy a world unless one destroys the people who make it up: language, habits, tools, and much else—all the essential components of culture—remain unless a people is totally destroyed. Culture changes, but it cannot be destroyed in one blow. Men live in culture, but culture lives in the people who compose it. And even if one allows that a world can be totally destroyed, one has to realize that the destruction of the world planned by the Communists is an inadmissible catastrophe, since what they would put in its place, it is already obvious, is much worse than what they would do away with.

But that only means that a dream of a society altogether free from exploitation and entirely ruled by equity has to be abandoned; it does not mean that efforts to do away with specific defects are futile. The fight against evil has to be carried on relentlessly, steadily, without rest, with constant awareness that it will never end and that the hope of a perfect world is a false hope. Trotsky was not altogether wrong: The notion of a permanent revolution, taken literally, is fantastic, absurd; one cannot live in the midst of total upheaval indefinitely; but a permanent war against injustice is as essential as a permanent war against dirt.

As Alonzo gave up utopian dreams, he also began to perceive that his philosophical convictions did not have the solid basis he had thought they had. A number of questions presented themselves to him which demanded answers. Alonzo accepted naturalism because he had taken it to be a complete philosophy; not necessarily one already completed, which therefore could be formulated in a summa in which all the questions that could be asked were answered, but a philosophy within which answers could be developed for questions as they arose. Truth was cumulative: Additions to it were to be expected, indeed, welcomed. Truth was corrigible: Corrections to it should be welcomed by the man who sought it. For naturalism our possession of the truth is never complete, indeed the notion of a complete substantive truth was an illusion: There was no such thing about substantive matters. All the chambers of naturalism would always require extra work. But the mansion was already up and many of its chambers could be occupied in comfort. While in principle it was possible that the mansion might have to be demolished and an altogether different one built in its place, the probability was not large since it was built on the rock of Nature itself.

Naturalism claimed to give an account, consonant with the sciences, and therefore in harmony with the spirit of the age, of the whole range of human experience, an account that was not only as complete as that of any other philosophy but one that was better; better because it was fully adequate or could be made adequate to the diverse modes of human experience, to the institutions that they had produced, and the values these institutions anchored.

But somehow Alonzo began to suspect that naturalism was indifferent to some aspects of experience, that it was myopic or utterly blind toward some, and that it misunderstood others. Some it undervalued, others it denied altogether as the product of human error; while vociferously protesting that it successfully avoided nineteenth-century materialistic reductionism, it reduced some modes of experience just as much as nineteenth-century materialism had done.

It could not be denied that naturalism had made important contributions to the philosophy of science and had insisted, as no other philosophic movement had, on the important role science played, and increasingly would continue to play, in the development of our modern world and the melioration of life. It was one of the strong straws of the broad and powerful broom of Western culture that had swept superstition from the civilized scene; it had fought obscurantism in a perpetual battle and had put it in the end on the defensive. But while making contributions that, in fairness, had to be acknowledged to be immensely valuable, Alonzo began to suspect that naturalism had also helped to erode the foundations of a truly humane existence; it had shrunken the possibilities of a full human life. It did its destructive work without knowing it was doing it, but its work was destructive nevertheless. Because it claimed to be superior to other ways of looking at the world and because it was proud, and rightly so, of its methodological sophistication and insisted on its relevance to the modern world, it was by these criteria that it had to be justly judged.

In theory the possibility that naturalism might be inadmissible had to be granted, since this possibility held for all empirical, substantive knowledge. Actually, during the flood tide of Alonzo's̃ faith in it, the possibility of its error was not really conceivable by him. But the flood tide did not last forever; imperceptibly, slowly, a suspicion began to drift into his mind like fog, silently but persistently, that he might have been holding false doctrine. Did naturalism meet the exigencies of the modern world? What were these exigencies and why should the modern world call for a philosophy that was special to it? How could one tell what is "the modern world"? Did naturalism really give a better account of the essential values of human experience than any other philosophy? History was a succession of errors—until 1859 and after, until John Dewey, until the very present. But the present was an exception—somehow. Was this a reasonable assumption?

But what was the modern world? Alonzo used to bring the subject up in his classes—it was an effective propaganda tool. He would draw a circle on the board and divide it into horizontal strata; this was the world of today; but surely all our contemporaries are not "modern," are they? Who could deny that the Australian aboriginals were our contemporaries but were not moderns? And South American peasants or the illiterates of Appalachia? But if these people were not modern but merely contemporary, would you assert that fundamentalists believing in the literal truth of Genesis were modern? They were, somehow, more or less medieval. By an easy extension, Alonzo included moderate religious believers and those crypto-religious believers, the philosophical idealists, among the nonmoderns, and finally all those who rejected naturalism, which was the only philosophy solidly grounded on science. But it was false to assume—he would add, to show how reasonable he was—that any man living today was a thoroughgoing modern. The diagram held for the individual civilized man as much as it held for mankind. We all had in us a bottom stratum that was thoroughly archaic and above that stratum there was the medieval and above that a thin layer of modernity.

This was good propaganda and he took it seriously until the question occurred to him concerning how we could decide exactly what made up the upper stratum. The answer was, genuine needs, which is to say, those that were acceptable to a valid conception of the world; which in turn was to say, those in harmony with modern science. All of this was plausible until he perceived that there were many aspects of experience of great importance that could not be in harmony with science simply because they had nothing to do with science or science with them; there were others against which not science but scientists and philosophers proclaiming themselves the friends of science had a bias.

Alonzo began to see that naturalism met the true exigencies of man and gave adequate accounts of the genuine modes of human experience because it defined modernity and genuineness and hence could not be caught off base. In short, it delivered; it delivered prodigiously; it delivered with royal generosity; but it delivered by means of a tricky argument: What was modern was what was in sympathy with science, and what was in sympathy with science was whatever the naturalist decided was in sympathy with science. Naturalism gave an account of what was genuine and not false by accepting as genuine those modes of experience it thought it could give an account of and by rejecting those it knew it could not give an account of. When it gave an account of experiences that it could not deal with in their own terms it reduced them, as it did with religion. It was a tricky argument; but it was the argument that was tricky, not the naturalists who were themselves the victims of their own argument and who argued in perfectly good faith.

2

After Alonzo began to question some aspects of naturalism, he still thought of himself as a naturalist and he continued to write as one. But gradually it became clear to him that it was necessary to enlarge the edifice of his thought. This shift he did not put into print. In withholding it he did not think he was being dishonest; his doubts were still too inchoate for him to make them public, and he had not altogether lost the hope that his questions could be satisfactorily answered within the framework of his naturalistic beliefs. He was energetically trying to find answers.

The ideal would have been for Alonzo to stop writing for publication until he was confident that he knew where he stood. But not even an approximation to the ideal was possible, since he had to publish or perish. Maxie Waxie had become chairman of the department after McGilvary and Sharp had retired within one year of each other, and he was determined to get rid of Alonzo. He had very good reasons for wanting to get rid of his former assistant: He saw clearly through Alonzo's bungling efforts to show admiration for him as man and thinker. When Alonzo tried to compliment his boss, it did not come off.

The dean, telling Alonzo once that he wanted Alonzo in the Department of Philosophy, suggested that Alonzo mention Klotz in something he wrote. The dean told him that Klotz had complained to him that Alonzo had no respect for Klotz and the evidence was that while Horace often referred to Klotz in his writings, Alonzo had never done so. As for the others the question did not arise, since eunuchs are sterile. Following the dean's advice, Alonzo mentioned Klotz in his next article and the latter was more angry than before.

Alonzo saw there was only one way to keep his job, and that was to gain local reputation by achieving a bit of distinction at the national level. He had to write. Since there were few things he enjoyed as much, it was not difficult for him to do so. The upshot was that every time Maxie Waxie looked at Alonzo, the latter handed him a reprint. Alonzo's strategy worked. Every article was a stone that made the small pile on which he stood a bit higher and made him more visible nationally and locally. In 1944 Alonzo's name appeared in *Who's Who In America*. This infuriated Klotz still more but there was nothing he could do and it made it more difficult to fire Alonzo.

The comparative quality of Alonzo's writing did not concern him; that was for others to judge; what concerned him was to do the very best he could of each job of writing he undertook. Whether it was good or bad when compared with the work of others, whether it attracted many readers or only a few, was something over which, having done his best, he had no control whatever. Although ambitious, he was not competitive in the usual sense of the term; but ruthlessly competitive with himself, self-demanding, he was. That some of his work was at least passable he knew, since it was accepted by journals and reviews of quality and he began to be noticed nationally. He took care that the work he was doing did not go unnoticed by colleagues outside the department at State.

Thus the contrast between Alonzo and his contemporaries in the Department of Philosophy was noticed locally. The upshot was that he made himself invulnerable and when he finally walked out of State it was on his own decision. Life was, of course, made miserable for him; why, then, didn't Alonzo find another job? This was the Depression. The alternative to his job was a job with the WPA Writers' Project. The universities and colleges were not hiring anyone. If a man retired or died he was not replaced. But there was another reason Alonzo could not find a job: Through his loud mouth and his uninhibited writing he had given a number of people—even personal friends—the impression that he was a member of the Communist party. He was not even considered for two jobs for which friends had recommended him between 1935 and the beginning of the war, and he knew from the inside why he was not. In those days no one known to be a Communist, or thought to be one, had a chance academically.

3

Of the questions, or doubts, about naturalism that had arisen in his mind, three were of decisive importance. These questions were important in themselves, but they gained in importance because a historian of philosophy had affirmed in an essay on naturalism, that this philosophy "is not unsympathetic to the genuine values of the human spirit on which anti-naturalists have heroically insisted. It is convinced that it feels them as strongly and understands them better." The qualification *genuine*, precludes all challenge, because if naturalism does not recognize a value it rejects it as not genuine. But one can let that go. The important question is whether naturalism had indeed been sympathetic to all the values of the human spirit and whether it has felt them as strongly. The claim gave one the right to ask, What does naturalism have to say about natural piety? Spinoza's *Ethics* was instinct with it, but he had written in the seventeenth century. As we come closer to our day, can one find evidence to match that of the philosopher of whom Heine said that he had ground the lenses of all future philosophers?

A contemporary naturalist reacts, as all men can whatever their theories, to a lively spring day or to a mellow day after the leaves turn, to the beauty of a face he glances at without desire, but if he feels gratitude for the joy of living he cannot trace it to its source and there seems to be a reason for his inability. If you tell the naturalist that in order to grasp fully the joy of living he has to trace it to its ultimate source, the creative mystery of the universe, he simply does not understand what you are talking about and he tends to write you off, in his puzzlement, as a man who spouts anthropocentric nonsense. He knows nothing of cosmic piety. His philosophy seems to preclude all knowledge of it.

But note that the word *piety* refers to much more than religious piety. Philip Rhav once wrote somewhere that he knew nothing of piety. He no doubt employed the term in its vulgar, narrow sense. A man incapable of piety in the Roman sense is not, to put it minimally, an admirable man. Such a man is a moral quadruped, to borrow a phrase from a master of insults, Pietro Aretino. *Piety* refers to the gratitude one has towards the sources of one's being; it refers to the awe the infinite spaces inspire, the terror they invoke, however courageous one may be, the gratitude for life. Contemplating the awful mystery of "it all," one shudders; remembering one's parents, one's city, one feels piety in the classic sense of the term. And one becomes aware of one's finitude. But the naturalist can only use the word *piety* pejoratively. What the Roman felt and called piety the naturalist can no more feel than he can feel terror at the witches that ring his door bell on Halloween and threaten him with treat or trick.

Pascal put in the mouth of the atheist that the eternal silence of the infinite spaces terrified him. But that was in the seventeenth century. The naturalist today knows better. He has deep-sounding *clichés* ready at hand: It's all evolution and adaptation. If *per impossibile* he could hear the explosions that take place beyond the reach of the naked eye, he would say that such events can be understood, that they will be fully understood, if not tomorrow, at some time in the future, if not in actuality, in principle. Terror of the eternal silence of the infinite spaces does not awe him—not to mention the fact that he knows that they are not silent. Indeed, he is already speaking in all seriousness of traveling beyond our own galaxy. Perhaps. If he has reached the moon he can in principle go beyond it, and beyond the furthest reaches of our galaxy, and further on.

It is not that naturalists felt no joy, of course they did. There cannot be many men, however unfortunate, who do not on occasion have a moment they would fix forever, not many who would not say to it, "Tarry a while." No doubt naturalists have as many such moments as anyone else; but they cannot refer these moments to their sources beyond themselves and cannot feel compelled, therefore, to give thanks to whatever it is that brings such moments about. They are inhibited in their depths from referring such moments to a source beyond themselves lest they be caught in one of their capital crimes, thinking in anthropomorphic terms. Were they capable of feeling piety they would understand prayer, in one of its functions: The spontaneous flowing from one's lips of thanks for whatever it is that elicits it. But they approach all experience with an unconscious assumption that precludes a sense of mystery, reverence, piety towards the cosmos. Their attitude is that whatever happens has causes and in principle these can be discovered. Nature has no mysteries; it has only secrets, and the keys to its secrets will sooner or later turn up, as they have begun already to turn, since we already know how to pry them up—in principle: We have the method. If science cannot discover the secret of things nothing can, except accident, which produces a solution that has to be tested by the method.

Mystery? *Mystery* is a term that belongs to the language of obscurantists, superstitious men, witch doctors, theologians, quacks, alchemists, spiritualists, politicians of the opposite party—in short the vast archaic rabble of paleohominids barely breaking into the human form, who honestly and dishonestly prey on themselves and their weak sisters, male and female, who crave to believe. Once you discover the cause of the secret you can control it—or you cannot and you submit to it since there is nothing else you can do. There is no more to be said about the secret: Either you explain it or you don't; if you do, either you can control it or you can't.

Leo Szilard, one of the distinguished scientists for whom we have to thank the Nazi barbarians, a man who moved from physics to biology, has left on record that what brought him to biology was "not any skills acquired in physics, but an attitude: the conviction . . . that mysteries can be solved. Classical biologists, he once said, "lacked the faith that things are explainable." By this he seems to have meant that they were astonished but declined to go beyond their astonishment, and this attitude of theirs implied a certain reverential pleasure on their part in contemplating the mystery of things, almost preferring the mysterious to remain mysterious. Szilard was right to criticize biologists, if it is true that they have the attitude he attributes to them. Biologists are scientists, and they have no business turning into pious men before they have busted a gut pushing their scrutinies as far as they can. If this makes them narrow—and it does not make all of them narrow—this must be the price they pay to be able to carry on their work. But the attitude that Szilard criticizes, if it controls a philosopher's thought, as is the case with naturalists, turns into a fatal plague. When they adopt it they turn into scientistic thinkers, and condemn themselves and those whom they influence, to be less than full men. How so, if philosophy seeks knowledge? Because the knowledge philosophy seeks—it has to be said no matter what curses the statement brings on one's head—is not "pure" knowledge, such as the scientist seeks, it is knowledge for man, for his use no less than for his delectation and for the slaking of his pure curiosity.

But the naturalist seeks to be a pure knower, and his philosophy contains what may be called a positivistic central ingredient. The result is a failure of development in the naturalist. He possesses no doubt important virtues, but his philosophic stance inhibits the development of an important component of the human personality. Lacking the capacity for cosmic piety, he is in that particular respect a thin man. The naturalist is either a schizoid or a shriveled man. If he can respond to the mystery of the cosmos he is schizoid, if he can't, he is a shriveled man.

It now became easy for Alonzo to see what was wanting in some of his friends. One of them was a man of Alonzo's age who already enjoyed a high reputation as a philosopher of science. In a second marriage he seemed to be a happy man; he had some knowledge of literature and painting, and music elicited from him a profound emotional response. That to use music as an emotional masseur was to misuse it, as Alonzo was convinced, was not an indictment he would bring up against this man, for it would involve a complex argument that would deflect attention from the point he wanted to make; namely, that this man's love of music was evidence of the breadth of his interests. Pleasant, personally friendly—personally, for in his reviews of books he disagreed with he was intolerant, brutal, an utter bully—this man was widely admired by his colleagues, and justly so, for he was without doubt an extraordinarily gifted man, as gifted as could be found in the academic world.

But Alonzo had felt for a long time that there was something lacking in the man. In his professional work he gave ample evidence of acuity and imagination, yet . . . yet he lacked something which Alonzo sensed was important and that after much searching, he was able to name: The universes of Bach, Beethoven, Mozart, Titian, El Greco, Cézanne, Hemingway, had made his life richer than it would have been had it been exclusively dedicated to probability theory and to the philosophy of science.

But men of such talents lacked a component that Alonzo was now able to see clearly was essential for full humanity: They were aliens in their community; they could not identify themselves with it, although they spoke of "us Americans," because they could not see any meaning whatever in the rites, rituals, and myths by means of which their fellow citizens carried on their lives; they saw the rational vacuity of the symbols in which the aspirations and the fears of their fellow citizens were expressed. Their rationalism led them to ask for the "cash value" of the ceremonials which make up the binding element of the national life; but to ask for the cash value of mythic symbols was to discover that they had a very low rational value; national symbols, cultural symbols, stood for nonsense, much of which was false and what was not false was trivial, misleading, and expensive—or so such people thought. Why waste money on ceremonials that could be put to research or the melioration of urgent human needs? Men who believed in their country right or wrong were men who put partisan interests above the claims of justice and humanity. Loyalty as a virtue was not denied but it was redirected toward rational objects: loyalty to truth, justice for the citizen, freedom from exploitation, from imperialism, from the arbitrary dominion of private interests.

Like this brainy philosopher there were many. Very few were as brilliant and creative as he was, but they were all of one kind, men who were thoroughly terrestrial, utterly sublunar, endowed with a completely secular, rationalistic mentality. If there were a few fine particles of sacred dust remaining in the corners of their souls from their infancy

and the tradition of their parents, the reason for their being there was
that they could not be reached with the vacuum cleaner of their rationalistic criticism.

Being highly literate, these men were acquainted with Kant's dictum
about the conscience within and the stars above. They understood
what the old pietist had meant, but they could not feel what he had
felt. The stars? We knew so much more than Kant did about the stars,
and knowing as much as we did how could we be awed by the heavens?
The conscience? Explain it as you will, and few of them made the attempt to explain its origin, it was a natural phenomenon, like a kitten's
attachment to its mother or the distress of a dog who commits an im-
propriety in the living room. Although no adequate explanation of its
origin was available in terms of their philosophy, they knew, knew with
an apodictic certainty to which their empiricism gave them no right,
that it was a natural phenomenon. Their conscience was not identical
with the distress suffered by the dog but the same kind of distress.

There was no essential difference between secular academic man
and secular nonacademic man in terms of fundamental attitudes towards their lives and culture. On the average the non-academic man
may not have been as well read as the academic, but as regards his attitude toward life, there was no essential difference between them. But
of a philosopher and a learned academic man you had the right to
expect more. He could not be excused as the ordinary man could be;
his task is to peer beyond the known into the unknown as far as his
sight can go, although ultimately, he knows, he is doomed to be de-
feated because the unknown is impenetrable mystery. But the philosopher somehow senses that the unknown is the source of what makes
our lives joyful or sad, tragic or pathetic, sometimes hateful, sometimes intolerable. If the philosopher is anesthetic to what lies beyond
knowledge, he is no better than the thin man, his unacademic brother.
For him his philosophy fosters thinness.

4

Once Alonzo became aware of this omission on the part of naturalism other omissions came into the range of his awareness. What did
naturalism have to say on tragedy? The place to look was in Dewey's
Art As Experience. He had read this book with a thoroughness with

which he had read very few other books. There was only one other book he knew as thoroughly, and that was I. A. Richard's *Principles of Literary Criticism*, which at one time he almost knew by heart. Dewey's interest in the arts other than painting was exiguous, as can easily be confirmed by a hasty leafing of *Art As Experience* or a look at the index; but in this book a theory of art was presented that Alonzo found quite adequate to such knowledge of the arts as he had and such questions as he had asked about the relation of the arts to the rest of life; the theory was, incidentally, very interesting also because it was evidence that in some fundamental sense Dewey had never abandoned certain important elements of his early idealism. In Dewey's aesthetics, as in his theory of knowledge, the constitutive role of mind in the act of perception is of the essence. For this reason, no doubt, there are no radical differences between Dewey's approach to art and Croce's—the operative word in this judgment being *radical*.

But Alonzo had not read Nietzsche and Unamuno in vain. It must have been from the German and the Spaniard chiefly, but also from his own background and temperament, that he had acquired the conviction that a conception of life that denied or ignored the tragic ingredient of experience was incomplete and shallow. However, although Alonzo had been interested in the subject since the early twenties, and had read among other things Krutch's chapter on tragedy in *The Modern Temper* with deep sympathy, it was not until Franco invaded Spain that Alonzo realized that his interest in tragedy had never led him to ask what his borrowed philosophy had to say on the subject. He was shocked to find that apparently his Dewey *cum* Carnap borrowings had nothing to say about it.

In the index to *Art As Experience* there was only one reference to tragedy, in page 36, but when you turn to this page you find that what Dewey was interested in was the reconciliation that tragedy, since the days of Aristotle, has been said to produce in the spectator; Dewey was not interested in the nature of the tragic, its place in art, and probable source beyond art and perhaps even beyond human existence, as the Greek poets and Shakespeare had obviously been. Alonzo himself could ignore the problem of tragedy as a literary genre; lack of interest in genres one picked up from Croce and Dewey almost in an unconscious way. But the question of what in the technical language of Dewey's aesthetics would be called "the matter for" tragedy, the tragic vision, the stuff of human experience and possibly the cosmic stuff out of which a literary tragedy was made, remained: What had Dewey, what had the naturalists to say on this topic? The answer was, nothing, nothing whatever.

The omission of this important topic could be explained in a number of ways, the easiest but not necessarily the worst was that the varieties of contemporary naturalism, reared in a climate of opinion in which the notion of progress and the belief in the perfectability of man are fundamental articles of faith, philosophies all of which are futuristic and hopeful, not only lack sympathy but lack even the sensory equipment, so to speak, to attend to topics that are too easily dismissed as the concern of romantic softheaded dreamers, who have not yet made their entry into the modern world. But explain tragedy in any way whatever, so long as you do full justice to the vision of the great Greek poets, a philosophy that has nothing to say on the subject, once Alonzo noticed the omission, could not be acceptable to him.

Before Franco's invasion one could be interested in tragedy and espouse naturalism without awareness of incoherence: The question of the harmonious relationship of one aspect of his beliefs to other aspects did not arise since he had somehow managed to keep them in separate compartments. But after Franco's invasion, Alonzo could no longer ignore the topic and overlook the fact that his borrowed philosophy had nothing to say about it. That the topic was universally ignored by American philosophers at the time and that some of them did not become fashionably aware of it until their attention was called to it by Alonzo's own critique, long before the epidemic of *angst* hit the leaders of intellectual fashion, made no difference. The defect was there, and a serious thinker had to pay attention to it. Philosophically the subject could not have wider and more profound ramifications. For tragedy may be the means by which the spectator turns his mind to certain human catastrophes and detects in them something he had missed before their impact on him: that their source is somehow to be traced beyond man, to the universe itself. This impression must be explained and not explained away. To trace human catastrophe to a cosmic source may be an exercise of superstition or of mythomania. It may also be explained as a component added by the poet to his drama in order to increase its tension, although this explanation is one that anyone who knows anything about the wholeness of the great tragedies would dismiss out of hand. But however the connection is explained, it cannot be treated lightly.

It could be, as Alonzo soon came to see, that tragedy is the exception that probes the validity of naturalism. Apply the criterion furnished by the historian of philosophy and ask whether the naturalist is at all capable of the tragic vision; forget about his having as profound a vision and about his capacity to explain it better than his opponents. If his philosophy ignores the sense of tragedy it is unacceptable. Welcome the tragic vision and you become aware of the fact that it leads you to see truly an aspect of the experience of man in the universe, and thus denies the Neo-Pelagian doctrine that is an indispensable component of naturalism. By the Neo-Pelagian doctrine Alonzo meant, as he has indicated somewhere, the view that denies the validity of the notion of original sin, whether interpreted literally or mythically. In opposition to this doctrine stands the doctrine that can be called, in an extended sense, Augustinian, and that asserts that human evil has its source not only in the social arrangements of man but beyond, in an aporia that is somehow lodged in the heart of the cosmos.

Alonzo was aware that the tragic vision cannot claim that it leads to a purview of the whole of human experience. Such a claim would be tantamount to asserting that human life is wholly evil because it arises from a wholly evil universe, and this in turn would be tantamount to asserting that man is utterly incapable of joy. He also knew that there are very few tragedies in our Western literature. The Greeks produced them; Aeschylus' *Agamemnon* and Sophocles' *Oedipus Rex* are supreme examples. Not very many have survived. Shakespeare wrote four great tragedies, of which *King Lear* is no doubt his most profound achievement.

Something like this, Alonzo thought, can be said of heroism: It is one of the prominent virtues yet prominent for its absence in naturalistic moral philosophy, although the disregard of heroism in naturalists does not lead to the grave consequences that the naturalists' blindness to the tragic sentiment leads to, since room can easily be made for it if the need to add it should make itself felt. What the omission of this virtue did was give the naturalists away. They could be serious moralists. But they were open to Nietzsche's jeer. Theirs is a morality of shopkeepers. But it was worse. European events had forced on Alonzo an attitude that was radically different from the one he had entertained toward social questions during the halcyon days of his untroubled liberalism. The topic of heroism had thrust itself into Alonzo's attention since young men, some of whom he knew, were volunteering for the International Brigade and some of them were dying or being wounded in Spain. There were important elements missing in the philosophy in which Alonzo had placed full, passionate trust; it ignored two essential values.

5

Alonzo would not have been himself had he kept his discovery of the defect of Dewey's philosophy to himself. He had to get a little juice out of it; so he took himself to Klotz and asked him what the instrumentalists had to say about tragedy as an ingredient of life and an embodiment of it in literature? Klotz had a polished genius for conveying pity and contempt for anything that did not enter his awareness or that he disapproved of, and on this occasion he gave an outstanding performance of his talent. "Tragedy? Much tragedy is unnecessary," he replied. "The rest must be borne as best one can." But he was not through; what can a philosopher do with questions of literary criticism but treat them with the scorn they deserve? He picked up the nettle with bare hands, and replied with deep, obviously specious, pity: "I have always known, Alonzo, that you are really a literary man. Your question is not a philosophical question." Alonzo retorted in a manner meant to be seen through, "No doubt, then, the same holds for the epic and for heroism?" And he added, as an afterthought, something he had planned, "Homer, Aeschylus, Shakespeare—they are not figures in which a philosopher could be interested?"

"I didn't say *that*," replied Klotz. "Of course some of the topics with which they deal are matters of serious interest to the philosopher, murder for instance. But you've got to approach these topics carefully and not rhetorically." As far as Klotz had gone, he was, of course, right, but he had avoided the problem, namely, that the naturalist was not interested in tragedy or heroism. But the Philistine heart has reasons that ordinary reason knows not of. Instances like this added proof, although by now Alonzo had more than enough proof, that Maxie Waxie's contempt for literature was deeply rooted; it probably grew out of the character that had led him once to put on a blue uniform and pick up a tambourine.

Not content with his little victory over Klotz Alonzo took himself to Lakaitel Holzkopf. "Holley" was the oldest of Maxie Waxie's family as well as a teacher in Mieck's college. He had been a teacher of speech in a high school until Littlemieck rescued him and brought him to State. Because he had only an undergraduate degree Holley was working for his doctor's. Tall, extremely handsome, he exuded charm and knew it. The girls drooled over him. Among those who knew him he had the reputation of being lazy, stupid, and one of the most ignorant members of the faculty. Since he had been a high school teacher he was not quite a mere Margites, but he was a reasonable facsimile thereof. For Alonzo, Holley's greatest distinction was that, because of his extraordinary servility, among the members of Klotz's family, a group of accomplished *derrière* kissers, he was without competition Maxie Waxie's and Mieck's "Pooh-Bah without portfolio." His spinal column violated the laws of physics: it had such a high coefficient of elasticity that it was fatigue proof, so that no matter how frequently it bent down to perform his favorite form of *derrière* kissing, it was incapable of breaking.

Expecting some sort of stupidity about Dewey on death Alonzo turned to Holley. "I am puzzled," he said, "but I have looked everywhere in Dewey for what he has to say about death and I can't find a word on it. Could you tell me what Dewey has to say on the subject and where I can find it?" "That is easy," replied the big man brimming with charm and confidence. "Dewey is not a biologist. What can one say about death except that it is a biological event and that it often leaves those who knew the deceased in grief?" Alonzo said, "You are right, that is all he could say." Alonzo stressed the *he* but Holley did not realize that he had been had.

A defender of Dewey will argue that Dewey can't be blamed for the myopia of his followers, particularly when they are not very bright. Alonzo agrees heartily. He does not hold Dewey responsible for the two men. But he had put the same questions about tragedy and death to the two most distinguished disciples of Dewey in New York and had gotten totally inadequate replies. Too intelligent and sophisticated to pull the same foot-in-mouth act that Maxie Waxie and Holley had pulled, these eminent lovers of the truth, these Cardinals of the Scientistic Church, were stumped by the questions and when they tried to answer them they showed not only that they had not thought about them—that Alonzo knew since he was acquainted with their printed "wisdom"—but that within their philosophy there were no resources with which to improvise an answer. If the midwestern suppliers of "wisdom" had shown themselves fools, these two Eminences had exhibited the fact that when asked critical questions beyond science and Philistine moral problems, they were caught with their breeches down.

X

Pragmatism and
the Tragic Sense of Life

1

SHORTLY after Alonzo discovered that naturalism had nothing to say on tragedy, that naturalists ignored heroism and that what they had to say about death was trivial, he was asked by a literary quarterly for a report of the "new" naturalism about which there was a great deal of interest among the intellectuals at the time. In the last short section of the essay he submitted, Alonzo succinctly sketched the doubts he had begun to entertain about the adequacy of naturalism. The response to the essay was much stronger than he had anticipated. He received a number of letters that indicated that the essay had been read with dismay by his friends. I asked Alonzo for a full account of the reaction to the essay. I seem to remember, I said, that the reaction included more than letters. Yes, more. But a complete account of the indirect consequence it brought about, besides getting us into too long a story, is not quite relevant to your job. I insisted it was because I remember vaguely what had happened. More interesting than the letters he received condemning his "defection" was an indirect response that, he thought at the time, was flattering. A Left literary review announced the forthcoming publication of an essay on pragmatism and tragedy by one of Dewey's chief disciples, Professor Disney Haten. I insisted that the story was certainly relevant to my job.

He told me that when he submitted the essay he had expected his friends not to like it. Naturalist philosophers are human. Their claims to impersonality and objectivity were not to be taken as rigorously binding on them as on those with whom they disagreed. Some of them were more impersonal and objective than others, but the majority, and certainly Haten, reacted to disagreement with their views as religious believers do. Alonzo, however, had not anticipated the implacable way in which they would open up on him. They proclaimed the virtue of tolerance, but they acted as if he had changed sides in the middle of a war. He had "defected." Haten told a friend who passed it on to him that Alonzo had betrayed his naturalism. This way of putting the matter was interesting to Alonzo because it gave away their attitude. A man who defects gives up his allegiance. But Alonzo had never asked to be received in their church or sworn fealty to their flag. He had been a Deweyian, but only a Deweyian of sorts, as a serious thinker must be, whether he is a Deweyian, a Kantian, or a Will Durantian. He had been a Deweyian naturalist because he found in some of Dewey's writings what he took to be, at the time, the truth about the relation of man to the universe.

But he had never accepted all of Dewey's theories. Some he considered incoherent: Dewey on truth wavered. Dewey on education simply did not interest him. Alonzo ignored these views. And Dewey on human nature was, for one who had learned about man through the eyes of the great "poets"—some of the Greeks, the Elizabethans, Cervantes, Dostoevski, George Eliot, and the others who had nourished him—irrelevant; it was, at best, a sample of what the "science" of man could do: to offer elaborate academic dog-do. Further, Dewey knew nothing of religion and was prevented by temperament and theory from learning about it. He ignored the fundamental objects that elicit religious experience: the heavens, the complexity of living things, the potency and the creative energy of large and small things. For these reasons and others, Alonzo had never been and could never be, a true Deweyian. A wholehearted naturalist he had been, but never in a religious way. If his belief in naturalism was "faith," it was not the kind that would have satisfied an inquisitor. He had never had occasion to state this in print or in public, but those who knew him personally must have known that he was not a trustworthy disciple, since he had never concealed his partial disagreement with thinkers who had influenced him. But was it necessary to say this? A thinker who defects or betrays the thought of a man from whom he has learned may be a most meritorious father of a family and citizen, he may even be a hero to his valet, but he is no thinker. The question was not whether he had defected or betrayed any views or any one. It was whether the grounds for abandoning his naturalism and whether the views he put in its place held or not. He was loyal, he had always been loyal, but not to a philosophical party or school (which is self-evidently a contradiction in terms) but to his commitment to an objective search that promised to carry him as close to the truth as it was possible for him, given his handicaps, to get. This was the reason he had moved from one philosopher's counter to another till he found the views he had confidence were the best available.

The response to his criticism I remembered, but I wanted to get his present attitude to the essay in reply to his criticism, written by his former friend, Professor Haten. Haten's essay had been announced immediately after Alonzo's criticism of naturalism appeared, and it finally was made public a number of years later.

First I wanted to have his reaction to the man, for Haten had published a virulent diatribe against Alonzo, and second I wanted his present views on Haten's claim that pragmatism did have a theory of the tragic sense of life. Well, Alonzo replied smiling, Haten's attack on me was his response to a review of mine of his book on education in which I showed up his doctrine for the tawdry Philistinism it was. But you must look at the original edition of the book, for I was told by someone who read a subsequent edition that he had deleted several passages I had criticized. To me Haten's furious diatribe was interesting because it showed that I had put my finger on a spot where his vain soul hurt.

So, in a way, I had it coming. The virulence, however, I did not have coming, but I should have expected it since I knew Haten well. A man as vain as he is wouldn't put up with what he called my betrayal. Add to the betrayal the truth of my criticism about the lacunae of naturalism and the exposé of the vulgarity of his views on education and you arouse the murderous anger of a vain man. If I had not sized up the situation as I did, he might have hurt me. But all he managed to do was to confirm my judgment of the intellectual vulgarity of the man —something I had suspected long before I saw how it expressed itself. This does not dispose of him. In many important ways he is a very generous person with those who think well of him. He once did me a great favor, which I have never forgotten. But this does not make the picture he has of himself true. His view of himself is only partly true. Unbeknown to himself he is an implacable dogmatist. Disagree with him and you bring out the vast aggressive energies he is endowed with. So much for the specific corrigibility he preaches. I trace his intolerant dogmatism to a sense of insecurity he has no reason to have, because in the field of political journalism he has made a deservedly good name for himself. His journalistic talents aside, Haten is a very human animal, I would say. But I have said enough on Haten the man. It is his essay on the pragmatic tragic sense of life on which you should focus. In this essay he asseverates, first, without proof, that Dewey does have a sense of tragedy. How could he lack it? If the tragic sense is a good, Dewey must have had it and indeed he did. How could the *capocosche* of Naturalist Families, the *capo di tutti capi* of contemporary Wisdom Lovers, the cornucopia of as much of the ultimate truth as is given to men to attain—how could a man like that lack the tragic sense of life? Moreover, Dewey grew in the shadow of the Civil War, and like all men who grew in the shadow of the Civil War, he had the tragic sense of life. The historians who give you a different idea of the age are wrong. Mary Baker Eddy, for instance, ached with the tragic sense of life, and so did the railroad builders and those who after the Civil War trekked west into the unknown, leaving behind them a strong spoor which is characteristic of those who have the tragic sense of life, as animals are said to emanate the smell of fear. Even before the Civil War the United States lived in the grip of the tragic sense, as shown by the fact that when Brigham Young descried the valley into which his people were to settle he exclaimed, here we shall build a kingdom dedicated to the tragic sense of life. Of course Dewey's tragic sense of life was no ordinary tragic sense of life, but how could it be, since it was Dewey's? It was nothing like the tragic sense you find in Aeschylus or Sophocles or find giving force to *King Lear*. It was a pragmatic tragic sense of life, as you would expect from him. And make no mistake, it was not an instrumentalist tragic sense of life, it was a pragmatic one. And it was pragmatic because it worked.

Haten adds that although what the phrase describes is implied in Dewey's account of the moral experience, nothing of moment depends on whether the view is actually Dewey's, or Hegel's or William James's or Nicolai Hartmann's, in all of whom it can be found, for he takes the responsibility for its interpretation and its application. One cannot decide whether it is the phrase or the view that is found in those philosophers, but let that go since it is Haten's view that is in question.

But if nothing of moment depends on whether the phrase or the view is found in Dewey, why is the matter brought up? The statement that Dewey, because he was born in the shadow of the Civil War, felt the tragic sense of life is as relevant as if we had been informed that Dewey had been born with right-angled big toes, like some Nepalese, and during his adolescence he had lived with a sense that he was a freak which, of course, accounted for his humanitarian concern for the underdog. Dewey might have felt the tragic sense of life. But how, in the absence of a discussion in print by Dewey himself of the nature of tragedy, or as second choice, of lecture notes taken by a student, can students of philosophy know that Dewey did indeed feel the tragic sense of life and not an ersatz tragic sense, and what is at least as important, that feeling it in his own life, he incorporated an account of it in his philosophy?

The word *tragedy* is notoriously used in all sorts of ways. It is used in the classic sense to apply to the lives lived by the heirs of Pelops and the heirs of Oedipus. But it is also used in a cheapened sense to refer to the death of one of Mrs. Goodall's chimps, or to the catastrophic death of seabirds killed by an oil spill. But let us accept the irrelevant fact that Dewey felt the tragic sense, how can the reader bring Dewey's radical optimism, his futuristic outlook, instinct as it was with secular hope, his Pelagian denial of "original sin" that he probably absorbed with his mother's milk, his patented pedagogical cure-all bottled in Teacher's College, his faith that science and social engineering can reduce the evil among men, his faith in progress expressed in the first edition of Dewey and Tuft's *Ethics*, his rigorously restricted sublunar purview—how can the reader bring these central components of Dewey's faith into harmony with his tragic sense of life?

No student of philosophy can be expected to take seriously apologetics based on such a biographical assertion; it proves nothing. But even if its irrelevance had not been acknowledged by the author, the question remains: where did Dewey's subjective experience find expression in his published philosophy? If it did not, why didn't it? Do we then have here—a case common enough in the history of humane letters—a thinker who fails to express an important aspect of his vision of the world in his philosophy? This is possible; if so, the fact may be important to a biographer of Dewey, but it is totally irrelevant to the student of his philosophy. For the latter, it is only his thought as expounded in books, essays, letters, or student's lecture notes, that is of interest.

2

So much for Haten on Dewey. How does he himself show that the pragmatic purview includes the tragic sense? Since he takes responsibility for the interpretation of the phrase and its application, he is not required to quote what other pragmatists have written on the subject. He cannot go to what he himself wrote before his attention was called to the omission, since before that sad event our warrior, who is fond of asking where were you when he was in the thick of the battle, somehow missed that scrap. Nor can he go to the tragic poets to show that their vision is a component of the pragmatic purview. This door is closed to him, since he has advised young people who want an education for modern man to read the *New York Times* instead of Herodotus —by which one can take him to mean, not the author of the inquiries exclusively but himself and his fellow ancient men of letters. How then does our empiricist sage show that there is within the pragmatic purview room for the tragic sense of life? It is hard to believe, but this advocate of empiricism stipulates the meaning. So much for our empiricist's use of the scientific method.

He asks, "What do I mean by the tragic sense of life and what is its relevance to pragmatism?" He answers that by the term he means "a very simple phenomenon of the moral choice." What is tragic in the moral choice? The fact that when we ask, "What should I do?" we find ourselves in a situation where good conflicts with good, or our good with the good of another, or others, or between goods and rights, or between rights and rights. On the stipulated definition of our pragmatist, life turns out to be through and through tragic, since even for the most powerful and most fortunate of men, even for the best regulated routine, even for the most customary and well habituated existence, it involves choice. But our pragmatist escapes the meaninglessness of the universality of tragedy by pointing out that just as there are little deaths there are little choices. It is only the big choices that are truly tragic. We are told that it is where the choice is between goods that are complex in structure and consequential for the future, that the tragic quality of the moral dilemma emerges more clearly. The reader no doubt will be relieved by the quantitative criterion and especially by the fact that the criterion makes tragedy a choice that is consequential for the future and not for the past. This makes it easier for us to decide when we are caught in a tragic choice.

We have long had Humpty Dumpty's authority, now indirectly re-inforced by *Webster's Third*, to the effect that we can use words as we choose to and not as someone else does. This is a little tragedy which is no tragedy at all, but a great boon. But if we define tragedy as our pragmatist does, how do we distinguish serious human catastrophes, a profound but honest error in a moral decision, and an unfortunately erroneous but honest practical choice from a choice that is complex and consequential—or complex in structure and consequential for the future, if one must have the bafflegab and the pleonasm—how does one distinguish these sufferances and endurances, from truly tragic events, which is to say, from events called tragic in the classical sense? If one of these events is complex and consequential it is tragic by stipu-lation. But are there no choices that are complex and consequential that can hardly be called tragic except by our pragmatist's stipulation? Let us see.

Consider a man trying to choose between two women to whom he is equally attracted as far as he can discern, who are in every respect equal: equal in his affection for them and their affection for him, equal in their beauty, charm, grace, personality, in their intelligence if that is a factor that counts with him, in what they may contribute toward a future home economically, although that factor may not be one to which he gives great weight—in short in every trait that for him is im-portant. Such a man is faced with a choice that is complex and conse-quential. But shall we say, Humpty Dumpty aside, that whomever he chooses, his choice is tragic? He may regret that he cannot marry both of them; sometimes, not often, he may regret that both women being equally moral, he cannot suggest to both that, since he cannot choose between them, the satisfactory solution, since they both love him, is for them to set up a *ménage à trois*; he may, in an idle moment, wish he were living in Utah in the days of old when men were men and women were plenty. But are we to say that he is confronted with a tragic choice? A sensible man would not allow himself such a melo-dramatic statement—even to himself.

A man who calls all choices, of whatever kind, however complex and consequential, tragic, because they involve renunciation and sac-rifice, is like a child whose mother finds crying disconsolately. What are you crying about, Johnny, my pet, asks his mother gently. I am crying, he says between heartrending sobs, because I ate one of my lollypops and now I have one less. But Johnny, his mother says, still gently, if you ate one you have one less, and if you wanted as many as you had before you ate one, you should not have eaten one. But I want to have it and I wanted to eat it, and I can't have it if I eat it, and I can't eat it if I want to have it, he cries, stamping his foot now, his mood turning to rage.

In serious discourse, one of the implicit duties of the thinker is the preservation of the health of the language he uses. T. S. Eliot and Allen Tate have written that the preservation of the language from the erosion from which it constantly suffers is the duty of the poet. But it is also the duty of all responsible writers and thinkers. And this, for reasons too obvious to state explicitly. Erase distinctions for the sake of making a point and you wilfully and irresponsibly contribute to the erosion of your instrument. A man who leaves his tools overnight on the lawn is not a man for whom a fellow worker can have respect. A man who erases necessary distinctions is open to criticism. And come the revolution, by and by there will be a classless state, and in such a utopia men who destroy language will be considered enemies of the people.

3

Let me turn next, Alonzo went on to say, to the substance of our pragmatist's definition of the tragic sense. It does not call for a profound or extensive knowledge of the history of philosophy to recall that what our pragmatist has presented us with is a rip-off from Hegel. You recall that for Hegel the essential nature of tragedy—and Alonzo pointed out that he was following Hegel here almost verbatim—resides in the opposition worked out in its finest way by Sophocles following Aeschylus, in the body politic, between the ethical life in its social universality and the family as the ground of moral relations. This is the reason that for Hegel the *Antigone* is the most perfect of Greek tragedies. That other ancient masterpieces can be subjected to the same misreading should not surprise anyone who has witnessed an intelligent interpreter force a poem down on the Procrustean bed of his a priori definition and chop off its legs to make it fit his bed. Thus Hegel tells us that the *Agamemnon* is a tragedy because Agamemnon, by sacrificing his daughter, shatters the bond of love between himself and his daughter, which his wife, Clytemnestra, retains in the depths of her mother's heart, and in revenge prepares an ignominious death for her husband on his return. True, or almost true—so far as it goes. With the *Antigone* Hegel has an easier time. The tragedy consists of the conflict between Antigone's reverence for the ties of blood relationship and Creon's exclusive recognition of Zeus, the paramount power of public life and the commonwealth. Again, true, or almost true—as far as it goes.

This is not the occasion, Alonzo continued, to examine exhaustively the inadequacy of Hegel's reading of these two tragedies. Suffice to indicate in haste that the defect consists of overlooking the transcendent or cosmic element in both tragedies. The origin of the *Agamemnon*—the matter for it—is an ancient myth with which, in its various forms, we can assume the spectators were acquainted. The tragedy began with the crimes of the heirs of Pelops which led to a conflict among the gods, a conflict as important an element of the tragedy as the crimes of the heirs of Pelops and Agamemnon's sacrifice of his daughter. It is therefore erroneous to overlook the fact that the tragedy takes place on two planes, the human and the divine, which the reader remembers, merge in the last play of the trilogy. In the *Antigone* the transcendent element is made explicit by Antigone in the opening lines of the play when she reminds Ismene that they are the victims of the curse of Oedipus. Hegel's interpretation maims both tragedies by overlooking the transcendent element, conveyed later by Scheler in the statement that tragedy is an essential element of the universe itself—a fact that only a very careless reader or a Great Thinker armed with a Definition that he wrongly claims he drew from the ancient tragedies, can overlook. But tragedy is an essential element of the universe in a sense that a naturalist—who believes that everything that happens is part of Nature—would deny. What Scheler means is that the human events that constitute the tragedy are connected morally and not merely by means of value-free causal connections with the universe.

Antigone was punished, if men of today can call it punishment, for a crime she did not commit. But she was also punished by Creon because she wilfully violated his edict. Less evidently than in the *Oresteia*, but obviously enough, the *Antigone* takes place on two planes. This may create a difficulty for contemporary logicians who may hold that if Antigone was fated to be punished as a victim of the curse of Oedipus, she could not have defied Creon's edicts freely. If we seek what is to be found in the play we can either ignore the contradiction or ignore the play.

If we remember that for Hegel human history is part of the procession of the dialectic toward a cosmic end, one can argue in his defense that his understanding of tragedy is not totally crippling, for the events that take place on the human stage are, in the context of his system, related meaningfully—and not merely in terms of value-free cause and effect—to the ongoing movement of the universe.

Alonzo went on, You can see why I say that Haten's version of tragedy is a watered-down rip-off from Hegel. Since for the pragmatist the phenomenon of moral choice arises from men's needs and desires and the conflicts these generate within man and among men, the tragic sense for the pragmatist is indeed a very simple thing, that under no circumstances can be taken to be an essential part of the universe itself as Scheler means it. If you take the tragedy to be an essential part of the universe itself, you give the enlightened pragmatist evidence that you are a victim of anthropomorphic superstition. The grasp of the relation between tragic events and the universe itself has been widely taken to be, again somehow, by victims of anthropomorphic superstition, evidence of profound vision. A few men in a few cultures—for not all cultures and not all men in those in which tragedies were produced—have grasped, or thought they grasped, the tragic relation; *somehow* because it is not a question of knowledge in the narrow sense, about which there is on principle a causal explanation. It is a question of obscure and complex responses of a profoundly disquieting nature to human events that elicit cosmic terror, reverence, and piety, and that somehow elicit expression and find relief through genuine tragedies—which is to say, in tragedies through the classical sense.

When a critic calls attention to the fact that there is no room within the purview of naturalism for the tragic vision and for the modes of expression for which it is the matter, he refers to considerably more than conflicts, however stubborn and however productive of human woe, within man or among men. For this reason the pragmatist's reply is either intellectually irresponsible or myopic. The critic of naturalism may be wrong. If naturalism is true the universe is value free and human conflicts cannot have an essential, moral relation to the universe itself; they can only have a causal relation. Tragedy, in the naturalist's view, unless he is a follower of Humpty Dumpty, is ruled out by his conception of the universe.

Because this is the node of the issue it is desirable to show up the phony empiricism of our pragmatic sage. Men capable of the tragic

vision in the classic sense of the term, and not in the *ad hoc*, Humpty
Dumpty sense our pragmatist stipulates, derive their conception of the
nature of human life from experience. It is what they learn about life
at first hand or from reflection on the vicissitudes of others that forces
on them the conviction that life seldom if ever permits a permanent
union with the bitch Happiness who, when she happens to pick them
up for a moment of joy, soon abandons them. From this bitter lesson
the majority of men seek escape by turning their eyes on a life to come
after the miseries they endure here and now. Others turn their hope to
a Golden Age in the future, a utopia free from iniquity and avoidable
pain. But some men—not many and only in a few cultures of our
West—for how it is in the East Alonzo did not know—free from secular chiliastic delusions and perspicacious enough to see that human
catastrophes cannot always be traced to failure of human judgment,
leap mythically or literally and attribute the condition of man to the
nature of the universe in which they think they discern a flaw which
denies the Whole to be a Cosmos and to which they trace the source
of human misery. It is a leap prompted by what they observe men endure. The leap may land them in an egregious error; if the universe
is value free, it does. But it is no more of a leap than that which the
pragmatist takes. For this man, along with his fellow naturalists, ex-
tends the demands of physical science to the Whole and declares that
it is value free. Such an assertion about the Whole cannot be based on
experience, for the obvious reason that it is given to no man, not even
to a scientistic pragmatist, to survey the Whole.

The man endowed with tragic vision in the classic sense lashes out
at the Whole; it is not a Cosmos, for at its heart there is a flaw. He is
only an empiricist of sorts, but he is an empiricist nevertheless, for he
starts out from the observation of what men endure. In this important
respect, the pragmatist is not an empiricist, for he rules out the classical notion of tragedy a prioristically on the basis of a nonempirical
theory about the Whole, namely, on his scientistic theory that it is
value free. This faith of our pragmatist is probably what leads him to
his inability to see human life against the background of the Whole.
Hence the banality of his notion of tragedy. Did I say *banality?* I did.
No, much worse than that; it is more like infantilism, since a man in
his maturity takes in his stride the fact that to live is, among other
things, to lose one choice for the sake of another.

And the horrors of history? the misery of men? the indignity of so much that is living? the helplessness before the essentially untoward universe?—what does our sage say to this? He probably dismisses it. It is rhetoric, and meaningless rhetoric at that, since by applying our reason, aided by the scientific method, we can avoid many of the evils that until the appearance of John Dewey and his enforcer visited men.

4

The defect of our pragmatist's effort to meet the criticism of naturalism is obvious; moreover, it is disingenuous. In order to show its disingenuousness, Alonzo invented a fable. Let's imagine, he suggested, an argument between a patriotic Englishman who cherishes the monarchy and an American jingoist. The Englishman criticizes the United States because it does not have a queen. This is not difficult to imagine when one remembers that *niaiseries* of which narrow partisans are capable are apt to bloom with tropical luxuriance. But the fable need never have had a real model, since its purpose is to show how disingenuous our pragmatist is.

"We have no queens?" the American jingoist snarls. "That shows how ignorant critics of the greatest country in the world are. You know nothing about us or you would know that we have dozens of queens, literally dozens, whereas you English have only one, a plain faced skirt that wouldn't have the smallest chance of placing in a contest with one of our queens. The beauty and the sexual power of our queens must be seen to be believed. No queen in English history has ever come close to any of our queens. What is more, our queens are crowned yearly and are universally admired. We have a queen of potatoes, a queen of onions, a queen of oranges, a queen of frankfurters, a queen of tulips . . . you name it and the chances are I can show you we have a queen to fill your bill. And you say we have no queens!"

Obvious as it must be, Alonzo continued, we must look at what the American jingoist has done. He has pretended to himself and anyone silly enough to take him seriously, that there is a substantive equivalent between what in the United States are called queens and what traditionally have been called queens in monarchies. But as Giovani Sartori puts it in *Democratic Theory*, "To make two things verbally alike only makes them *verbally* alike."

Alonzo turned to me with a face that did not succeed in concealing his sense of triumph and asked, Elementary, my dear biographer? Of course, utterly elementary, but not unnecessary, since what the jingoist wants to do is to me-too himself into a class where he does not belong by means of verbal alchemy. What he should have replied to the English monarchist was something like this: "You are quite right, we have no queens—not consecrated janes like your queen. We abolished that kind of useless ornamental ribbon-cutter and king-breeder when we kicked you out. We have dames we call queens. But these dames are not queens in your sense of the term. What we have done by calling them queens is to borrow the prestige of the old word. This is not an illegitimate trick; it fools no one and it makes our queens feel happy. But no one in the whole extent of this blessed cotton-picking land is so ignorant as to believe that what we call queens are queens in your archaic and, to a democrat, ridiculous if not odious, sense of the term. The word endures and the prestige that it had originally and still has among you monarchists still clings to it among us. For that reason we use the term. We call our young women, selected competitively, queens, to indicate they are superior. But a queen, like the woman you call queen, the woman who is married to a king or to a stud quasi king and has been consecrated according to ancient ceremonies—that kind of luxury we do not have. What is more, I dare say that outside of a small minority of kooks and weirdos, were anyone to propose seriously that we should change our form of government and bring in a monarchy in order to have a real queen, he would be laughed at."

This is the kind of answer our pragmatist should have given the critic when the latter wrote that within the purview of naturalism there was no room for tragedy, the sentiment, the vision that informs some kinds of acts and sufferances, and some aesthetic spectacles. He should have said: "Naturalism excludes the tragic sense because it holds that the universe is value free and value is result of human desire and need. We have abolished tragedy in your sense, because you hold that tragedy is an essential part of the universe itself, and such a belief is anthropomorphic superstition." The pragmatist could have added that since words are not copyrighted, there is no dishonesty in using the term *tragedy* as anyone wishes to use it, so long as the user makes fully explicit that in using the word tragedy in his way he is using it in a totally different way than it was used in the classic sense, and so long as he makes it emphatically clear that he is not claiming for what he calls tragedy the virtues that are claimed for it by the old users.

Had he been fully honest he would have admitted that his philosophy cannot claim for it virtues it does not have and that for him are not virtues but expressions of superstition. A serious thinker does not cheat; he avoids giving the impression of cheating. To claim that pragmatism is capable of the tragic sentiment without a full and emphatically explicit clarification of what he can claim for his philosophy as well as what he cannot, is objectively—whatever his subjective motivations—cheating. A serious thinker has no need of me-tooing his philosophy where it does not belong. He accepts the limitations inherent in his position, aware that no philosophy is under the obligation of doing in any one respect what other philosophies do. He might remind his readers that claims to the contrary not withstanding, all philosophies entail limitations. Indeed a serious thinker should glory in the limitations of his philosophy. He defends the truth of his views without inventing for them virtues they cannot have and that from his point of view are indeed not virtues. To defend a philosophy *à outrance* is to put himself on the plane with lawyers who argue to win, not to discover the merits of a case.

5

Alonzo added that this is not all he had to say about the pragmatist who had tried to refute his criticism. He came back to the fact that pragmatists are neo-Pelagians and that our pragmatist had called himself a Pelagian in print. But Pelagians, neo- or paleo-, are optimists in principle who believe, as our pragmatist argues, that "the method of creative intelligence" can reduce at least in part if not entirely, the evil that makes the warp of human history. This in turn means that what our pragmatist calls tragedy is a very simple thing that is only waiting for social engineers to do away with or to meliorate. But even if human conflicts are found in practice to be ineradicable, are they not at quite a distance from the myths the great tragic poets wove into their tragedies?

Why do you keep on rubbing in the business of tragedy being a very simple thing? I asked Alonzo. You know that the man you call our pragmatist does not mean by *thing* a physical thing and that he calls it simple, probably, in order to remove it from the cosmic plane and keep it within the body politic in which the ethical life in its universality comes into conflict within man and among men. The reason I rub it in, Alonzo replied, is to call emphatic attention to the flat-footed language of the man. Whatever the exact relation between language and thought is taken to be, this much we can say with confidence, that he who writes without grace, he who writes in a flat-footed way, thinks in that way. Our pragmatist writes without grace, without inspiration, always at sea level or below it, never above it. When he feels inspired —have you ever seen a hen trying to fly? It's a sight. It flaps its wings in desperate vigor, it runs, it jumps, it reaches the height of a foot or two, and still trying desperately it falls to the ground. Our pragmatist has no sense of history or of the value of history, or he would not have advised a young man in search of an education to read the *New York Times* instead of Herodotus. The advice gives superfluous evidence of how much you can learn about the nature of man from the best daily newspaper or the worst.

Alonzo changed his attitude. The seriousness of naturalism's failure to recognize the tragic component of experience, using the term, not in an *ad hoc*, me-too sense, but in its classical sense, cannot be exaggerated. An adequate philosophy, one equal to the requirements of a whole man, not of a man with vision dimmed by scientistic faith and Pelagian optimism, should have something to say about the cluster of values and disvalues that men cannot successfully turn their face from. If a philosopher ignores these values and disvalues, sooner or later the dour components of human experience will catch up with him.

XI

Naturalism's Theory of Value

1

NOT ONLY was philosophical naturalism blind to two important values, thus preventing in theory the development of a rich personality, but its theory of value, when reflected on, turned out to lead to two appalling consequences.

Since for naturalists the universe was value free, Alonzo had no doubt that they were right in discarding the various definitions of the good supplied by Aristotle and keeping only his definition of the good as the object of desire. The majority of naturalistic philosophers had discarded the term *desire*, but the terms they put in its place made no radical difference to their views. On this doctrine, the meaning of life was to be found in human existence, if men gave their lives meaning by entertaining desires that they were able to satisfy. There was much argument among naturalistic moralists about which desires could be satisfied and how they could be satisfied to produce value. But they agreed on the basic notion that it was desires that constituted value and therefore each in and by itself was neither good nor bad; desires were capable of producing goodness or badness when they began to interact with one another, furthering or obstructing one another's satisfactions, thus leading to acceptable or frustrating consequences. But whose desires made up the good? Ultimately, of course, those of the individual, for to assume that society by itself, as an entity, was capable of desiring anything, was to reify society; social desires emanated from individuals and had their locus within them.

If you asked a naturalist whether there was a good life *par excellence*, a *summum bonum* for man—not for the individual but for generic man as distinct from angels and brutes—he replied that there could be such a *summum bonum* if one could speak of a universally shared desire that had primacy over all others—allowing for its absence because of perversion, or criminal tendencies, or physical accident. This desire had to be the strongest and the longest lived of all desires and took in fact precedence over all desires. But a naturalist could not take the notion very seriously; if he was not a thorough-paced relativist he was at least keenly aware of the pluralism of values among societies and among the individuals making up a society, and he did not seem to be able to go beyond the pluralism; he was also, as a rule, a nominalist; he had to reject the view, therefore, that there were desires that were not someone's desires; disembodied desires that were not someone's love, or friendship, or charity, or pity, or loyalty, or hatred, or envy, or hunger, or lust added up to the geometrical figures rejected by Berkeley: triangles that were neither right angle triangles, isosceles, nor scalene. Such figures did not exist. In the absence of an actual concrete desire shared by all men that was dominant in all, the *summum bonum* was a nonexistent abstract figure. Naturalists were able to think about happiness as much as anyone else; but the only thing that could be meant by such talk was the satisfaction of specific and, in principle, distinct desires for man, taking the term *man* distributively—for each man. They could not mean inclusive goals for all men taken collectively, unless they were actually operative.

There was no point in asking positivists what was the meaning of life; for reasons that were sound in terms of their views, they could not make any sense out of the question: The meaning of life, if you allowed the term *meaning* when a much better term was *goal*, was what each man sought to make out of it. What did Dewey have to say about it? Dewey had a great deal to say about the part that intelligence should play in the moral life and showed that the good was not merely the desired but the desirable; that is to say, that which, after the intelligence has subjected desires to criticism, was still desired. But when the question about what Dewey meant by the good life occurred to Alonzo, he recollected what Unamuno had said about pragmatism; in spite of the profound influence that William James had on Unamuno, the Spaniard was a sharp critic of James. The pragmatist, Unamuno pointed out, sought to make the world better in order to make it better in order to make it better, in order to continue to make it better and better forever, in an endless beaver frenzy of perpetual improvement which, since there were no terminal values, could not be known to be an improvement and which, therefore, no one could cash in on. True, Dewey had much to say about consummatory experiences. But ultimately each of these experiences had to satisfy the individual—with emphasis on *each* and on *individual*.

What did improvement mean? In theory, Dewey was emphatically not a hedonist; he had written against this view. A good society was not one in which there would simply be an increase of pleasure and a decrease of pain for everybody; but when you unraveled the technical argument against hedonism and asked what was the pay dirt of Dewey's criticism of a life of pleasure, it turned out that a good society was conceived as one making possible secular satisfactions of an essentially bourgeois character whose true hedonic nature was decently camouflaged by abundant verbal branches and leaves and painted burlap, the whole thing speciously looking like a monument to the "higher values." But what were these higher values if they were not satisfactions which brought with them pleasure? What did this add up to? A glorified bourgeois society. On a naturalist theory of value a good life in a good society was a decent, well ordered, successful life, in the sense of Kierkegaard's "aesthetic stage." At this point it became clear to Alonzo that he was using the term *bourgeois* in order to avoid a stronger but more accurate term. On the naturalist theory of value what a good life adds up to is a thoroughly Philistine affair. It was a life of satisfactions enjoyed by honest men; satisfactions that were not called pleasures.

What then were the values that made up the good life? A visit to church fully *endomingue*, of course, on Sundays, where one hears a sensible sermon on social melioration, and meets one's friends; a little wine for the tummy's sake, but not so much that it leads to an arrest for drunken driving; no heroics, no dramatic self-sacrifice, no extremities of the kind that David Hume dismissed contemptuously as monkish virtues, no sweat—since coupons can be clipped without much effort—no exaltation, and if one is lucky, good health.

There is no question whatever that this is one kind of good life—it would be stupid to deny it. But was it the only kind? Hardly, anyone who has read history knows about others. Was it the best? For the bourgeois, yes, but certainly not the best without qualification, since it was not a life in which men could display their greatest, although conceded, their rarest powers. The smug provincialism that assumes that this is the only kind of good life men can live is proof of—what is it proof of? What of, but a deep rooted Philistine rationality that asserts that it is folly to go for broke, that the only way to live is to be prudent and stick to the middle of the road. Alonzo pondered what he had read about the lives of Moors and Spaniards before the victory of the latter, and arrived at two insights that showed him the limitations of the conception of the good life of Santayana and Dewey. First, that in spite of the romantic madness of Nietzsche there was a heavy component of truth in his repudiation of his world and in his yearning for the superman. The other was that to repudiate as barbaric and to deny the value of the Spaniards's heroic life was to repudiate our own world and its notion of the good life, for it was the incredible heroism of the medievals that had made possible the world of today—with its undoubted values and its serious defects.

But what if, after traveling the road of prudence you approached the end and you were forced by the aching emptiness of your life to acknowledge that something had gone wrong, that somehow your life had been a radical failure in spite of its apparent success? Such an event happens, and not rarely, to men, and often happens when it is too late. One runs into people who have succeeded but whose success, when it comes, tastes bitter. The possibility that this is an event that waits for you when you reach the top is not a suspicion that is pleasant to entertain, since it forebodes despair. If it comes on you, you'd better chalk it up to the evil daimon in you that succeeded in defeating you.

2

One had to distinguish between Dewey's doctrine of the good life and the life Dewey himself lived. His own life, if Alonzo could tell from information readily available from those who knew him, was admirable. Dewey's life was a creative life of the highest order and greatest intensity; all one need to do to verify this fact was to look at the card catalogue in the library. His was not a mean Philistine's life outside his professional activity. Albert C. Barnes had introduced him to painting, and his book *Art As Experience*, which could more accurately have been called *Painting As Experience*, since the book has little to say on either literature or music, is evidence of his serious interest in the art of painting. One also had to consider the broad and profound influence he had had on several areas of the intellectual and to some extent the practical life of the nation. Looked at from the standpoint of philosophy Dewey's was a dominant figure, however baneful some of his critics might consider him to be.

Once you got over your distaste for his fuzzy prose, you discovered important truth behind his verbiage. If a life dedicated to thought was worth living—something that Alonzo would not think of questioning —Dewey's life was as worth living as any. There was more: Alonzo had firsthand evidence of Dewey's generosity. One of Dewey's students had fallen mentally ill and Dewey footed the expenses. But Alonzo could see that the life that Dewey lived was not quite the life his doctrines recommended. His doctrines were not defective merely because they had nothing to say about heroism, tragedy, and death; they were defective because they prevented—if one took him seriously—the development of piety; and what was worse, they did not stress nobility and dignity, and when Dewey mentioned the latter, he gave a fuzzy and inaccurate picture of it.

Dignity was one of the concerns that liberals complacently thought they had a corner on; but in naturalism there was no foundation for human dignity, and naturalists did not give evidence that they understood what the demand for a foundation meant. Dewey wrote of democracy, equality, freedom, opportunity for everybody to better himself; he was eloquent about education—as much as a man could be eloquent who had such a tin ear for language; he had a profound faith (indeed much too much faith) in the corrective part that intelligence and science could play in human well-being; he put great emphasis on values that made for moral decency. The values he insisted on were no doubt true values, certainly moral decency was urgently needed, since it had never been a distinctive characteristic at any period of Western history about which Alonzo knew anything. But when you acknowledged what was desirable about Dewey's conception of life and took account of the values and experiences that it placed stress on, there was something missing in it which robbed it of possible amplitude and catholicity. It was a class philosophy.

The essentially Philistine nature of the naturalistic philosophies with which Alonzo was acquainted, even that of Santayana, was not easy for him to perceive all at once with clarity. A man as deeply committed to naturalism as Alonzo was could not recognize its defects easily. However, the evidence against it was slowly mounting. In one of his visits to New York, he showed an old friend, Dick Blackstone, a saying

of Stendhal: *La vie, c'est une affaire d'âmes impériales.* "What do you
have to say to that?" asked Alonzo. Dick's reply came without pause:
"Imperial souls? Fascist nonsense!" And he continued with passion:
"Life is for anyone who knows how to live it. Some can't ever learn to
live, because social circumstances prevent them." Irritated, Dick followed up: "Who said that?" "One of the greatest novelists of the nineteenth century," said Alonzo, "Henri Beyle." "Henri Beyle? Who was
he?" "The author of *The Red and the Black.*" "You mean Stendhal."
"The very same." Dick now felt on firmer ground. "Surely," he said,
"you don't expect me to take a literary epigram seriously, do you?"
"Well," replied Alonzo, "no, I guess I don't."

3

For some time Alonzo had been dissatisfied with naturalistic moral
philosophy; he had a number of minor objections to it, as for instance,
that not all things one found valuable one desired prior to discerning
their quality or that one could discern value in things or events for
which one had no desire and could not expect to develop it. An instance of the first case occurs when one runs into an arrangement of
flowers unexpectedly, has had no previous desire to see one, but finds
it lovely. Another instance occurs when one says of a woman that she
is beautiful but does not attract him. By an elaborate explanation, one
can bring such cases into harmony with the naturalistic theory of
value. One can say of the flowers that one's response to them was a
trained response: One knows that some arrangements of flowers are
lovely because one has somehow learned what is considered beautiful
in flower arrangements. The same can be said about one's judgment
of the woman. Which is to say that the judgment elicited in either
case is the result of stereotyped standards. One does not desire the
woman. But does this not mean, on the naturalistic theory, that one
does not really think her beautiful? One knows what men take beauty
to be in women and one recognizes these qualities in her. But for oneself, she is not really beautiful, since one does not desire her.

On consideration it appears that this explanation exhibits an *ad hoc*
quality that makes it unconvincing; it seems to have been contrived to
make the cases fit the theory. Objective harmonies and disharmonies
in the acts of men and in nature, cannot be said to be valuable unless
they arouse desire. But when they don't, are they still valuable? Not if

value is the product of desire or aversion. Yet, one can say, with full sincerity, "I find what X did right, although I regret that he had to do it," or "I wish he had not had to do it." In the case of a man who shot his son recently in self-defense and was found not guilty by a jury, one can say, "It was right for him to do it, he had no alternative, but I wish, and I am sure many others also wish, that he had not had to do it."

This means that on the naturalistic theory our response to values often lacks spontaneity or genuineness. The naturalistic theory introduces into the moral life, and into axiological experience in general, duplicity and turns one into a systematic fake. One does not really respond to an object directly, one does not desire or feel averse to it, one puts aside one's response or lack of it, and falls back on borrowed standards that one believes are employed by others—one's group, or party, or class. That this is often the case cannot be denied; most human beings, and perhaps all, in one respect or another, habitually, without thinking, put aside their authentic reactions and adopt, or pretend to adopt, what they take to be the reactions expected of them by others. But such judgments are not prompted by a direct desire for an object; at best they are prompted by a desire to be a member of a group; when this happens, the judgment is a falsehood, a judgment of an object lacking in genuineness.

4

Alonzo had not yet formulated adequately the most serious objection to naturalistic moral theory. Two factors led finally to the discovery of this defect: his own precarious situation in the philosophy department at State and the growing threat of Nazi Germany. Naturalistic philosophy could not meet an essential requirement of a moral theory: No moral theory was acceptable, at least to him, unless it provided a moral means of resolving radical moral conflicts—with emphasis on the term *radical*. If a moral theory neglected this requirement one could conclude, as some philosophers had concluded, that in the last analysis the right was made by might.

Why? If a thing was good because it was desired, desires by themselves were neither good nor bad; a desire became good or bad if it promoted or frustrated the satisfaction of other desires when satisfied. This was granted. The difference between one desire and another, then, taken each by itself, can only be quantitative; one desire might be immediately strong but short-lived while another might be weak but long-lived; still another strong and long-lived, and yet another might make itself felt intermittently but in a manner that brooked no rejection or could be easily suppressed. Since there were no intrinsic values, one had to scan the future in an effort to calculate what would be the result of present decisions.

Loyalty, honor, integrity, honesty? Loyalty was desirable when it kept a group together. But if anyone did not desire to belong to a group and knew what he was doing, what rational ground—as distinct from undisguised force—could persuade him—as distinct from compelling him—to be loyal to his group? Honor? All honor meant was the pleasure of being thought superior in some sense; but if instead of deserving the honor one could somehow get it without deserving it, what was the difference? If what one wished was to be considered superior, did it matter how one obtained the reputation? If reputation for superiority was the object of desire and desire was satisfied, the value residing in the object was obtained. Integrity? It meant moral consistency; a man of integrity was honest, kept his word, was a whole and not an unrelated or loosely related collection of parts, was recognized as reliable, was known to stand firmly on principles. But was this valuable? Its value was not intrinsic and if you could obtain a solid reputation for integrity by somehow faking, why not? How could you, on naturalistic grounds, reproach a man who successfully faked integrity or honesty? He simply replied that he did not desire to have this virtue; all he desired was to appear to have it, and so far he had gotten by. And that put an end to the argument. One could, of course, argue that men cannot get away with lack of virtue forever, but that was nonsense. Alonzo never forgot that Gomez died in bed.

For the sake of the argument, grant that it is impossible to achieve a reputation for integrity unless one possesses the virtue, allow that in the social process one was bound to be caught faking and the smell of dishonesty would spread slowly all around; allow that men were not such good actors that they could live a life lacking integrity without being found out. But this was not the point. It might be impossible to fake social virtues consistently throughout a lifetime. The point was that the virtue did not reside intrinsically in an act or a set of acts that made up character but in obtaining the satisfaction of a desire—the reputation for integrity or honor or honesty. Indeed, men actually bought honors all the time and got by with enormous swindles.

Alonzo remembered the story of a man who was one of the most distinguished and honorable men of his community. Prominent in church, a successful banker, known as a good father and husband, a pillar of society: He had a sterling reputation. But a maid found him smothered in bed with his mistress in a hotel room. There was evidence of heavy drinking before they got into a foldaway bed. For some reason not disclosed the bed folded up and this honorable man and his mistress were not able to crawl out of it in time; they were probably too drunk or in some way both stunned. If an expert on furniture were to object to the story, as one once objected, on the ground that the accident could not have happened because foldaway beds are so made that they cannot close accidentally, the answer is that the only impossibility is a contradiction in terms, and that the bed in the story did somehow fold up accidentally. But whether foldaway beds can or cannot fold up accidentally is irrelevant, since eminently respectable people are caught in crimes.

How many respectable men, honorable, prominent in church affairs, deacons, leaders of charity drives, judges or bank presidents, are metaphorically speaking unable to crawl out of a foldaway bed? Probably not many. But again that is not at all the point. The point is that if desire makes value, if all you desire is the appearance of honor and not honor earned through genuine merit, no one who desires the latter and scorns the former can criticize you, if he holds the naturalistic theory of value. Indeed the idea of real honor as distinct from one that is not disappears; if it is desired, it is real no matter how one comes by it.

5

If this was the case, how could a man appeal to another for justice when the latter had no desire to be just? This led directly to a question that began to concern Alonzo more and more deeply, as his situation in the Department of Philosophy became worse and the international situation became more and more threatening: How can radical moral conflicts be resolved morally? If a moral theory could not answer this question it was saying that in the last analysis might establishes right, exactly what some philosophers had said from Thrasymachus down to McGilvary and Charner Perry.

The naturalist—usually a liberal—had a ready answer: "Let us rea-. son together." But of course this was no answer, since if your opponent does not want to reason with you what can you do? And if you do manage to get him to reason with you, how do you show him that your own desires have as much a right to satisfaction as his? . . . Prolonged silence. There was no answer to this question; there could indeed be no answer on the view that value is constituted by desire. What was there to say, if the ultimate appeal was to desire, or interest, or drive and your opponent had no wish, or interest, or drive to reason with you? If you pressed the naturalist for an answer he was forced to say: "Ultimately you have to fight for your rights." He assumed, as men nearly always assume, whatever their philosophical affiliation, that he was always right. Of course if one was right his opponents were wrong. And since the right was on one's side it would win. Or so it was hoped.

But it was hoped too soon, for the right was on every side of the conflict or there was no right at all, until either a moral resolution of the conflict was achieved or one of the contending rights was eliminated by force. It turned out then that the majority of these men did not know that they stood on the side of Thrasymachus. A few of them knew on what side they stood and stated frankly that might makes right; not that it is right but that it makes it, that it establishes it; there are a number of contradictory claimants to the title of being right, and might eliminates them and proclaims right the one it backs; this is then the true and only right.

The majority did not know that this is what their doctrine led to. These men, great thinkers all, balding, bespectacled, paunchy, bent under the weight of knowledge—for the weight of the dandruff on their backs could not account for their round shoulders—bedoctored, as radiant with self-esteem as any class of men ever was, and indeed human, no more nor less human and kindly than their less learned fellows, but above all, believers in the abstract, in the dignity of man— these erudite eminences, effulgent with intelligence and superior wisdom, when your need was greatest and you asked them how you were to resolve radical moral conflicts morally, had no answer. Their great philosophical acuity had not drawn the consequences of their position and had it drawn them, the majority of these men would not have liked it, since it erased the distinction they drew between themselves and the Hitlers big and small with which the world pullulates.

6

Alonzo could now see clearly why naturalistic philosophy could not furnish the basis for an adequate moral theory. According to naturalistic moral theories—for he did not forget that there were many varieties of them—experience indicates that some human arrangements do not work, but all this can mean is that they did not work in the past. Experience had no authority to dictate in advance what a given organization should be like; the realm of human experience, as distinct from that of physics or even biology, was the realm of contingency; it offered no laws.

The good was the desirable and the desirable was made up of those desires that were long lasting and which therefore brought prolonged satisfaction. But which desires did actually bring prolonged satisfaction? Here ignorance played havoc with naturalistic moralists and they were not aware of their ignorance. The stronger were not those given fake citizenship papers by social expedience; the stronger were those that had shown themselves to be strong and this also held for the longer lasting; among the strong and longer lasting one found not merely the holiness of the saint, the decency of the stock character of all historical plays written by moralists, not merely the *homme de bien*, but one also found the respectable thief, the stinker, the hypocrite, and he whom you would never know about because he possessed Gyges's ring and was not burdened with a heavy conscience; you also found the pirate, the accomplished liar who got a hold of the social controls, . . . the list was endless.

The naturalistic moralist was an empiricist by assertion; but had he been a practicing empiricist he would have given a different picture of the good life from the pretty rosy one he offered. He selected a list of desires respected by respectable men, or more precisely, he chose desires acknowledged by respectable men. But for all his empiricism the naturalist did not look at life as it was actually lived, and the reason was that he dwelt in a noble world of aspiration and hope and dreams of high endeavor, radiant with ideals which he took were rooted in desire: He condemned the political corruption; he repudiated imperialism, and the exploitation of workers; he was a reformer, and there was no question that he was a well-intentioned and decent man; but there was something that he could not see, and that was that his doctrine sanctioned the *status quo*. For if that which men desired was

good, and you wanted to find out what was good, you had to look at
what men actually desired, not at what they said they desired. Which
were in fact the strongest and longest lasting desires? As Al Smith
would have said, "Let's look at the facts." But who could tell us what
the facts were? Historians could, and sociologists, and psychologists,
and anthropologists, and students of criminal law—these men knew
the facts no less than optimists, Pollyannas, and hagiographers. But
one did not have to undertake a colossal job to see how value was constituted by desire; a few pages of recent American history were sufficient to observe the theory at work. Prohibition taught a very good lesson. It was an excellent illustration of the theory. Indeed when you
looked at it, it turned out that Prohibition was a fountain of values
back of each one of which there was a strong desire.

Let us look at the facts: It satisfied the desire of the old biddies of the
WCTU who rammed the amendment through while the boys were
"over there" fighting to make Wilson's world safe for democracy, this
was one value; but the citizens desired alcoholic beverages and had no
great difficulty in obtaining them, this was another value; the law carried sanctions, but the desire of the citizens for their hooch set these
sanctions aside, because Prohibition agents and policemen had a
stronger desire for graft than for enforcing the law, another value.
Bootleggers and rumrunners had a strong desire for the overnight
riches that Prohibition brought them, still another value. The fact that
bootleggers murdered one another off brought with it a situation that
was difficult to analyze. Some citizens thought that it was a good thing
they were eliminating one another, which is to say that the citizens
desired their murder and found value in it, while others took a different
stand, and thought that murder was bad, this was a disvalue.

In any case, although not a complete inventory of the values Prohibition brought with it, this hasty look at it was sufficient to give us a
clear idea that Prohibition aroused and satisfied enough desires to increase the values American citizens enjoyed during the time it was in
the law books. Repeal brought with it two principal disvalues: the
wishes of the stalwart ladies of the WCTU were frustrated, and frustrated also were the wishes of the Prohibition agents, bootleggers, and
rumrunners who lost a rich source of easy money. Some of the agents
and operators no doubt went on to fulfill their wishes for easy money
in other activities; they became members of "organized crime." But
whether the net result was a serious disvalue or a trivial one is of no

importance since all the example of Prohibition seeks to disclose is how wishes make values and the frustration of wishes makes disvalues.

To make up for the disvalues that repeal brought about, one value took their place; old drinkers who knew from pre-Prohibition days what well-aged liquor tasted like regained in a short time their taste and were able to get the liquor they preferred—for which they wished more strongly than for other liquor—for less money than during Prohibition; and young drinkers who had never known anything but what bootleggers supplied learned to wish for the legal stuff in preference to Prohibition alcohol.

The law could have been enforced (at least in theory) although given the values that disregard of the law brought forth it would have been very difficult, but the rigorous effort on the part of the federal agents might have done away with bootlegging. That it might have resulted in the inception of a police state did not worry the members of the WCTU, who were clamoring for enforcement; nor did it worry legislators and ordinary citizens, who did not have imagination to develop desires for a nation free from the goods Prohibition had brought with it.

It should be quite clear from even this hasty and utterly inadequate sketch of the wishes that created value when the WCTU rammed through the Prohibition amendment that they not only created a great value for themselves but also created a large number of values for the rest of their fellow citizens. Since things are good because they are desired, Prohibition brought innumerable goods to America.

But didn't this account ignore the distinction between the desired and the desirable? Wasn't this an account of what men desired immediately and not in the long run? True. In the long run the story was not, prima facie, quite the same. Let us look again at the facts. In the Midwest, until Capone regularized the industry, there was chaos and you sometimes ran the risk of drinking wood alcohol—a disvalue, since it blinded you. But this early period was put to an end by Capone's business genius, his ruthlessness, and the strong arm of his enforcers. The elimination of bootleggers by one another continued until repeal, but since, as already noted, the public had conflicting desires about bootleggers' murdering one another, one could not tell whether their murdering one another created more value than disvalue or vice versa.

Indeed the argument can be made that their murdering one another did create value, since their funerals were magnificent. Alonzo knew well a poet, a man of literary distinction, whose father had run the funerals for the Chicago gangsters: There was no question that their funerals had created a high value for their undertaker. In Chicago there were only two "respectable" men killed by gangsters during Prohibition: one was an assistant district attorney, William H. McSwiggin, of whom Capone said, "I paid him plenty and I got what I was paying for." The other was Alfred "Jake" Lingle, a *Tribune* reporter, who after the murder was shown to be connected with crime. In terms of wishes satisfied and thus goods constituted, since very few people mourned the murdered men, the evil that could be pitted against the good constituted by Prohibition was very small.

One could point out that in the longer run the results of Prohibition were seriously damaging, since it strengthened organized crime and lowered respect for the law. But this overlooks the fact that there is no strong aversion to organized crime on the part of the American public. Evidence? The fact that there is a great desire for the services that organized crime provides. Every time a citizen patronizes a cafe on the Near North Side of Chicago the chances are almost without exception that he is patronizing organized crime or, as it is as often called, the syndicate. This goes for illegal gambling, prostitution at professional and business conventions, and much else. True that some moralizers point out that the situation lowers respect for the law and seem to believe that this is a disvalue. But if only a few have an aversion to lowering respect for the law it cannot be a grave disvalue.

7

Another consequence of the theory that value is created by desire is of great interest. As the theory became popular—and it was received as gospel truth among college people—men seriously began to demand that morality should keep up with the times, that there were moral codes and values that were not up to date and should be discarded—since they stood in the way of creating new values by satisfying new desires that until then had been denied satisfaction. This was another expression of the assumption, deeply hidden in naturalistic moral philosophy, that what is, is what ought to be.

This was naturalistic moral philosophy. A thing was good because it was desired; strip social phenomena of their hypocrisy, discard merely habitual and purely verbal respect for conventional rights and goods that had once been taken to be objective in nature, find out honestly what men desired and not what they said they desired, and what you got was a description of the actual state of affairs. Whatever was, was right because it was, and anything else was a deceiving dream dreamed while one was awake. If one looked closely enough, morality turned out to be a description of how life was actually lived; the prescription emerged from the actual resolution of conflicts, which indicated retrospectively which desires had succeeded in eliminating conflicting weaker desires. So long as there was a discrepancy between the ideals men honored verbally and the goals actually pursued, the good and the right were what one found them to be and not what some old decalogue claimed they ought to be. It was the drives that actually pursued real goals that defined the ought since they expressed effective forces and not verbal masks. For naturalism, not altogether successfully concealed, if one looked sharply, what ought to be was what actually was.

But what of the eternal yearning of the human heart for justice? Mostly rhetoric, little more than stereotyped rhetoric, to hide the brutality of human life. Who in hell said that the yearning of the heart, whether eternal or ephemeral, had a right to be heard in this court? Of course men who are kicked and abused appeal to justice. Sometimes the appeal is answered; but it would seem that more often than not force, mitigated by self-interest and prudence, guides the affairs of men. The unseemly foofaraw, the unconscious balder twaddle, that moralists have carried out throughout the ages, what has it produced? For the last two centuries there has been some melioration in some areas of the world: Human beings do not get ground up as they did before, or so it would seem. But brutality, cruelty, selfishness, indifference to the dignity of others, these qualities still flavor the daily bread of human relations.

From which it follows, does it not, Alonzo asked me in derision, that Thrasymachus could be right. Why not? If experience meant anything he probably was, not in the sense that brutality was the sole or even the predominant quality in the relations between men but that brutality and iniquity have as dominant a hand in directing the course of events as had justice, and charity, and a recognition of the dignity of others. Thrasymachus could be right; the Athenians speaking to the islanders of Melos could be right; mad old Nietzsche could be right; McGilvary could be right; Charner Perry could be right; might was not right, but it established one's interest which, once established, and so long as it remained backed up by might, was accepted by men as the right or forced itself on them as right. Which proves, as men have always in their hearts known, that God is on the side of the big battalions, *n'est-ce pas, mon petit cochon, mon ami?*

And sympathy, and love, and kindliness, charity, pity, the capacity of a man to sacrifice himself for others? What about them? Naturalistic moral philosophy did not have to deny them. And Alonzo did not have to paint its picture in charcoal black. All of these qualities were fibers in the texture of human existence. The point was, not that they were not present in human relations but that there was no objective obligation to give them primacy and to deny those that had always been theoretically considered bad qualities. If the good was what men desired, even if it was what was desired in the long run, after critical intelligence brought out the results of satisfaction of desires, unless one felt obliged there was no obligation for him. If one did not feel obligation it was not a good for him, and it was not a good for him because he did not desire it.

At this point I broke into the flood of words. I have heard you dispose of those you contemptuously call the *bien pensant* before. Your argument has all the appearance of being clever but it does not dispose of the claims of respectability. You can't dismiss it as if it were merely hypocrisy. No, you can't, he replied. The matter, let me say first, is too complex to cover here *au fond*. I am emphasizing one aspect of the theory of value as interest that naturalists have overlooked. The conflict between the respectable members of society and the others or within each member on any side can be traced to the splits that exist in any group of men or within each member of the group. But if the good is defined as the desirable, it is simply false to overlook what we learn from historical and contemporary experience about the desires of men. And what I have said is that if the good is what men find desirable in the long run, Prohibition is a good example of what the good added up to until the Fourteenth Amendment was repealed.

XII

The Question of Origins

1

I T WAS NOT pleasant for Alonzo to have to acknowledge to himself that his philosophy was worthless. But it was even less pleasant to have to acknowledge that as a result of that error he had been living two lives that had nothing to do with each other. His philosophy had condemned him to schizophrenia and this condition became intolerable once discovered and had to be put an end to immediately.

His philosophical life had been intense, exciting, fulfilling in generous measure; it could not have been more rewarding. He had thought honestly and had gone way beyond the days when his experience was fertilized by the thought of Nietzsche, Unamuno, or Santayana. But his theories were defective. His other life, a life in which such topics as tragedy, heroism, death, could be given the consideration they demanded and deserved, a life in which a full and passionate experience was not hedged in by all sorts of arbitrary, self-imposed, and artificial limitations, had also been lived by him. But the two had no commerce with one another. The question came up quite naturally: Had he been living his life fully? Could one live a full life when his experience was divided and the two parts into which it fell had no connection with each other?

It was time to begin to live fully; nor was the decision one over which he had much choice. Whether he liked it or not events over which he had no control had begun to exercise their power over him, compelling him to turn his mind to dark topics. It was bad enough to have to carry the deformity he carried, his lack of a rigorous education; it was bad enough to drag his intellectual clubfoot, to have to find his way with his intellectual myopia and the multitude of defects and shortcomings, the limitations, that his past, his character, and his bad luck had cursed him with. These had to be endured; he was learning to live with them, had been learning all along, so to speak, to walk without limping, in spite of his intellectual deformity. But two separate lives it was not necessary to live; he would not allow his existence to be split into halves, each enjoying its own order and adequacy by virtue of the impassable wall that he had unwittingly erected between them.

What had sent him to philosophy was not a desire for a career; had it been that he would have majored in Spanish, for in this field he would have had a much faster and higher rise. What had sent him to philosophy was an urgent, a passionate need to understand the world and his place in it, and to understand them truly. He had given up his church because it asked him to believe a lot of fables which made no sense as truth. His need for answers to his questions could not be stilled, as Hume had stilled the questions he could not answer.

Alonzo's deepest "instinct," so to speak, told him that Hume, great thinker as he was, was wrong. Hume was not only wrong but when you looked at the matter, it turned out that this great thinker was, as a man, not at all admirable, because he never caught on to the fact that his premises and his method led, not to skepticism—that was honorable enough—but to the acceptance of the irrelevance of thought.

In a well-known passage of *A Treatise of Human Nature*, Section VII of Book IV, Hume had asked, "Where am I, or what? From what causes do I derive my existence, and to what condition shall I return? Whose favor shall I court and whose anger must I dread?" Hume re- plied that while his reason is not able to "dispel these clouds," and to cure him from his philosophical melancholy and delirium, Nature suffices. And how does Nature cure him? By leading him to dine, to play backgammon, by conversing and being merry with his friends. He continues that when, after three or four hours of amusement, he re- turns to his speculations, "they appear so cold, and strained, and ridic- ulous, that he cannot find in his heart to enter into them any further." But Hume did not quit speculating and he was very disappointed when his work fell, as he put it, dead born from the press. Later in life he re- wrote the *Treatise* into two essays in order to make his ideas more ac- cessible to the public.

No, this would not do for Alonzo. The protracted trauma that he had undergone when he rejected religion was still a vivid memory. The conclusion that terms like *heroism*, *tragedy*, and *death* were philosophically irrelevant, was inadmissible. If a philosophy found no room for these terms, it was the philosophy that had to be discarded, for the terms referred to matters of transcendently vital importance. Alonzo could not accept a philosophy that condemned him to schizophrenia, such a philosophy was false both theoretically and practically. Philosophy is or tries to be, a coherent grasp of human experience and ought to point to a satisfactory goal. It need not promise happiness but it cannot deny it in advance by inadvertence. If it fails to give a coherent picture it ought to give evidence that the universe is cracked with faults. But naturalism did not offer such evidence and indeed it could not, since it was a monistic view of the world. Its failure to recognize values like the tragic and the heroic, and events like death, was no mere error that could be corrected when attention was called to it. It was inherent in it, and what naturalistic definitions of tragedy pointed to missed the truly radical San Andreas fault in reality.

2

Having discovered a serious defect in his borrowed views, it was natural for Alonzo to suspect that they might contain others and he soon came upon them. One important group clustered around naturalism's failure to solve in its own terms, which was to say, empirically, three problems: the starting point of the universe, its initial source, a problem which until now seemed to remain within the domain of theologians, the question of the so-called First Cause; the second problem was the beginning of life; and the third was the transition from a prehuman animal to a fully human one. Contemporary astronomers, biologists, psychologists, anthropologists, and philosophers offered a number of solutions to these problems none of which proved acceptable.

At the biological level the fact of evolution was not in question. It presented a small difficulty but Alonzo did not consider it damaging to the theory. The distinction had to be made between the fact of evolution and its factors—the *that* and the *how*. The fact was proved as well as a scientific hypothesis could be. The factors were under discussion and their nature was an open question. The majority of biologists seemed to accept Neo-Darwinism as an account of how evolution had taken place and if the truth were arrived at by counting heads the Neo-Darwinians had won. But even if there was no knowledge of the way evolution had come about that was up to the quality of the knowledge that it had, it was too late in the day to hold out against evolution.

But evolution started from life. How did life begin? How did the universe begin? How did the human mind begin? On these problems naturalists permitted themselves unrestrained coltish gambols in green fields of pure speculation that were scientific in name only; when one turned one's critical mind on them they turned out to be purely speculative thinking founded on the solid rock of faith in their creed.

For naturalistic philosophy the problem was this: It could not fall back on the nothing-but arguments of nineteenth-century materialism and it had to reject supernatural agencies. But before it could make the claim that there was only one nature and nothing beyond it, beside it, under, or above it, it had to supply an account of how that nature had begun; it had to supply an account of how life had begun; and it also had to supply an account of how the human mind and the culture it created had begun. These accounts had to meet naturalism's own basic methodological criterion: They had to be empirical. Only if naturalism met this criterion did it have the right to assert that there was nothing mysterious about the universe, about life, and about the human mind and its culture; or, to put it positively, that these events had come about through natural causes. Only then could it sweep into the rubbish heap of mystic religious accounts and the purely speculative accounts of the metaphysicians. Religious accounts could not be taken literally: No educated man today could take Genesis literally and even when you did take it literally, it gave rise to a number of questions that literalists did not pose. Metaphysical speculations did not have the force of science. Until the demand for empirical accounts had been met, naturalism could not make the claims that its followers made for it.

These demands were rigorous but just, since naturalists themselves had laid down the rules by which thought could be accepted and since they claimed that their philosophy had nothing to do with faith, that it was empirical. Since the demands were rigorous they did not allow any old John, Sid, or Ernie of a theorist to argue in favor of his views. The naturalist had to give a nonreductive account of the various modes of human experience that did justice to their inwardness. But he was not called on to reinforce claims that were made for their prima-facie value. Thus, if a mystic or a lover of music should assert—as mystics and some lovers of music did—that he enjoyed moments in which he had access to a higher kind of reality than he came by in his pedestrian experience, the naturalist was under obligation to seek to understand fully, with sympathy, the experience of the mystic or the lover of music, in its inwardness, and to lean over backwards to discover the mystic or the lover's meaning and what modicum of truth it might contain. But he was under no obligation, none whatever, to accept the mystic's or the lover's interpretation of his experience at his words.

The nature of the problem was such that it left room for the exercise of a large amount of intellectual tact. For the critic of religion, let us say, could go about his job with the spirit of a bouncer in a tavern brawl, hitting right and left, throwing the battered bodies into the street; or he could go about it with the sincere sympathy with which a good surgeon listens to the account of symptoms of a patient whom he believes is exaggerating but not lying; the surgeon does not believe all he hears but he is aware that from the rigamarole of self-pity and exaggeration of painful symptoms his own knowledge and experience can extract information of value for his diagnosis.

When Alonzo looked into the accounts of the origin of the universe —something he did at second or third hand, since he did not have the scientific equipment to read the monographs and study the scientific papers of astronomers—and when he studied the accounts of the transitions from nonlife to life and from prehuman forms to the distinctly human, it became quite clear to him that naturalists not only could not meet their own criteria of truth but that they did not even recognize the critical nature of the challenge. They were as indulgent towards their theories as some parents are towards the depredations of their children in their neighbors' yards. And the reason was the profound faith they had in their way of thinking.

3

The first demand was for a cosmogony. Astronomers, it seemed, disposed of the problem in one of three ways. One was to turn it over to metaphysicians with an ironic smile. The specious politeness—if it could be called politeness—could clearly be seen through and said (1) that they could not do anything with the problem, and (2) that it was therefore best left to zany pates given to playing verbally with dotty puzzles. Those who took up the question, as far as Alonzo could tell from the science sections of the Sunday newspapers, solved it in one of two ways. Both were stories and the evidence for one was insufficient and for the other nonexistent. In this respect there was no substantive difference between astronomers on the one hand and on the other, the authors of Genesis and of the fantastic stories produced, it seemed, in great quantities, by gnostics immediately before and after the founding of Christianity. The difference between the older myths and the new cosmogonies was that the former were the product of imaginations gone wild, while the latter were sober. As to evidence, both were on about the same plane.

One gnostic story, for instance, had it that Agathos dwelt in Light, and Elohim, the male principle, mated with Eden, the female-viper principle, giving birth to two gaggles—or is it flocks—of angels of a dozen each, one batch for the male and another for the female. The story went on, gaining in elaboration as it descended toward man, who is in this world stranger and sojourner, a pilgrim in a land unknown and who yearns deeply to find the way back to his true home, the way to salvation. Another story started with the Perfect Aeon, Proarche, and carried on the same unfettered inventiveness, till it reached man again. The kind of salvation the various stories said man yearned for differed, but there was always a way. These mythographers, it seemed, took their fantasies seriously; but if they didn't, their followers did. They believed their gallimaufries literally. Not all of it was nonsense. The yearning for salvation was an expression of a deeply felt need. Contemporary astronomers did not intend their stories to be taken literally. Part of their sobriety consisted in taking their fancies to be hypotheses. This made a difference. But it made no difference in their capacity to explain empirically the origin of things.

According to one of the stories told by the astronomers, once upon a time Energy was concentrated in one Big Lump—the Perfect Aeon, maybe? And then came the Big Bang, sending Energy or whatever it was that the Big Bang sent, flying off in all directions and accelerating to beat hell. The evidence for the whole hypothesis was the theory of the Expanding Universe. The other story told how Energy just appeared out of nowhere and apparently for no reason, no reason at least that the science reporter told his Sunday readers. The first story had an immense melodramatic quality. It must have been a terrific Big Bang. Imagine watching it—as *per impossibile*, and from a safe distance, of course. A cosmic Fourth of July sort of bang, to end all Fourths—in the cosmos, that is, not on earth. The other story cut up the melodrama into bits: Energy here, Energy there, Energy yonder, popping out of nowhere and for no reason. Had gamblers been watching, they would have had themselves a picnic, for no one among them could have had any ground for a guess where Energy would appear next. When Alonzo thought of this theory he thought of a supracosmic magician taking an endless number of energy rabbits out of a cosmic top hat. A beauty of a story. Yes, a beauty of a story, but it begged the issue, since it assumed the energy. Clearly the astronomers were of no greater help than the grand old mythographers.

If the astronomers were of no help, could the naturalistic philosophers do better? Alonzo was ready to settle for a purely speculative hypothesis which could account for the origin of things, or could show in acceptable contemporary terms what Kant had shown, namely, that the question of origin shouldn't be asked.

When you turned to the naturalistic philosophers you ran into three kinds of answers: The first answer was given by a small number of people who said that they did not know how the universe had begun; the second asserted that we must begin with the fact—the universe is there —and we must not try to go to its cause; the third group was made up of crypto-Kantians, who said that the question could not be asked because it was not meaningful.

The first group should, first of all, be honored for their honesty. Given the irritating habit of so many philosophers of being able to answer any question asked of them, it was refreshing to run into men who did not know, knew they did now know, and admitted it. But one had to add that naturalism made categorical affirmations and denials about the whole of Nature. It affirmed there was only one Nature and it denied that there were causes beyond it or above it to account for it. But if you could not answer the question about how Nature originated, what followed from your ignorance was that you could not tell whether there was only one Nature or whether there was something behind it or beyond it that accounted for it. To call it "cause of itself," as Spinoza had called it, was merely to cover the mystery with a phrase, the old technique of covering the shame of our ignorance with a verbal fig leaf.

To those who argued that we must begin with the fact that the universe is there and we must not go beyond or behind it to its cause, the answer was that they were Humeans, but incoherent Humeans, whereas Hume was coherent and lucid about the shortcomings of his philosophy, and did not conceal those shortcomings from his readers.

Naturalists did not share Hume's temper; they were not resigned schizophrenics who at the same time did and did not take their philosophizing seriously. They were certain; they were men of faith; they were convinced that those who did not agree with them were not genuine truth seekers. Naturalists knew with a great deal of certainty, that there was only one Nature and everything in it could be known by empirical means.

Professor Sidney Hook says somewhere in his first book, Alonzo remembered vaguely, that about the universe as a whole nothing can be asserted. Alonzo does not remember whether Hook had shown that the statement that about the universe as a whole nothing can be said is a statement about the universe as a whole. It would seem that one thing at least can be said about the universe as a whole, namely, that nothing can be said about it as a whole. But there is at least one other proposition that can be asserted about the universe as a whole, namely, that it is. Still Hook and his fellow naturalists believe that all there is, or has been, or can ever be, is collectively known as Nature and that all the questions that can arise refer to natural events and must be answered in natural terms and must be answered empirically. But if one cannot say anything about the universe as a whole, how can one know about Nature as much as naturalists know? That there is only one Nature and that there is nothing beyond it or behind it or beside it or under it cannot be known empirically and the conviction that the naturalists hold arises from faith. Historically, Alonzo knew, the story of how naturalists came to their faith was more complex. They were heirs of a theological tradition that had led scientists like Galileo and Huygens to declare that mathematics or geometry was the alphabet of God. But however they came by their views they were men of faith.

There is, then, one question that cannot be answered in principle in any terms whatever: that there is one Nature and nothing beyond it. But why not?

Naturalists have much to say about the whole universe. Why do they exempt from scrutiny the one critical question about Nature, the one question to which, it would seem, they should be most eager, if they are really looking for knowledge, to address themselves? Alonzo did not say that their certainty about the universe and their inability to answer the ponderous and critical question were in contradiction. What he did say was that these gentlemen, for all their appeal to science, for all their protestations about the empirical nature of their beliefs, for all their anger when their faith was called to their attention, were rank fideists. And he added that their philosophy hung in midair, unsupported.

4

But even if we waive the question about the origin of the universe, Alonzo continued, we still have to face the question of the origin of life from nonliving matter. When naturalists came to this problem the games they played with themselves and their readers began in earnest and were fascinating to watch. There were two games or two ways to play one game: One was to draft a hardworking, honest term, that normally earned its living by doing an honest day's work for an honest wage, and promote it to perform miracles that are not called miracles; the other was to mortgage, as a naturalist himself once put it, the future of science.

The first way to play the game, or the first game, is done by taking the term *to emerge*, and giving it the job of accounting for the break between nonlife and life. Now this term is as hardworking and as decent a blue-collar term as you can find in the labor force of any philosophy. Thoroughly decent, thoroughly respectable. But when it is made to work in defense of naturalism it turns out to display capacities one would never suspect; it turns out to be as sleek, as facile, as purely verbal as any term has ever been. In its original meaning *to emerge* means to rise from the sea. Used in defense of naturalism it means that life rises from nonlife. Higher forms rise from lower. Fine. But how? Until we are told how, what we have is a sophisticated form of the old explanation made famous by the candidate from Montpelier— we are offered the old *vertus dormitiva* dressed up for the twentieth-century parade. But the steps by which living processes are said to emerge when certain nonliving processes take place are either causal steps or noncausal. If they are causal, the steps should be shown; if they cannot be shown, we can believe they are causal only on faith. If they are not causal, what the word *emergence* refers to is a miracle. But miracles are not a method of explanation on which the naturalist can fall back. The naturalist must believe that the steps are causal; he has no alternative. But he does not know what they are. How then does he know that they are causal? Because he believes that all that happens happens naturally. But how does he know that all that happens happens naturally, that each and every event is a natural event, when at a most critical point he cannot find the cause of an event he cannot deny? Alonzo realized that at this juncture he was confronted with the naturalist's unshakable faith. He wants us to believe that his philosophy is based on empirical evidence, and at the point at which that kind of evidence is most sorely needed he confronts us with his unsupported belief in his generalization. Alonzo did not for a moment believe that the naturalist wanted to deceive his readers any more than he wanted to deceive himself. But the objective result was deception—deception of himself and of others.

But couldn't you argue that the explanation was valid, since it was the sort of explanation accepted in science? Water emerges from the reaction of oxygen and hydrogen and the reaction of an acid on a metal leads to the emergence of salt and hydrogen. In the same way life emerged when certain conditions were present and certain materials were available, and mind, when certain other conditions were there to lead to its emergence. But it did not take arduous reflection to see that the analogy was false. There are important differences between the emergence of water and the emergence of life. One is that chemists know considerably more than the single isolated fact that when hydrogen is burned in oxygen water emerges. The emergence of water was one event or fact among a large number of other events which were referred to hypotheses interrelated in such a way that they hung together systematically; and it was this interrelationship between facts and hypotheses that made any one fact intelligible. A fact is understood when it is referred more or less explicitly to a whole system of facts and hypotheses. The whole which is chemistry is not, of course, a finished whole; it is a body of knowledge in constant growth; constant adjustments, revisions of hypotheses and reinterpretation of facts were going on as research went forward. Intelligibility was the result of a fact or hypothesis finding a place in the growing whole. There was much more to it. But rough as it was, this was a good enough account of scientific inquiry, since the purpose of this account was to show that there was no analogy between an explanation in chemistry and the alleged explanation that was given of the beginning of life.

Another difference between the emergence of water and the emer-

gence of life was that in respect to their antecedents the emergence of
life involved the appearance of a phenomenon different in kind from
the appearance of water. Water was a physical substance made up of
two other physical substances. It could be made out of its components
or broken up into its components by chemical reactions, and this
seemed to be the case with all purely chemical reactions. When the
chemist made up water or broke up water, he used the same methods
he employed in bringing about other chemical reactions. Chemistry
was a homogeneous realm of inquiry unified by its laws, its language,
and its subject matter, in spite of the fact that pioneers both from the
side of physics and from that of biology were tearing down the fence
that separated it from them. If the time ever came when scientists
could do in the realm of living processes as they could do in the realm
of chemistry it would be soon enough to speak about the continuity of
both realms. Until then what they seemed to be discovering was the
purely physical conditions of life—conditions that Alonzo had never
dreamed of denying.

There was still more to it. Naturalists did not know what nonliving
processes bring about living ones. But if they didn't, the appeal to
emergence is worse than an evasion of the problem; it is a positive
obfuscation of it; for it gives the reader the false feeling—shared by
naturalists who use the term—that an explanation has been supplied
when all that has been supplied is a cover-up word that deceives the
philosopher and his uncritical readers.

A bolder variant of this game is played by pronouncing by fiat that
Nature is such that processes of one kind give rise to processes of a different kind; thus chemical processes give rise to living processes and
living processes to mind—and mind to angelic processes perhaps? This
way to solve the difficulty was adopted by the scientific philosopher in
the East with whom Alonzo had a brief discussion about faith at the
time he was beginning to suspect his naturalism. It was not difficult to
see that the solution assumed that there was only one Nature and
everything in it took place naturally. No doubt one kind of process
leads to the other kind and the other to the last, but how? And how
does the empiricist know that it does so naturally, if he does not know
how it does?

The second way of playing the game, or a second game if you prefer,
was—as a naturalist once called it—to mortgage the future of science.
The game was simple and the rules easy to learn. The naturalist ap-

pealed to knowledge usually said to be around the corner. Biologists, or their public relations men, had been asserting with exemplary regularity and persistence that someone was on the verge of pulling off the feat: Any day now he was going to synthesize life in a test tube. *Mañana-itis*, you could call it, if it were permissible to coin a hybrid. Every time the news came out that biologists were on the verge of synthesizing life, naturalists, with understandable triumph in their eyes, turned to the doubting Thomases and said, "There, I told you so! Give them a little more time and we'll see a biologist make a Newton or a Darwin in a test tube!" Alonzo replied that he had been waiting for a biologist to pull off the trick for quite some time. As far as he was concerned they could take as long as they needed. What was more, there was no need to make a Newton or a Darwin; no need even to make a village idiot. What he would like to see them make was a tiny bit of living matter, a cell, with its chromosomes and genes, capable of maintaining itself, reproducing itself, and passing on to its heirs, its own traits, as any decent little cell does, if she is a well brought up cell and not the dream of a public relations man. But of course a cell made out of pure chemicals, not out of quasi-living matter and its compounds.

When confronted with this argument the naturalist replied that it rested on a dichotomy that the progress of biochemistry had made obsolete: the distinction between living and nonliving stuff. But on the naturalist's assumptions, not on those of his critic, the naturalist was committed to take materials that are as distinctly inert as the graphite in Alonzo's pencil, and construct from whatever kinds of chemicals he needed, stuff that bridged the gap and at that point destroyed the distinction between inert matter like graphite and living matter of the humblest kind, whatever at the moment that might be said to be. Until the biologist turned the trick all the naturalist was doing was asking us to share his faith and hope. A pity he did not follow the example of that resigned schizoid, David Hume.

Alonzo knew, at second or third hand, that biologists were going deep into genetics and cytology and had made wonderful discoveries about the way a pair of animals passes on their traits to their offspring. He also knew that they had taken gigantic steps toward an understanding, in increasing detail, of the physical conditions of life. He also knew that they knew a great deal and were learning daily more and more about those purely physical (or chemical, if it be preferred) aspects of biological phenomena. But this fact did not blunt the cutting edge of his argument, since Alonzo had never denied that life was grounded on physical conditions. However, he insisted that from that premise no philosopher or scientist could draw the conclusion that living processes were the product of purely physical processes whose nature biologists were on the verge of fully elucidating. The conclusion could only be drawn when they were able to synthesize life. And until then the philosophy of naturalism was intrapolating unjustifiably. Until the breach was closed by synthesis, it was closed not by science but by faith. If the naturalist had been willing to admit that this was the case there would have been no argument. For the argument was not that biologists would never be able to produce a cell out of nonliving stuff. That would be to claim to know more about the future than anyone could know. He would not argue against the future. The argument was that until they did, the naturalist could hope as much as he wanted to, but hope was no ground for a philosophy that claimed to be empirically grounded.

But why do some naturalists sputter with rage when it is suggested that their philosophy is grounded on faith? There are no doubt many reasons, some of which their psychoanalysts could tell us about. But one of these is surely that their bleached rationalistic minds consider faith to be the enemy of science—as, indeed, religious faith has often been; another is probably that they do not want to be chained to a rowing bench in a *galère* bound for heaven.

XIII

From Protohominid to Homo Sapiens

1

ONCE ALONZO saw through the argument from biology it was possible to sit back and enjoy anthropologists putting on their act. It was done by denying the distinction between men and animals. The denial was accomplished by two tactical moves. The evolutionist minimized human intelligence and interpreted the intelligence of animals as favorably as he could. There remained a break. Here the comedian went into the climax of his act, as beautiful a vaudeville performance as one could expect to witness, fully worthy, indeed, of the high tradition of the greats among the philosophers. If Leibniz, as Coutourat had argued, drew the whole universe from A = A, why could not a post-Darwinian anthropologist-magician pull a more modest trick? With the spotlight on him, the anthropologist showed a pongid-looking thug that was the spitting image of the character that had sat down for the portrait of the ape-like beast reproduced in every textbook on human origins, said to have the distinction of being the honorable ancestor of man: a hefty, shortish, low-browed beast, tailless, of course, with a jaw that could crack a petrified coconut as easily as a peanut, and as ugly a character as you would like to see on the safe side of the cage in the zoo. With the spotlight on himself the anthropologist would say, "Watch him now, see? Look carefully!" The spotlight would shift to the ape. It would shift back to the actor who would say, "Watch carefully! As I pronounce the word, he will be transformed before your eyes into a human, a real human." The light shifted again to the ape, and the anthropologist shouted, "Emerge!" The beast turned into a short-armed, hairless biped that looked like a man. No, he did not look like a man, he was a man, the thing itself, the real McCoy, homo sapiens himself.

How had it happened? Adaptation, of course. By now enough jaws and pates and pieces of pates and bones said to be pates, and for all Alonzo knew, whole skulls, real old ones, not planted ones, were available to trace the line back. No fideistic skullduggery could keep us from worshipping at the altar of Saint Charles, canonized by Bishop Huxley—T. H., of course. It would take the unmovable faith of a William Jennings Bryan to stand up against the irresistible avalanche of bones that bonediggers had dug up. Alonzo was no Bryan.

But neither did he have any longer the faith he had had in the halcyon days of his naturalistic period. Could all the bones already dug up and others to be dug up in centuries to come account for the evolution of man from a prehuman animal? The answer to this question was a rotund no, but an explanation of this categorical negative was complex. One had to note, first, what was at issue. Alonzo did not deny biological evolution. What he pointed out was that all the bones dug and to be dug could not prove or help prove the evolution of man. The problem presented itself under two aspects. On the one hand, evolutionists could try to solve it in general terms, arguing that somehow man had evolved from a prehuman animal. Or, on the other hand, they could try to solve it by giving an account of the development of the human mind or human consciousness, or what would be about the same, they could try to solve it by giving an account of the development of human culture.

An argument for the evolution of man from a prehuman animal was offered by a distinguished zoologist from Cambridge, England, G. S. Carter, who wrote: "Man is an animal, and, however greatly his present state differs from that of the rest of the animal kingdom, we must accept that he arose from subhuman ancestors by a process of evolution. And, since the life of those ancestors must have been very like that of other animals, the process by which he evolved must have been similar to that which other animals undergo. If so, it is clear that some consideration of the general theory of evolution is required before the special case of the evolution of man can be discussed."

This statement sounds unexceptionable on first reading. And it cannot be said to be fiction. It is merely a deduction. If man is an animal, he must have arisen from subhuman ancestors by a process of evolution. In what other way could he have arisen? This would seem to be self-evident. But the reason is that we readily supply the implicit premise of Mr. Carter's enthymeme, to the effect that whatever happens must happen by natural means. This assumption is not a scientific proposition, but a philosophical one.

That this implicit premise is an unsupported assumption can be noticed when we look with care at another paragraph of Mr. Carter's article. He tells us:

> We must now consider how far man's evolution since he arose from his primate ancestors can be interpreted as governed by the same controls as those we have seen to govern the evolution of other animals. There can be no doubt that his evolution has been in many ways most unusual and it is to be expected that unusual factors may have taken part in its control. But man is an animal, and he arose from animals much less unusual than he himself is. Also, his geno-type is similar in its organization to those of other animals, and there should be no great difference in type between the variations that form the raw materials of evolution in him and his animal ancestors. His ecology, at least in the earlier stages of his evolution, must have arisen by modification of that of the Primates from which he arose. Changes in ecology undoubtedly occurred in the course of his evolution and must have largely influenced its course, but he must have arisen from a primate life, probably arboreal, very like that of many of our modern primates. I shall assume, for the sake of the argument, that he early gave up his arboreal life, coming to live an omnivorous life on the ground; that at first he lived in small groups not much larger than the family; and that the size of his communities was enlarged only later when he began to develop a social life.

What was of interest to Alonzo in this paragraph was the style in which it is couched. "There can be no doubt . . ." we are told, and "there should be no great difference in type," and "he must have arisen," and "changes in ecology undoubtedly occurred." And finally: "I shall assume." As a student of philosophy, Alonzo found himself utterly at home in this kind of reasoning, for it is the rhetoric philosophers use when, as is so frequently the case with them, they want to persuade their readers and have little more than belief in their doctrines to help them achieve their end.

If "there can be no doubt" of something or other, why are we not given the evidence that makes it indubitable? And if man "must have arisen" in a particular way and not in another, why are we not given the facts in the case, the how? And if changes in ecology "undoubtedly occurred," why are we not forced to accept the proposition that they occurred by being confronted with the evidence? And why is it necessary to "assume" for the sake of the argument what ought to be the conclusion of an empirical demonstration that has to be accepted whether we like it or not? The reason Mr. Carter uses the persuasive form of address rather than an argument based on evidence is that he cannot point to the causal process by which an animal that was the primate ancestor of man finally became a human being. Or, changing the expression, Mr. Carter has to cross from the subhuman to the human and, lacking factual stepping stones, he pole-vaults by means of his sturdy and trusted conviction that the change could have come about only by natural means. He extrapolates but does not see—men of faith are usually blind about their beliefs—that the extrapolation begs the issue.

How does Mr. Carter know the truth of this proposition? He cannot profess to have examined all the processes operative in the universe or even a representative number of the kinds of processes that are known about, nor can anyone else have done this for him. Neither he nor anyone knows by what means man acquired his distinctive powers and developed his institutions. It would seem, therefore, that before we can hold that man is nothing but an animal, we shall have to establish by scientific means that whatever happens can happen only by natural means. But how can the latter statement be established scientifically? You can't prove a negative, and if you turn the proposition into a positive, you can't prove it empirically. The proposition that all that happens happens naturally is beyond empirical knowledge since what we know is a very small part of what has happened, happens now, or will happen in the future. The belief is nothing but pure speculation grounded on the assumption of the uniformity of nature. It is indeed the most succinct expression of the philosophical *Weltanschauung* of naturalists. Note carefully that the belief would be beyond the reach of criticism if those who hold it acknowledged it is a speculative belief and not, as some philosophers claim, scientifically grounded.

Note also that Alonzo was not denying that man was an animal; man was an animal that had somehow or other managed to add to his animality capacities that enabled him to transcend his sheer animality. Alonzo believed that man had come by his talents in some sort of non-miraculous way. What he was insisting to himself—and to himself only, for no one would listen to him on this point—was that the kind of reasoning that proved the hypothesis of biological evolution at the prehuman level up to but excluding man, and the arguments in favor of human evolution, were different in kind. Biological evolution was defended by solid arguments; the evolution of man was not argued; when you looked into the problem you discovered that it was pleaded for. It was not a question, therefore, of filling in the facts by scientific investigation. It was a question of acknowledging that as far as the speculations of evolutionists were concerned, the evolution of man was not defended with hard scientific arguments. Whether in the future, near or far, the methods of science could be brought to bear on the evolution of man, could only be answered today by hope and faith. At the present nothing but this kind of argument could be offered. Mr. Carter's rhetoric was eloquent. But his statement was a pleading, not a scientific, piece of discourse.

2

If there was no scientific proof of human evolution in general terms, was there a proof of the evolution of the human mind? A lady thinker who had offered a philosophy that she claimed was in a new key, presented an interesting argument. An argument? Hardly. An interesting plea then? Yes, just that—quite honest, but only a plea. At the time the book came out Alonzo had got it for review because he had read that it offered an alternative to the Dewey-positivism philosophy that he was finding inadequate. Here there was supposed to be naturalism with a difference. The key, however, was not new. The lady thinker had borrowed it from Cassirer who had in turn borrowed it from the sage of Königsberg and had thoroughly modernized it. In this book the lady philosopher says that she knows that man came by his faculties in a natural way, although she does not know how he pulled the trick. How does she know? She knows it on faith. Alonzo read, rubbed his eyes, and looked again. The assertion was hard to believe, but there it was in cold print before his startled eyes: "What causes this tremendous organization of forces [that constitutes man] is one of those things these tremendous organisms do not know; but with their organization, suffering and impulse and awareness arise . . . . Now this is a mere declaration of faith . . . ." Alonzo read again: "Now this is a mere declaration of faith . . . ." Mere? There are little meres and big meres and this one was a big whale of a mere. Eight words. Here was a tremendous organization of forces at long last telling the truth. A little word *faith*, five letters, to let the cat out of the bag. And what a cat and what a bag! "Wouldn't you say," Alonzo asked himself, suppressing by a tremendous organization of his own forces a tremendously forceful Rabelaisian guffaw, "that in this mere declaration of faith there was a whale of a cat let out of a teeny weeny bit of a bag—that is, a five-letter bag?" Well, he said to himself, if a cat can't be a whale of a cat it surely can be a Siberian cat, and that was enough of a tremendous organization of forces. But there was a bit of a problem the lady thinker did not explain. How could she know by faith? Know, by faith? And if she knew that by faith, was that all the knowledge faith gave her? And was the knowledge she got from faith the same kind of knowledge scientists produced when they stuck to their lasts and did not fancy themselves philosophers—like, say, Julian Huxley? And if she could know by faith, why couldn't his Grace, Soapy Sam, or the Great Commoner, Cross-of-Gold William Jennings himself, know by faith that every work, nay every comma of his English translation of the Bible was true knowledge and that Saint Charles and T. H. were advancing a pack of lies? The answer to this question is easy: My faith is good faith and produces truth, while yours is bad faith and produces falsehood when it contradicts mine. In fact faith does not give knowledge, what it gives is certainty, conviction, unyielding belief. Call what faith yields anything you like, what it gives and knowledge are two different states of mind.

There are all kinds of men, and women too. You have to learn to live with them—no, not with them, but next to them. Some put their faith in the classless society and some in free enterprise; some in the commissars and some in the New Deal; some in Mao and some in the Mau-Mau. The Simbas put it in *dawa*. If men have faith in *dawa* and in figurines, why not in naturalism? Surely what is sauce for the goose is sauce for the gander? But it isn't. Naturalism repudiates faith and claims to be founded on scientific evidence. What is *dawa*? you ask. Let me tell you. If you rub it on you, bullets can't touch you.

3

What was needed was an account of the appearance of the kind of consciousness man possessed and that apparently animals other than man did not possess or possessed only in a most rudimentary way. This was the reason Alonzo had once waited so eagerly for the publication of G. H. Mead's *Mind, Self and Society*. Here at last he would find a solution to one of the most serious difficulties of naturalism. But in the end Mead proved to be as disappointing as everybody else.

Mead argued, with great ingenuity, that when a dog met another dog and growled, the other growled back and the fight started; but when a man meets another man, his behavior is quite different from that of the dog. He may gesture in an angry fashion, shake his fist, say; but he does something that the dog does not do. He internalizes his own gestures and the anticipated gestures of the other man. In the notion of gesture Mead included what we call language in the narrow sense. The internalizing consists of the reproduction of muscular movements, telescoped subcutaneously, images and words, which the gesturing man performs and which he anticipates the second man will perform. The difference between the behavior of two men and of two dogs is that while one dog growls and the other responds by growling, the growling leading to a fight, in the case of the men, whatever the upshot of the threat, the gesture was mediated by the internalizing process.

When man developed the capacity to internalize gestures, consciousness developed. Men often respond to stimuli as dogs do. A well-trained squad responds to the orders of the sergeant. Nothing but stimulus-response is involved in the squad's act. But when man internalizes the gesture while making it, consciousness has developed.

Mead wrote: "The gesture is that phase of the individual act to which adjustment takes place on the part of other individuals in the social process of behaviour. The vocal gesture becomes a significant symbol (unimportant, as such, on the merely affective side of experience) when it has the same effect on the individual making it that it has on the individual to whom it is addressed or who explicitly responds to it, and thus involves a reference to the self or the individual making it." And he had written: "Gestures become significant symbols when they implicitly arouse in an individual making them the same responses which they explicitly arouse, or are supposed to arouse, in other individuals, the individuals to whom they are addressed. . . . Only in terms of gestures as significant symbols is the existence of mind or intelligence possible; for only in terms of gestures which are significant symbols can thinking—which is simply an internalized or implicit conversation of the individual with himself by means of such gestures —take place."

Mead was interpreted by his readers to be offering a genetic account of mind; and that they were right is shown by the fact that he wrote to that effect. For instance: "I have constructed two situations to show what a long road speech or communication has to travel from the situation where there is nothing but vocal cries over to the situation in which significant symbols are utilized."

For quite some time Alonzo found Mead's theory satisfactory. He took it to shed light on the most critical and most baffling problem. Explanation, he said to himself, when it is causal, consists of the discovery of invariant relations, as Morris Cohen called them. Given a combination of antecedents—physiological changes in the animal that was to become man—the capacities of the body changed, which is to say that mind appeared.

The solution was plausible because Mead argued in favor of emergence. Mead performed a meticulous analysis of the growth of the mind in its full complexity. He analyzed the self and distinguished between the *I* and the *me*, and he went on to do much more. But one of the fundamental stones on which his argument was reared was his conviction that the mind emerged from a condition in which mind had not yet appeared and this emergence was no different from the appearance of water when hydrogen and oxygen were combined in a chemical reaction. When Alonzo saw through the notion of emergence Mead's explanation collapsed like a Homeric hero struck by a spear. Its knees bent and it fell to the ground.

Mead's theory suffered from another defect; one that, once noticed, seemed utterly obvious and crippling, although it took Alonzo a long time to notice it. Mind was the capacity to internalize gestures. Very good. This explained the nature of an idea and threw light on the process of thinking. Mead had written that "Only in terms of gestures as significant symbols is the existence of mind or intelligence possible." Good. But if the symbol is significant the mind is already there or, if you prefer, the body is already minding. You were not explaining the emergence of mind, you were merely positing it. All Mead did, then, was beg the problem. However, the account was far from being worthless. It brought forward emphatically the notion that thinking was more than a purely cerebral process, that it involved awareness of kinesthetic activities, ideas being these activities mediated by stenographic verbal processes, telescoped verbalizations, slurred images of all kinds, not merely visual, incomplete symbolic activities that the requirements of communication dressed up in complete grammatical speech—more or less.

To internalize one's gestures was to become aware of them, and to become aware of them was a complex process, the awareness factor of which was not explained by the kinesthetic processes or by the incantatory word *emergence*. One could gesture, one could dance, one could talk and even talk meaningfully, and not be aware of what one was doing. But for symbols to be significant, awareness was involved either by the one who used them or by the other, the awareness being distinguishable from the symbols although not separable from them. To be aware is to identify internal processes for what they are, and that is already to be capable of giving them a meaning. To grasp a sign symbolically is to find meaning in it. The animal who internalizes a gesture does not respond to it as he does to a mere stimulus. In one sense, of course, a significant gesture is a stimulus, but it is different from the kind involved in other stimuli. One can respond to a large number of stimuli more or less automatically, without the mediation of awareness of them, without identifying them in consciousness. This is the way an experienced driver responds to a traffic light, doing the right thing unaware or barely aware—since it is a matter of degree—of what he is doing. But a man who shakes his clenched fist at another makes a gesture of which he is aware and which is meaningful to him. The dog makes gestures: He growls or wags his tail. But he is not conscious of what he is doing, nor do his acts have any meaning for him in the sense in which they have for a man who shakes his fist. Or at least that is what, until recently, has been universally assumed. If he is conscious in the way in which we human beings are, the fact merely pushes the problem farther "down the evolutionary scale," or brings Fido up. But it does not solve the problem of awareness.

To become aware of a gesture is identical with the internalizing of it. In asserting that mind or minding is the capacity to internalize gestures, Mead was right and he was making an important advance on Dewey, who never explained, or so it seemed to Alonzo, the nature of an idea. For Mead an idea was made up of kinesthetic, imagistic, and vocal events: But the idea was the awareness of these events, not the events as such.

The internalized gestures make up an interrelated system, which taken together is language or conscious thought, and expressed vocally is what is meant by language in the narrow sense. Otherwise stated, the act of internalizing a gesture is the act of grasping a symbol or the act of identifying the gesture. We can speak of meaningful signs and of mere signs. But it is better to speak of signs and of symbols, although the terms' usage is prescriptive and arbitrary. The distinction is Cassirer's.

On this usage, the distinction between sign and symbol, however, does not explain the emergence of mind any more than Mead's elaborate account of the internalizing process explains it. Which is to say that Cassirer's theory suffers from the same defect as Mead's if taken as a genetic explanation—which it is not intended to be. The distinction simply marks the fact that an animal capable of engaging in the symbolic process or an animal who internalizes gestures is an animal who minds or is capable of dwelling in a universe of meaning. When we respond to a mere sign no minding is occurring.

We can, and much of the time do, act automatically; the behavior of the experienced driver when he approaches the traffic light is a good example of a purely automatic act. To respond to a symbol is to enter a universe of discourse, or meaning. It involves more than stimulus-response activity. It involves the use of a system of symbols that are interrelated and which are said to be meaningful by the way they are grasped. These symbols are meaningful when the animal identifies them. The identification involves awareness. Traffic lights can function both as mere signs and as symbols. In *Art as Experience* Dewey marks the difference by means of the terms *recognition* and *perception*, and for aesthetics it is an indispensable distinction without which we cannot make any headway in the understanding of the response to art qua art.

Further, the grasping of a symbol is the performance of a constitutive mental act. The mind does not receive impressions passively—not even British empiricists can do that, although they are extraordinary men who make up the world entirely out of impressions and three simple laws of association, thus coming close to rivaling Jehovah, who went them one better and made it out of nothing. On their theory of perception empiricists claim all they do is receive impressions. But even their minds are active and add to the impressions they receive.

Leibniz pointed out that ideas are mental processes, acts, not mere passive receptions. The constitutive mind receives impressions or intuitions, but it synthesizes them. The process of synthesis consists in part of the selection from among the received impressions in terms of interests, followed by the act of identification which involves placing them in classes and thus referring them to an organized universe of discourse made up of interrelated symbols. There is much more to the act of synthesizing impressions than this. An act of perception—as distinct from a mere stimulus response—is possible because the symbolic structures reared prior to the act function categorially. This is, of course, knowledge that comes to us from Kant.

The nonhuman animal is able to perform successfully the recognitions necessary for his life. Man perceives: He identifies selectively and symbolically inward or outward contents thus building around himself a meaningful universe in which there is at least a minimal amount of order. Man is encased in a sphere of symbols, outside of which he cannot step—encased, not imprisoned, since it is his dwelling in this universe that constitutes his first liberation. He can only get away from his symbolic universe by letting consciousness go, either through drugs, or sleep, or death.

This Alonzo did not begin to understand until he began to read Cassirer. His understanding of *The Philosophy of Symbolic Forms*, such as it was, revealed to him not only the defect of Mead's theory but of much writing on mind and language which systematically confused signs and symbols. But Cassirer had not explained how men came by the power to use symbols. He simply was not concerned with the problem.

XIV

Darwinians on Human Culture

1

NOT ONLY were there no accounts of the evolution of mind, as a distinctive human capacity or faculty, but Alonzo could not find acceptable theories of the beginnings of human institutions such as morality, religion, art, the gathering of knowledge and all those others that, taken together, make up culture in its sociological sense.

The Darwinian hypothesis had triumphed in biology in a very short time in spite of eminent biologists like Agassiz, of distinguished and sometimes notorious theologians like Soapy Sam Wilberforce, of statesmen like Gladstone and Disraeli, in spite of the vast hordes of believers, often led by brilliant but ignorant obscurantists, who tried to stop its advance—to no avail.

Once it won out in biology it began its imperialistic expansion all around its frontier: It carried on a triumphant lightning campaign, blasting old edifices of theory and belief and rearing new ones before the dust had settled. Writers of all degrees of competence began to write treatises on the evolution of this, that, and the other human institution. Distinguished scholars, full of atomistic erudition like Hobhouse, Westermarck, Edward Caird, Herbert Green Spearing, and lesser lights wrote books on the evolution of the family, marriage, the state, art, the idea of God, morality. If it was a human institution or activity it had an evolution and someone had written a book on it.

In short, social evolutionists had themselves a picnic. They applied the theory to all culture and everything in it. What was offered were scientific accounts—or so the men who produced these theories thought. It had already been shown that somewhere some time in the past, an ape had decided that, since there appeared to be no future as an arboreal trapeze artist, he'd better de-arborealize himself, hard as it might be to learn to use his hind legs to walk or run. It had already been shown how, after the first monkey started walking he had begun to act in a rudimentary way that dimly foreshadowed the elevation of tea-drinking English High Churchmen of the nineteenth century, toward which the whole of evolution had from its dark beginnings in a single cell pointed, when it did not point to the German state with Hegel on his Chair in Berlin. There had been setbacks, stoppages, meanderings off from the main road. The accidents had been many. But at last evolution had reached its goal with the perfection of humanity in either of the two classes mentioned above.

Here the plot thickened and something that seemed to be a bit of a confusion entered. For while the monkey and his group were descending from the trees into manhood, the theory of biological evolution was transmogrified into a theory of progress—down from the trees was up from the monkeys. Or more exactly, like Hermes and Aphrodite, the two theories became one. How did the consubstantiation occur? Both theories had been around for a long time before Darwin. Kant had thought of the evolution of the heavens. Hegel of the evolution of everything with Hegel himself as the culmination of the German state, which in turn was the culmination of history. And seven years before *The Origin* the formidable Spencer had demonstrated to his satisfaction that evolution was progress.

The truth of the theory of biological evolution was laboriously and successfully established by Darwin; but progress apparently needed no laborious proof: It was obvious. All you had to do was to line up a monkey, an Australian aboriginal, a Mediterranean, and an upper-class Englishman or German in a row, to see that evolution was progress: Here was an order of rank evident to anyone who was not prejudiced. You looked at the series and if you had any brains at all and eyes that saw you could see the increasing excellence, culminating in the self-evident superiority of the last member of the series—an upper-class Englishman or a German, depending on who was looking at the row.

You saw, clearly, with your own eyes, how high progress had reached, from its lowly origins in a one-celled organism, through an adventurous fish who took to land, up through an anonymous simian who decided to leave the trees, through an Australian aboriginal, through a Mediterranean, till it came to a nineteenth-century Englishman or German of the upper class. If evolution was taking place, progress was also taking place, and that gave us two names for one process. Darwin had not boggled at the con-fusion of the two processes into one; in the last page of *The Origin* he expressed the pious hope—in the form of a statement of fact—that natural selection must lead to perfection. There have been a number of spoilsports who have found fault with this scientific theory; you always run into such types, but they can be ignored.

But how did social evolutionists prove their theories? Once it was done one or two times, it was easy for an ambitious young man who wanted to pick up a reputation as an advanced thinker to get into the act. All he needed was industry. All he had to do was to accumulate a large number of facts in any field the evolutionary origins of which he was interested in proving. Suppose he wanted to write about morals in evolution. He ransacked the library and filled several filing cabinets with data. Much of what he gathered was extremely interesting because it was odd. The practice of couvade had to go in, and the way certain peoples mourn their dead by cutting off their fingers. There was headshrinking (physical, that is) and head shaping . . . There needed to be, indeed, no end. Once he had what looked like enough facts— the more the merrier, of course—he ordered them in the evolutionary scale. If it was marriage it began with all the men having all the women and progressed through a horde in which one brute monopolized the women, through polygamy, to the strict monogamous relationship enjoyed in theory at least by your nineteenth-century middle classes, English or German. As for the upper classes, it is well known that they were exempted from sexual restrictions.

About the arrangement in between the beginning and the end there might be some differences of opinion, but about the starting and finishing points there could be none: The simple facts are the oldest, the more complex the later ones, the older were lower, the later were higher. Thus primitive communism came first, in which personality had not yet "emerged," and at long last came individualism, which, early in the second decade of our century, we were told by Dewey and Tufts in the first edition of their *Ethics*, was the peak toward which the moral evolution of man had been climbing. These two American philosophers thus proved—it was never too late to correct errors—that progress had not been finally pointed toward upper-class Englishmen or

Germans but past them towards the American common man, as represented by the uncommon Robber Baron.

But was this ordering of cultural data proof? Once the question was asked you could not very well miss the fact that the theory of social evolution had not been proved. Evolution had been proved in biology and had been applied to culture where it was taken to be self-evidently applicable. Why? Because there was no other way of conceiving how men and their arrangements for living had come about. Social evolution was not proved: It was illustrated or exemplified.

But the illustrations of the evolution of art and religion and marriage and the rest suffered from a number of defects on two of which Alonzo pondered. The first was that many of the facts about the alleged remote past were not pristine facts at all. They were collected from the study of contemporary primitive societies. But savages now living have a history as old as that of any missionary or anthropologist who recorded their strange and often profoundly repugnant customs. To assume that present savages were like the earliest men was about as unwarranted as to assume that their institutions had come about by acts of special creation. This fact or, rather, this error, was not noticed because the social evolutionist assumed that while primitives might have back of them as long a history as his own, their "development" had been "arrested" somewhere along the line; they were supposed to be "living fossils."

The second defect was sufficiently crippling by itself. The alleged proof was no proof at all. It was no more than illustration of the theory of social evolution, which theory was presupposed in the progressive or evolutionary ordering of the facts and in the bland ignoring of those that were embarrassing. As Alonzo became better acquainted with the literature of anthropology he learned that the ordering of the facts assumed that their relationship to a culture was mechanistic and atomistic. One fact was taken from one culture and another from a second, as if by themselves they could retain the significance they had when they were components of the cultures from which they were drawn.

It was not until Boas and his disciple Goldenweiser came on the scene and called the anthropologists to order, that the game was stopped—in the sense that hefty accounts of the evolution of human institutions were no longer written. Goldenweiser's devastating analysis was a beautiful instance of lucidity and elegance. Boas and Goldenweiser pointed out that the anthropologist's business was to study primitive societies. They could have added that he was to leave fairy tales to Grimm, L. Frank Baum, and other pros who had superior talent for the job. But the belief in social evolution did not prove easy to eradicate. The notion continued to be used. There seemed to be something like the spirit of an age. After Darwin it had become impossible to think of an alternative to evolution since belief in special creation was . . . well, what was it? It was not nonsense; it was simply repugnant to the intellectual climate of the day.

Social evolutionism had survived all criticism because there was a legitimate philosophical need to account for human origins, if naturalism was to make the claim stick that it was more than faith, and because there seemed to be a deep-rooted need in men to know about their origins. In Russia, social evolutionism, coming from Engels and L. H. Morgan, was official doctrine. In the United States it was not official doctrine, but like the young lady in the Jewish joke, it was just a little bit official. As Alonzo began to see, the social evolutionism of our day was considerably more sophisticated. But it was still based on faith and hope, which generate heroic efforts to stretch the known facts from genetics, biochemistry, and anthropology, patching up the holes with speculation not always acknowledged for what it was, in order to give the doctrine the appearance of scientific respectability.

2

How had human culture come about? If evolutionists could not give an acceptable account of the appearance of the human mind, could naturalists, starting from it, give an account of those distinctive products of the human mind, the institutions of culture? Human culture was made up of a number of institutions, some of which were universal, in the sense that they were to be found in every human group—morality, religion, art, knowledge gathering, the family, a complex system of taboos and other forms of human expression—which were interrelated for each group and which differed from group to group according to a large number of factors some of which were at least in part understood.

These institutions could be studied wherever animals that could be called human were to be found living in interrelation; the various modes of life they made possible were the forms through which the substance of living found expression; forms and instruments and substance were transmitted from one generation to the next, thus giving the life of a group continuity; because of the social transmission of modes of experience men did not live entirely by means of unlearned instinct, and they did not have to start from scratch with every generation. The question the naturalist had to answer was, "How have the institutions come about?"

Evolutionists were fond of discovering in what was known in the ways of life of other animals analogies to the ways of life of human beings. But when the analogies were examined critically, one had to conclude that the differences between the ways of life of nonhuman animals and those of the human animal were at least as essential as the similarities, and that the latter could not bridge the chasm. Alonzo was willing to concede, for the sake of the argument, that evolutionists could explain how the animal species had come about and developed the organs and intricate patterns of behavior and adaptation they exhibited. The evolutionists were satisfied with their explanations, and Alonzo was too ignorant of biology to put his skepticism against the biologist's knowledge.

Adaptation seemed to be the all-purpose word that functioned as a kind of incantatory om term, the unctuous utterance of which led the believer to bend his knee, join his hands in prayerful gesture, and sink his head in reverent assent. But Alonzo had to let the biological problem go, keeping his doubts to himself while uttering a silent prayer, "I believe in thee, oh Saint Charles, and in thine Apostle, Thomas Henry; help me in my unbelief." But the problem of the origins of human institutions he did not have to keep silent about. Obviously inadequate when you looked at it, appeal to biological adaptation did not explain the development of any distinctively human institution.

Alonzo had read a literary critic who wrote that when he considered "the staggering sums spent organizing the materials and the human energy necessary to produce floods of art throughout the history of man," he decided that "the only way to approach the matter was to consider artistic activity as a mode of biological adaptation." Why? Because, for this writer, "the ultimate question about any kind of human behavior is a question about why any human being should trouble to do it. That is, what is its *function* in biological adaptation? Ultimately this means that there is a physiological basis for artistic behavior, that creating works of art and the looking at them serves some physiological need."

This kind of thinking, said Alonzo contemptuously, is utter non-sense. What physiological need does art serve? Obviously, I replied, the need for art. Alonzo did not notice my irony and retorted, irritated, that he was not kidding. What is the difference between the dormitive virtue of the seventeenth-century student of Montpellier and this? Why, a big one, I said, since the critic is scientific and the Montpellier student was not. If Malinowski can invent an obscure "instinct" to account for the widespread desire for immortality why can't this literary critic assume a physiological basis for artistic behavior? There is a need for food and a physiological basis for it, I continued, and for sex and a physiological basis; there is a need for art, and it must therefore have a physiological basis even if we can't see the organ which meets the need. But Alonzo could not yet see that I was pulling his leg. He retorted that if I was satisfied with a vague reference to biological adaptation and a physiological need that art meets, I was not to expect him to join me.

In addition to this objection, there were two others: This kind of thinking was purely verbal and crudely reductionistic. Back of it there was nothing but the nothing-buting of nineteenth-century materialists. That there is a physiological basis for artistic behavior we need not doubt, in the sense that we need sight and hearing and hands before we can make art. Note, however, that *basis* here means some of the conditions for it. But to argue that through art man adapts himself to the world or the world to himself was mere talk and crude talk at that, until you went on to show step by step how the adaptation took place, in answer to distinctly prehuman, merely biological, needs. Aesthetic contemplation and the making of art are distinct ways of being human, a mode of activity that goes so far beyond survival as to make the prehuman stage altogether irrelevant to the human.

I did not see how I could cool him off, so I said to him that I had often suspected that he was a card-carrying member of Soapy Sam's party, American branch, headed not so long ago by William Jennings Bryan.

Not at all, he replied, his objection, as he had already pointed out, was not to the theory of biological evolution, the fact of which was as well established as one could want, although the how was still open to question, in spite of the broad consensus among biologists about Neo-Darwinism. The objection was against the extra-polation of biological evolution to cultural evolution. But of course he knew that he was in opposition to the orthodoxy of the day and did not expect anyone to agree with him. Please get it clear, my argument is not against biology but against the philosophy of naturalism, he said. The argument is this: The naturalist claims that there is nothing but Nature and that everything human can be explained in natural terms. But how can he make the claim when he cannot give us an account of the origin of human institutions that does more than argue in the crude way the literary critic argues? What right does the naturalist have to assert that he knows on empirical grounds that there is only one Nature and everything that happens happens through its agencies when he cannot tell how the distinctly human institutions originated?

All right, forget the crude literary critic with his cliché appeal to adaptation and the biological basis of art which he does not exhibit. Take a scholar who could make a strong claim that he was a scientist. This man had been trained in philosophy but he had achieved an enviable reputation as a theoretical anthropologist. Discussing the origins of human culture he wrote: "Culture is primarily a mode of human behavior acquired by man in the course of his experience of nature to promote his survival as an individual and as a member of society."

It did not take a broad and profound knowledge of history to show that the generalization did not at all stand up. To assert that it was for the sake of survival that man created culture, is to repeat uncritically a late nineteenth-century cliché. One would expect an anthropologist in mid-twentieth century to know that the human animal, animal though he be, is more than a mere animal because he employs unique gifts in order to discern values and to devise institutions by means of which to give them a relatively permanent anchorage. Heroism in war and peace, religious martyrdom, patriotism, self-sacrifice, loyalty, and much else, prove that survival often has to yield to other values. Man's pride, his dignity, his singular achievement consist in this capacity to espouse values that from the biological standpoint are burdensome and often too costly. These values man does not hesitate to espouse, at however high a cost. It is their espousal that makes him the singular animal that he is.

The longer Alonzo thought about it the more convinced he became that adaptation for survival did not explain the development of man. Let us see why. Consider man's incest regulations. Some of them seem to make sense eugenically, as for instance the universal taboo against sexual intercourse between mother and son. But many of them did not seem to have any survival value. If it was claimed that they did, the burden of proof was on the scholar who made the claim. And mind you, Alonzo said to himself, these presumptuous ex-apes married; something that their stand-patter relative who persisted in his old arboreal ways, had he been able to understand the institution, would have split his sides laughing at. One takes any female that one can when her bottom swells up and all these human-shines about marriage and about keeping your wives exclusively to yourself—what in the name of decent apehood is the point of that? Besides, it is unspeakably selfish. And the business of being proud of the bambino—who among us respectable apes ever heard of that? All of this did not seem to make things easier for the ex-ape who, not content with his former lot, decided that he would be superior to his conservative relatives. But why superior? Because he had a talent for complicating his life and making matters quite difficult for himself and the members of his group.

Alonzo was thinking of "mere survival," because if we are thinking of the survival of the animal who created culture, we cannot appeal to culture to explain its own existence. Once culture was created man, now fully human, may not have been able to do without its burdensome instrumentalities. But the assumption that he created them in order to survive is a generalization that will not bear examination.

One did not need to have read *Civilization and Its Discontents* and the relevant paragraphs in the second chapter of *The Future of an Illusion*, nor need one have more knowledge of history than an intelligent undergraduate to become aware of the heavy burden that culture places on man, and the frequency with which the defense of cultural products—beliefs, values, institutions he feels threatened—lead him as an individual and as a group to extinction.

But if religion is a means of survival, we shall also have to add up carefully both sides of the ledger to see whether we come out in the black or in the red. But the CPA who balances the books will have to know universal history, for he has to add up the victims of religious intolerance—the witch burnings, the religious persecutions, the massacres of holy wars and crusaders, the countless victims of inquisitions, the martyrs—in short, the whole red page, or more precisely, the bulging stacks of ledgers from all over the world, soaked in human blood, in which the butcheries caused by religion have been recorded. Does it seem as if religion aided survival? It may aid sometimes by maintaining the morale of a group, its conscious identity, by giving its members hope, and by fending off despair. But whether it helps more than it hinders no one knows. By falling back on a vague notion of survival all we are doing is helping the survival of the nineteenth-century notion that Boas and Goldenweiser did in quite a number of decades ago.

What shall we say in terms of human survival of the misery, hunger, and death which must have been the cost of building the great monuments of art in Asia, Egypt, Europe, and Central America? Is it not likely that the energy put into rearing the Maya temples—without draft animals and the wheel, remember—might have done more for survival if the laborers had been raising corn? Alonzo remembered vaguely an account of the building of a cathedral somewhere in France. It was at the time when the cathedral-building rage, that if Alonzo remembered rightly, began in France, swept through Europe like fire over a dry plain. As the rage spread, the Gothic bishops, it appears, contended with one another to see who could build the greatest, most stupendous building.

To this madness we owe the monuments celebrated by Henry Adams in his famous book and the other glories of that age. But to build them, Alonzo remembered reading that at the height of the furor, lords and ladies joined their peasants to pull the stones. Later, the bishops' overseers had to ride forth to collect the peasants, and drive them with the knout to the quarries. Pulling hard and probably not too well fed, the peasants brought the stones to the building site.

A factual answer to the following question would be required before we accepted the claim that culture helped man to survive: How did the building of the great architectural monuments of the world help those who built them to survive? Who survived and who perished? If we are going to accept the notion of survival we have to answer these questions with care, and not for one building alone but for a representative number of them. And not for one art alone but for all the arts. Alonzo did not know the answers to these questions and he did not know who has sought to answer them. Apparently no one. In view of our ignorance it will not do to accept the survival theory, no matter how respectable it might have been considered during the second half of the last century and for a number of years during our own.

But this is not the only difficulty to be found in the explanation. The same writer who wrote that culture promotes survival says that, "Culture is organically conditioned, and the universals of human culture may be explained by the needs and potentialities of the human orga-

nism, individually and collectively, in coping with his environment."
In this kind of argument what the writer is doing is deceiving himself
and his readers with a scientistic cliché that explains nothing.

The following passage from the same author gives rise to another
criticism, "Culture, in particular, as an emergent from human nature
acting upon its natural, ecological environment, requires the creative
activity of man, not only for its genesis, but also for its continuation in
existence and its progressive development." The criticism that Alonzo
thought the statement was open to is best put in the form of a question:
Was the man referred to in the passage already endowed with human
nature when he began to create culture? If the answer is in the affirma-
tive, as the passage suggests, man became human and was endowed
with creativity historically before he created culture. And the question
arises: How did he become human?

But is culture only a means of coping with the environment, a
means of acquiring power over nature? Alonzo saw that culture consisted of an elaborate, an obstinate effort on the part of the human animal to load himself with practices that by no conceivable means could
be accounted for in terms of adaptation and survival. Man was a self-
burdened animal. From the standpoint of adaptation, of biological survival, and of control of the environment he is an absurd, a fantastic,
a mad animal. Commands and prohibitions, beliefs, rituals, ceremonies, childish and elaborate taboos impede his life. He discovers
guilt and immediately uses it to inhibit the performance of acts some
of which are dangerous to him and his group but many of which would
not make any difference in his capacity to stay alive and prosper biologically either individually or as a group, and many of which would
bring biological ease, satisfaction, and success.

He discovers god, and proceeds to appease him by sacrificing his
own kind; he takes the fairest of his virgins and plunges them down
wells or undertakes wars to capture victims whose beating hearts he will
pluck as an offering to his blood-thirsty gods. One man fancies he
hears his god command him to take his son to the top of a mountain
and sacrifice him in obedience to him; he holds his hand just in time
and claims that the god that ordered him to sacrifice his son has promised him for his blind obedience a reward he'll never see. Man discovers beauty and spends hours, which he can ill afford to waste, in
such useless pursuits as painting his body, or putting a bit of an orna-

ment on a tool which would function as well or possibly better without it. From the standpoint of biological adaptation this was all insane, utterly and incontestably insane.

Look at any taboo from the outside, Alonzo said to himself, what can you tell about it? That it is childish or gratuitous; that it is senseless; that it is utterly useless. But look at it from the standpoint of the man who accepts it, and what must you now say about it? That many of these prohibitions are hung on to at the danger of life or at any rate at the cost of radical frustration, but that they are viewed as indispensable. Force a man to break one of these childish prohibitions and he sickens morally instead of rising from the broken chain triumphant and eager to live a fuller life.

Alonzo continued, let us assume that Jews—and the ancient Egyptians from whom they may have picked up the prohibition—discovered that pork was dangerous food. Let us assume that they hang on to the prohibition today for the sake of maintaining their identity as a group and forget also that the identity they thus maintain brought them only a couple of decades ago to the brink of extinction. Let us further assume that many taboos have a similar rational root as the Jewish taboo against pork. Are we going to say that all taboos are rationally grounded? When social evolutionists tell us that human behavior is in large part adaptive, we wonder how much thought they have put on that about which they are supposed to be thinking, the human animal and his ways. Hanging on to their theories, they overlook the fact that the human animal achieves his humanity, and thus pole-vaults over the rest of the animals, by burdening himself with biologically non-adaptive behavior. But the peculiarity of the animal is that on the surplus burden that he puts on himself he rests his pride and erects his self-respect.

Men are bent and have always been, in all cultures, Alonzo continued, on denying themselves the life of unclouded pleasure, particularly the life of purely somatic pleasure. That he has been forced to such denial by scarcity cannot be maintained, since he denies himself pleasure all along the line in the most ingenious ways, and since, for example, there have been few more taboo ridden societies than the Hawaiian before the whites took over, although it flourished in a land of plenty. Man may be a pleasure- and ease-loving animal—he is, in part; but he is also a pleasure- and ease-hating animal, and culture is a monument he builds to his hatred as much as to his love of pleasure. As to adapting himself for survival, isn't it clear from the facts that he seeks death as much as life and that his adaptation is always on his own terms and that his terms often mean his willing acceptance of death and his rejection of unqualified biological survival for himself and his group?

XV

On Human Origins:
Freud and Others

1

AMONG the several naturalistic accounts of the origins of culture available there was one to which Alonzo knew he need not give serious consideration, the Marxist. Since Engels had written a book on the origins of the family borrowing from L. H. Morgan, orthodox Marxists were stuck with the now obsolete anthropology of the American. In his day Morgan had been a most distinguished and powerfully influential writer, and the high place he occupied in the history of science was fully his due. But his views had long gone the way of Genesis, although Alonzo discovered that a highly intelligent and intellectually sophisticated friend, upon becoming a member of the Communist party in the thirties, had begun to read Morgan as if his thoroughly exploded theories were still worth taking seriously. Apparently when you swallowed the Marxist hook you also swallowed a long line and a big sinker.

The naturalistic account of the origin of culture that seemed to Alonzo to deserve most serious attention was the Freudian. In the course of developing his medical theories Freud had sketched an almost complete philosophical anthropology along genetic lines, or what is the same thing, an almost complete theory of culture. Freud and his followers claimed scientific status for their theories, using the word *science* in its narrow American-English sense. In this question Alonzo had no interest, although if forced to take sides he would have sided with the skeptics.

What could legitimately be claimed for the Freudian theory apparently no one, to Alonzo's knowledge, and least of all Freud, had claimed, namely, philosophic status. Freud's theory of human nature was a bold, and prima facie, a plausible combination of empirical

observation and unhobbled speculation about the etiology and relief of
psychic malfunctionings. But in the course of the development of his
views through a wide range of interests, Freud had worked out what
amounted to an almost complete blueprint for a system of philosophy.
It is true that Freud himself had stated that he carefully avoided any
contact with "philosophy proper," and had added that the avoidance
had been greatly facilitated by constitutional incapacity. This statement, one suspects, arises from Freud's concern for originality, and it
is therefore something we can altogether overlook. It is also true that
Lewis Mumford could not be contradicted when he dismissed Freud's
uncritical mediocrity as a philosopher because he accepted the atomistic materialism of his youth.

That Freud avoided what he took to be "philosophy proper" we must
take on his word. But what is philosophy proper? The word *philosophy*
has as many proper senses as any word in the dictionary. Whatever
philosophy proper may be taken to be, if we distinguish, as Alonzo did,
between the philosopher's mind and the philosophical mind, Freud
had a first-rate philosophical mind. His speculation and observation
about the whole range of human experience sprung from a well worked
out conception of man and was developed or sketched out by systematic reference to it. Freud did not actually leave us a complete and
finished system, as Hegel, Whitehead, or Dewey had done. But he left
us the blueprint for a vast edifice, some of whose wings were finished
and in satisfactory habitable condition.

Because Freud traced the beginnings of religion, morality, and art,
to the Oedipus complex, his thought was thoroughly systematic. On
all the topics he had discussed, he had either advanced reasonably
finished theories or left suggestions that could not be ignored. Further,
his thought had been powerfully influential. Its influence might still
be regretted by his adversaries, but in fighting him they often used
Freudian concepts and language, while showing at the same time a
strong prejudice or rank ignorance of Freud's theories. No one could
deny, however, that his ideas had spread throughout all of the humanities and the social sciences. They had spread because his views were
plausible and met a need. Although he was hated, vilified, denounced
as a dirty old man and a menace to civilization, indicted as a wrecker
of morality, dismissed for some very good and for some very puerile
reasons, no serious student of philosophy could overlook the contributions Freud made to the regnant naturalism of the day. That these con-

tributions were almost completely ignored by philosophers of Alonzo's generation and earlier, that only recently, as such things go, had Freud finally been taken notice of by philosophers, was philosophy's loss and spoke eloquently for the claims of philosophers to being adventurous seekers of the truth.

2

As regards art, Freud had little to say that could be of interest to a man looking for a complete account of its origin, nature, and function, and he knew it. If Freud's view of human nature was admissible, the tracing of art to repression and sublimation was probably, at least partially, correct. But artistic sublimation was no mere sublimation, whatever family relations there might be between dreams, neurotic disabilities, and art. A theory of art that had nothing to say about form and its relation to its in-formed substance was worse than worthless, since it was the origin of a confusion that ended up by erasing what gave art its distinctiveness. This was a confusion that Freud not only fell into but of which he had no inkling. He confused "the matter for art" with "the in-formed substance of art." The matter for art is whatever the artist makes art out of prior to his in-forming it: the whole of his experience, infantile and mature, including his knowledge of those artistic traditions in which he is interested, before he in-forms it, thus transubstantiating it into an organic component which is the finished object as it presents itself for aesthetic contemplation; this finished object is totally unlike the matter that the artist has digested and in-formed.

Alonzo iterated that there can be no objection in principle to the claim that the matter for art may contain childhood experiences, wishes the artist represses, the love of the male infant for the mother and his hatred of the father or of the female infant for her father, if on sufficient grounds these yearnings and hatreds can be established. But the radical limitations of the psychoanalytic theory of art cannot be denied. Art is more than the matter for art that the artist in-forms. Freud was utterly candid about some of the limitations of his theory; his well-known confession that "before the problem of the creative artist analysis must, alas, lay down its arms" was an important part of the truth. But his exclusive interest in "content"—in the in-formed matter of art, or as Alonzo calls it, "the substance of art"—in separation from its organic form—rendered his speculations about art inadmissible.

3

While Freud acknowledged the inability of psychoanalysis to solve "the problem of the creative artist" and hence to say something significant about the nature of the created object, he thought he was able to give an account of the earliest development of the moral faculty of the animal that became man, or the phylogenetic source of his moral faculty. He also provided an account of the way in which the human child, now fully human because endowed with the powers that as he grows make him human, acquired his moral sense, or the ontogenetic source. A complete account of Alonzo's criticisms of these two theories would detain us too long; all I can do here is to present a sketchy examination of his criticisms of them.

The theory of how the protohominid acquired the moral faculty—the acquisition of which, of course, contributed to the acquisition of its humanity—which is to say, the phylogenetic account, is presented by Freud by means of a fable that he tells us in *Totem and Taboo* (a book whose publication is variously given as 1912 or 1913 or even 1916). This fable has embarrassed Freud's followers, since it is wholly made up. But the serious objection to it is not that it contains as much truth as the stories of Parson Weems but that it begs the issue. After all, Genesis is a wholly mythical account of the creation of the earth and of man which has been taken seriously for centuries and is apparently still taken seriously today not only by analphabetic legislators but even by highly educated men.

It should be noted that Freud is aware of the mythical nature of the story, for he tells us that "The primal state of society has nowhere been observed." Nor could it have been, one adds, for reasons already stated in full.

How does Freud account for the pristine origin of morality or the sense of guilt—its phylogenetic source? He invents a primal horde in which the father keeps all the women from his sons. Finally the sons, perhaps through "some advance in culture, like the invention of a new weapon," which gives them superiority over the old man, get together and, as Freud puts it primly, "remove" the father. Since they are cannibals, they devour him, and thus identify themselves with him. Since they not only hated him and envied him before killing him, but also loved him, after doing him in the suppressed impulses of tenderness that they had earlier felt toward him assert themselves. Freud is certain that the brothers were dominated by a contradictory feeling towards the father because he can demonstrate contradictory feelings as the content of ambivalence of the father complex in all children and neurotics. Note in passing the assumption that the content of ambivalence in the past can be demonstrated because from the present the past can be inferred. But how does he know that the sons of the primal father felt ambivalent towards the old brute? This is as sheer a guess as is the notion of the primal horde which he took from Darwin. Note now carefully what follows: The emergence of their tender impulses, he writes, "took place in the form of remorse, a sense of guilt was formed which coincided here with the remorse generally felt." This is not the end of the fable but is sufficient for the purpose of showing how Freud fails to account for the phylogenetic or historical origin of the moral faculty, the sense of guilt, or remorse.

In order to examine the fable we must first eliminate from consideration "the remorse generally felt" with which the sense of guilt felt by the sons is said to coincide, since it is introduced suddenly, it is not accounted for, and above all, since if a general sense of guilt already exists there can be no problem of deriving the particular sense of guilt felt by the sons from the preexisting general sense.

This is the phylogenetic account. It suffers from a number of radical defects. Notice first that from suppressed tender impulses felt by the sons after the murder Freud asserts that a sense of guilt or remorse emerged. Perhaps it did, but assertion is not enough; we need to know in detail the process by which tenderness becomes remorse. In the absence of a moral faculty, the initial appearance of which Freud is trying to give an account, the sons could have regretted the murder because they needed and missed the old brute. But regret is not remorse. To wish they had not killed him is not the same as feeling guilty because they did. What Freud did was to posit the sense of guilt; he gave no account of the process through which it appeared.

Freud goes on to make a radical distinction between the commission of an immoral act and the violation of a taboo. He assumes that the commission of an immoral act gives rise to a response similar to that felt when a taboo is violated. In this he is in error, since a person who accepts a taboo does not distinguish, he has no means of distinguishing, taboos from moral imperatives or prohibitions. The word *taboo* is used by us usually in a pejorative sense; we apply it to the acts of others or even to our own acts, when we recognize prohibitions that are not morally binding. But a person or a people who accept a taboo have no means of distinguishing taboos from moral commandments, from imperatives or prohibitions that are morally binding. The distinction is a sophisticated one, made by rationalists who do not recognize how heavily they themselves and the members of their culture as well as members of other cultures are burdened by compulsions and restrictions that may have little to do with moral imperatives or prohibitions. The distinction, therefore, between taboo and moral imperative is thin —when it exists.

A primitive, or for that matter, that indispensable character without whose offices our thinking would be seriously impeded, "the man in the street," are not moral philosophers. This is the reason they respond to the commission of an immoral act as they do to the violation of a taboo; for them both taboo and moral command or prohibition fall under the undifferentiated head of prohibited acts. Indeed it takes a good deal of sophistication for anyone to recognize the distinction between taboos and moral prohibitions. For an orthodox Jew or a Mohammedan, is the eating of pork the violation of a taboo or the commission of an immoral or sinful act? Only a few years ago the eating of meat on Friday was prohibited to Roman Catholics. They considered it, I believe, a venial sin. Was the commission of a sin, even a venial one, the violation of a taboo for them? And the prohibition of incest between mother and son, is it a taboo or a moral prohibition? If one explains remorse or the feeling of guilt by violation of a taboo one is accounting for the origin of moral responses in terms already posited. One is begging the question.

This is the phylogenetic account found in *Totem and Taboo*. In 1930, in *Civilization and Its Discontents*, a more complex but considerably less clear account of the historical origin of morality is to be found. In this book the feeling of guilt is traced to two sources: "the dread of authority and later the dread of the super-ego." The latter we can altogether disregard as accounting for the origin of morality, since the superego, as he tells us in *The New Introductory Lectures*, we can, in a whisper, call "the conscience." The appearance of the superego cannot be explained by tracing it back to the superego.

When we turn to the dread of authority we ask how, without positing a moral capacity, this dread can produce a sense of guilt. In the absence of a moral faculty we cannot recognize authority in the proper sense of the term; what we recognize is force, arbitrary force. Authority appears when force is endowed with moral validity; guilt can then appear. A moral response to nonmoral authority is a contradiction in terms. If the response is moral, the force responded to has been recognized as endowed with moral quality. When arbitrary force, which is to say force we do not recognize as endowed with authority, which is to say, not recognized as morally valid, makes demands of us, two polar reactions are possible: If we are weak or helpless our attitude will be one of concealed rebellion and hatred, and we respond with a resigned submission, which may, nevertheless, remain alert to means of avoiding or nullifying the demand of force; if we are strong we respond with more or less open rebellion or defiance. Force that is not acknowledged to have authority will harden the heart, it will elicit cunning, it will repress any trace of remorse that may exist in the soul, and it will counsel resistance or evasion. In the absence of a moral capacity, tenderness may produce yearning, a desire for the presence of that which one has harmed or alienated. It may produce regret, it will not produce remorse or a sense of guilt.

In *Civilization and Its Discontents* the confusion of regret with remorse, which he did not fall into in *Totem and Taboo*, is plain upon the page. In the ordinary course of our lives we human beings are not helped by the language we use, hence we do not feel the need to distinguish remorse or moral self-condemnation from regret. And since often both are felt at the same time, the confusion is one easy to fall into. When we say that it is too bad that we did something we may mean that we regret it or that we condemn ourselves morally for doing it, or both; we can feel regret without remorse and more rarely, remorse without regret. Moral self-disapproval or remorse may be intense or light. But whatever we feel or however intensely or lightly we feel it, regret is not remorse, even though frequently it will take more psychological acuity than we are apt to put into such discriminations to grasp the difference.

4

Freud failed to give a satisfactory account of the pristine or phylogenetic origin of the conscience. Did he give a satisfactory account of how the child born of fully human parents acquired it, an ontogenetic

account of it? Ontogenetically the superego develops, according to
Freud, because the child introjects his parents' values. This theory is
open to three criticisms. The first is obvious: It raises the chicken and
egg problem. The child gets his conscience from his parents, who in
turn got it from their parents. But how did the first parents to have a
conscience get theirs? The ontogenetic account leads to the phylogenetic account, and it does even if it is said that to speak of a first time
when an animal got a superego is to overlook the fact that the acquisition took place gradually. The other criticism is that the child chooses
from among the values espoused by his parents some which he introjects while rejecting others. The ambivalence on which Freud is so in-
sistent is one of the factors accounting for the partial rejection of the
parents' values—assuming, what is likely to be contrary to fact, that
the parents' values are in harmony. But neither acceptance nor rejection is total or arbitrary. The values the child chooses are considered
by him truly valuable, those he rejects are taken to be disvalues. We
are told that the child begins to develop the superego at the age of two.
But from the beginning there is discrimination. This entails the exercise of a faculty whose development Freud is explaining ontogenetically. The capacity for discrimination is, in potency or act, the conscience, even if it is a matter of degree and not fully explicit. As the
child exercises it, he acts as a moral being. Again at the ontogenetic
level, Freud begs the issue.

The other defect of Freud's ontogenetic theory of morality is this:
Let us accept his view that at the age of two the child begins to introject
his parents' values and that the process continues so that his behavior
and judgments are nothing more than an immature copy of his parents'. Sooner or later, as he grows older, he will be faced with the problem of making a genuine moral choice, which he has not yet had to
make. A genuine choice is one in which the attitudes and modes of
response inculcated and introjected somehow fail to meet the demands
of the situation. The failure may come about because the introjected
values are in conflict and he must make a choice, or because they do
not apply to a novel situation that has come about through his growth,
or for some other reason such as his leaving home, or because he discovers that the values of his parents are ridiculed by his friends. It is at
this point that his moral life begins. The conscience is a faculty of
examining the ground of one's conduct and that of others and passing

judgment on them in terms of criteria that are capable of satisfying the moral sense of the examiner. It is not the capacity of acting like trained animals and talking like parrots. How this power comes about Freud does not explain.

But even if we were to accept the ontogenetic account of the origin of the superego, naturalistic philosophy could not make its claim if it did not provide a phylogenetic account. Assume that the child introjects the parents' values and that the parents in turn introjected their parents', the question has to be answered, how did the remote ancestors of man, leaving the hominid stage and becoming human, come to consider some acts right and others wrong?

More recent naturalistic theories of the origin of morality with which Alonzo was acquainted are no more acceptable than Freud's. One such theory was presented by Julian Huxley in his Romanes lecture. Huxley attempted to put Darwin and Freud together. But his explanation of the genesis of the conscience is a modified Freudian theory suffering from the identical defect found in Freud. We read in Huxley that "the proto-ethical mechanism," as Huxley calls the nascent conscience, is formed in the child's second year of life and arises from a special kind of conflict among the chaos of unregulated impulses with which the infant is originally endowed. The conflict is generated by love and hatred. The sense of guilt emerges out of suppression of the anger, aggression, and death wishes the child feels toward his parents. But how suppression becomes guilt we are not told. A child forced to repress his feelings and control his impulses may feel resentment. But how resentment turns into a feeling of guilt remains a mystery. Alonzo concluded that Freud's account of the development of the superego was inadmissible: Both the phylogenetic and the ontogenetic account of the moral faculty begged the issue. He further concluded that Freud gave very little evidence of understanding the nature of morality; he was a poor ethicist, however moral a person he might have been. A man can be profoundly moral and be no ethicist at all, just as he can be a good ethicist and be a scoundrel. Understanding the nature of morality and being moral are two distinct things. This was known by Aristotle, who recommended that ethics should not be taught to immature youths; only when a young man had acquired a moral nature should ethics or moral philosophy be taught to him.

5

Freud explained the origin of the idea of God by means of the notion of projection. God was the Father written large and thrust into the
heavens. That the notion of providence, the idea of the Heavenly
Father watching over each of us, has its source in the child's perception of the strength, authority, and providential nature of his father, is
altogether plausible. In the way of accepting this theory seems to be
Malinowski's criticism, arising from the fact that among some peoples
the biological father does not play the role the father plays in a Jewish
household. But this is not a disabling objection. What is serious is
that Freud was aware, and pointed out, that there was much more to
religion than his theory could explain. But Freud never gave serious
attention to those components. One of the finest minds of our world,
a subtle, perspicuous mind, a mind fully aware of the complexities of
human experience (if he was not, who could be, today?), as Alonzo
saw it, Freud was blinded by an intense animus toward religion. When
the subject came up he dismissed it with the coarse disdain of a village
atheist.

Freud, who was bold enough to trace his principles, Eros and Than-
atos, to the cosmos, did not respond to their mystery. If he did, he left
us no record of the experience that Alonzo knew about. For Freud religion was an illusion, and illusion was the product of wish to which no
objective reality could be attached. Naturalists were in the same boat.
Indifferent, if not inimical, to religion, they were anesthetic to the ultimate mystery of the universe and therefore devoid of piety, of gratitude
towards the ultimate sources of their being. And therefore, also, incomplete men, however well developed their enormous brains were.

6

Another naturalistic theory of culture with which Alonzo was acquainted was advanced by a man from whom Alonzo had learned a
great deal and for whom he had immense respect, Malinowski. In his
A Scientific Theory of Culture and Other Essays, one finds at least two
essays, the essay from which the book takes its title and another entitled
"A Theory of Human Needs," that constitute a serious effort to trace
culture back to biological needs. It is interesting to note that Malinowski disparages "the persistent search for 'origins' and 'historic causes,' in

the nebulous realms of the undocumented, unrecorded historic past or evolutionary beginnings of a people who neither have a history nor have left any traces of their previous evolution."

His intention is clearly stated by him: "It is clear," he tells us, "that any theory of culture has to start from the organic needs of man." What it seeks, he goes on, is to relate the organic needs to the more complex, indirect, but perhaps fully imperative needs of the type we call spiritual, economic, or social. Like everything Malinowski wrote, this book is full of valuable insights. But after reading it with care, Alonzo decided that Malinowski could not be judged more successful in his enterprise than the others. The weakness of the theory showed itself without shame when Malinowski, in the very brief essay, "The Theory of Needs," writes that "Survival after death is probably one of the earliest mythical hypotheses, related perhaps to some deep biological craving of the organism . . . ." If this is not a nebulous effort to relate spiritual needs to biological sources, what is it? Alonzo asked.

7

Why couldn't these writers see, Alonzo asked himself, that the thinking they employed in explaining human origins was shoddy? To the high quality of their minds the rest of their work testifies with eloquence. One explanation obviously was that the educated mind today thinks in terms of a disjunction for which it can find no third: either special creation or evolution. The first term of the disjunction, for intellectually sophisticated men, is inadmissible; therefore we must accept the second. But why must we? Because a third alternative is inconceivable. But why is it inconceivable? Alonzo suggested the reason was that the hypothesis of evolution is so deeply rooted in their minds that they are no more able to look at it critically than Wilberforce was able to look at the story of Genesis. Any other way out but evolution was inconceivable. But was it really inconceivable? He did not think so, since he could conceive of a third alternative to either special creation or evolution, and that was to admit with candor that no scientific answer to the question of the missing link was available although we had to recognize that it is a scientific question or one of fact.

But why is it necessary to explain the origin of culture? A scientist did not need to be omniscient—he is not a philosopher. Why was it not enough to say that on the evidence at hand we were reasonably cer-

tain of the fact of man's biological evolution but had no idea about
how the ape that became man pulled off the feat? One reason perhaps
was that the intellectual sophisticates were still scared of Wilberforce
and Bryan. The bitterness generated by the warfare that started with
the publication of *On the Origin of Species* has not been dissipated.
But why should the scientists be scared? Alonzo did not know. Darwin
and his bulldog, T. H. Huxley, licked the hell out of Wilberforce; and
a Bryan, in our century, is a perfect paradigm of intellectual backward-
ness and dogged religious faith. But over one hundred and ten years
after their triumph, the victors seem to retain the rancor towards their
beaten enemies. Another possible account of the reason these good
minds accept shoddy arguments is that while in some areas of interest
they are able to distinguish clearly between faith and knowledge, in the
area of evolution, they are not able to make the distinction. The first
possible explanation, however, does not exclude the second.

These reasons accounted, or helped to account, for the failure of scientists to acknowledge their ignorance. But it did not account for the
failure of naturalistic philosophers to see that the extension of the notion of biological evolution to cultural evolution was illegitimate, in
the sense that for the latter theory nothing like the facts that were offered to back the former could be offered. Back of the failure no doubt
was the faith to which the lady philosopher confessed, and perhaps
the knowledge that admission of the failure to explain the origin of culture was a serious indictment and conviction of the inadequacy of
naturalism.

XVI

Alonzo Too Was Guilty

1

ALONZO'S world was in ruins. His wife had died after five
years of pain and five radical operations for cancer and his
parents died shortly afterwards; Hitler was triumphant,
England in danger, and the United States was divided
between interventionists and isolationists who appealed
to a concept of patriotism with which Alonzo did not agree. Both
groups were led by eminent men. His job at State had been in jeopardy
since Klotz became chairman, but there had been no positions available in the academic world since the beginning of the Depression. It
would not be until 1945 that he had two offers, coming one day after
the other. And it would not be until he left State that he would be able
to return to a normal life.

The years between Pearl Harbor and his leaving State for Chicago,
painful as they were, were not fruitless. During these years he undertook a course of reading and hard thinking that led him first to discard
his former philosophical views and then to arrive, slowly, at a position
that he felt met the theoretical and vital conditions he decided should
be expected of a viable philosophical theory.

When Alonzo heard about Pearl Harbor he knew instantly that the
old world was suddenly finished and a new one had been born. The
death of the old and the gestation of the new had taken place at the
same time, and had preceded Pearl Harbor for years. On Monday he
spoke to his classes about the age that had begun that Sunday and he
was told subsequently by several students that he had been the only one
of their teachers who had commented on the fact. Alonzo did not by
then allow himself to make comments about political matters in his
classes; but he felt that this was a critical moment and that a few min-

utes were well spent in calling the students' attention to the event that
had changed the world and had changed their lives since last he saw
them on Friday. Whatever the world in which they lived until Sunday
had been like, it was now totally destroyed, and no one could tell what
the new one would bring. Of course, victory was not to be doubted
in the long run, but how long a run and at what price no one could
predict.

Alonzo's personal crisis had a component that was the chief cause of
the acute misery in which he was living. Shortly before Pearl Harbor
Maxie Waxie had mounted an all-out effort to get rid of him. Maxie's
intimate friendship with the governor of the state seemed about to bear
fruit. Anytime now Alonzo might find himself without a job. Several
friends advised him to get a job in Washington, something that for him
would be very easy; but Alonzo somehow knew that the advice had
been prompted by Maxie Waxie and that it was too risky to abandon
his job lest it be impossible for him to return to it.

But why might he not be able to return? Those were days before the
American Association of University Professors had promulgated rules
of tenure. In spite of his long teaching at State, Alonzo had no legal
tenure. No one had. Had he been fired there would have been a scandal at State that no doubt would have had echoes throughout the academic world. But Alonzo knew that to get rid of him Maxie Waxie was
quite ready to face a scandal both at State and outside. Academic scandals do not last very long and they never or very seldom seem to have
any practical consequences one way or the other—except perhaps to
teach the victimizers the need for a little prudence in starting scandals.
Gossip was not effective, and that was about all that a scandal would
add up to.

To his troubles two others were added. In spite of his concern for
the war, there was nothing he could do toward it except buy war bonds
—and save tin cans. And when he pondered the fall of France, he
began to realize that in his own way, and to his own measure, he had
a share in the responsibility for the catastrophe. For the fall of France
had been accomplished by the German armies in a very short time.
This fact had to be accounted for; it had not just happened. And as
Alonzo thought about it he had to face the ugly fact that the triumph
of Germany was not solely the result of the stupidity of the Allied
generals. They could not have been more stupid than they were. They
had been warned. An English writer had written on the subject of tanks

and Colonel Charles de Gaulle had written *Vers l'armée de métier*, a book closely read by Guderian. But in addition to the stupidity of the Generals another factor in the catastrophe was the demoralizing propaganda of the Left, to which, in his way, Alonzo had contributed to his full powers. Because English and French and American liberals had not wanted war they had decided that there would be no war, and they resisted preparation and denigrated the military and talked themselves into believing that the butchery that threatened could be averted. The term *men of goodwill* came into currency and of course the liberals claimed the title for themselves. The systematic ostriches who did not want to see the danger and tucked their heads deeply into the sands of their delusions, these were the men of goodwill. And they were responsible for the defeat. No, not they but we, since Alonzo had been one of them. Honesty compelled him to face his guilt. Fortunately his own share of the guilt had been relatively small. Or was it? He had had strong influence on his students. He had to face it. If you hated fascism, to make yourself weak before the fascists was treason to your cause. When Alonzo looked at the European defeat in this light he had to acknowledge that the clever propaganda he had been engaged in as a teacher had constituted a form of treason against the civilization for which he had pretended he stood. Treason—although luckily for him it was not a crime for which he could be brought before the bar of justice.

True, there had been many other factors contributing to the demoralization of France and the lack of preparation of England: The reaction to the butchery of the war of 1914, a thoroughly understandable yearning for peace, the bitter class conflict and the alignment of the liberal forces with the Marxists, the malfunctioning of the machinery of government, the basic moral corruption of the individuals that made up the Western democracies—one could not enumerate all the factors that contributed to the defeat. But the successful campaign of destruction carried on by his friends and himself at home was undeniable. It had been carried on by his personally unknown friends beyond the ocean, everywhere they could reach with their propaganda. This relentless work was not the product of impersonal forces; it was the result of rational deliberation and conscious effort. A group of individuals in harmony with one another had worked toward ends clearly in mind. Alonzo turned back again and again to the question of responsibility. He could not get it off his mind. Those were responsible who had spread the corruption at home and aided those who had spread it else-where. Their activity had been international. It had not reached Russia, it had been extirpated in Germany by Hitler and perhaps in Italy by Mussolini; but it affected men elsewhere wherever intellectuals existed. It affected men differently in one nation and affected the different nations differently, but in the end these differences did not much matter. The effect was the destruction of the values that sustained a people as a nation. And Alonzo had been engaged in this work of destruction.

2

As he thought of his responsibility for the disaster that faced the democratic world he remembered vividly a conversation he had had with Karl Heinrich under a lamppost in Frankfort on the Main late one night. They talked in German, French, and English, trying to express themselves if not in one language then in the others; but they managed to communicate pretty clearly. Karl Heinrich maintained that the Communists wanted the Nazis to come to power, for in less than six months they themselves would oust Hitler. Well, the Nazis had come to power and now they were the masters of Europe, they were threatening England, and the United States was at war. And he, Alonzo, had wittingly collaborated with Karl Heinrich's party.

He had no excuses. He was a member of a movement, a soldier of an army; he had not been press-ganged into it; he had not been drafted; he had volunteered. It was an international army whose operations took place not merely at home but in France, England, and in the rest of the democratic world; and its operations had been successful all along the line, on every front where the battles had been waged. He had known what he was doing when he cooperated with the Left; he could not excuse himself.

Of course liberals, when you told them they were responsible for the defeat of France, denied the charge, or laughed, or were simply bewildered: They were not wreckers they insisted; they were trying to prevent the destruction of the world by the Communists to whom they were opposed—or so they said, when pressed. And didn't Alonzo even now acknowledge that the world needed reform? Or had he changed his mind and did he now deny that it was imperfect? But here lay the trouble; for improvement consisted in trying to do away with evil by putting as much of perfection in its place as possible.

What was evil? Evil was superstition, ignorance, irrationality, deceit, oppression, exploitation; evil was repressive morality, authority, rules, law; evil was force, privilege, patriotism, tradition; evil was property, business; evil was the courts; evil was the military and warfare; evil was the institutions that maintained the disorder and iniquity of society; evil defined our social ethos and evil was the operative values of our society. When you got down to it, evil was nearly every thing that existed with the exception of the men of goodwill who knew what evil was and never saw evil in themselves.

What was good? Ah, when you came down to it there was very little that was good. Good was the ideal of a just society free from iniquity and oppression, and good was the blueprint that would help bring that society about. The blueprint—what blueprint? There was no blueprint; all there was was a pile of abstractions, vague notions of reform, shadowy ideals that had never been realized before and were not likely to be realized now or ever; dreams of reform inspired not by soberly considered potentialities but by rationalistic ideals forged out of frustration and resentment of a purely subjective nature that grew rank in a soil of rejection of what was. Blueprint indeed!

There was, of course, nothing wrong with wanting to reform the world; indeed there would have been something very wrong with not seeing the need for improving it, for doing away with its glaring defects, with the injustice, dishonesty, lies, oppression, and unnecessary repression that was to be found in our society. One could not, therefore, object to the liberal's intentions. The evil around one was obvious enough and Alonzo had not changed his mind about that. What had happened then? Hard as it was, he had to acknowledge to himself that until then he had emphasized the evil and had not looked at the good that actually abounded around him, that he had seen nothing but evil, and had deluded himself that in place of the evil, perfection or something close to it could be placed; it was hard to acknowledge that evil cannot be done away with, all one can do is replace one evil known for something that looked like a good that would either turn out to be an evil or bring its new kind of evil with it.

No, there was nothing wrong with wanting to make the world a better place to live in; but Alonzo's former condemnation, he could see now, was not acceptable because it had rejected what was, had not reckoned soberly with what was possible, and was not firmly grounded on what was desirable for men. Furthermore it had not considered that in bringing down working arrangements much that was of indispensable value would be done away with irreparably; the condemnation was wrong because it assumed that a new society could be created from scratch; it was wrong because it judged the existing world by a criterion of perfection that had not been drawn from reality; and one that could not be realized since all it was was a heap of hopes stiffened with faith.

Moreover, the liberal had faith in men who had all too much faith in themselves; these reformers were egregiously self-confident and their self-confidence pointed to an unlimited self-righteousness. True, they were well-mannered, charming and adroit, well brought up, they knew how to conceal their self-righteousness; but this quality came out sooner or later when you heard them disapprove of the existing order. When it came out you saw that under the critical attitude there was not only a desire for a better world—this was there, truly—but a deep resentment, a generalized animus against the existing order and a blank condemnation of the honesty of those who were not of their way of thinking.

To these faults was added another. They thought they understood how society worked and they just did not have any such understanding. In fact no one possessed genuine knowledge, extensive and deep enough, about how society works. If there were such knowledge, political theorists, economists, and sociologists wouldn't be at odds among themselves. To destroy the existing society, therefore, a society that worked, admittedly worked badly but worked somehow, in order to replace it with one dreamed out of hope and faith and resentment and a generalized goodwill was, objectively speaking, criminal, was criminally irresponsible.

The enormity of the crime became clear when you considered the cost of destroying the existing society. Alonzo thought of what the revolution had cost in Russia—the lives it had destroyed, the misery it had brought about, the destitution, the bleakness, the shabbiness that had been put in place of the old Russia and the new currents of hatred that had been added to the old currents; the arrogance and brutality of the new rulers, the lack of grace, their intransigence, their cruelty, their lack of generosity, the violent lust for power of the new masters—and he was now able to look with fresh eyes on those who until now he had thought of as his friends, in whose work he had co-operated. They were wrong. He had been wrong. Fortunately he had not done as much harm as some of his friends, although it would not do to minimize his influence on his students.

Able now to see after the fall of France his former convictions in a different light, he was appalled to realize what a credulous goose he had been. The Communists wanted quite frankly to destroy society. And after that? The dictatorship of the workers which was in fact the dictatorship of a minority. And after that? After that, utopia. The means of bringing utopia about, the classless state, had been used by Lenin and his men in Russia: blood and terror.

Liberalism, then, was responsible for the fall of France; it had its share in bringing about the Nazi onslaught. And the conclusion applied with perfect congruity to Alonzo. There was no avoiding the conclusion; insofar as he had been a soldier in the army of liberalism he too was responsible for the triumph of Hitler and the fall of France. Indirectly, of course, but responsible just the same.

3

The conclusion was not at all pleasant. To condemn himself as he now saw that he had to do was close to committing spiritual suicide, for it involved the examination of all of his convictions and the discarding of many of his hitherto sustaining values. But convictions and values are not things one throws away like cigarette butts; one's attachment to them is essential to their being one's values and to being oneself. But the difficulty presented one aspect that was the very opposite of unpleasant. He had been in error and he could now correct that error. Something to be welcomed. But how did one go about examining one's convictions and values to decide which were still valid and which not?

In general terms, this was not a difficult question to answer. One constructed a comprehensive philosophy, including a theory of value, a philosophy that gave an adequate nonreductive account of the whole and of its major parts; that was the only way to keep chaos at bay. The discovery of his errors had been the first step towards the acquisition of an acceptable philosophy. Alonzo had reared one once and he could do it again; he would borrow tools as he had done before, he would steal materials from the yard when the guards were not looking, he would hunt around in the shops and buy, steal, and borrow whatever he might need.

The most urgent part of the job for Alonzo was the development of a moral philosophy that avoided the radical defect of naturalistic value theory. The fundamental defect was its ineradicable subjectivism. Naturalists had tried to avoid it by introducing all sorts of considerations, like long-range knowledge of consequences, the distinction between the desired and the desirable, and other relevant factors. But in the end the subjectivism of naturalistic value theory could not be avoided. Naturalism conceived value as a quality or property of the individual who did the valuing, when in fact the relationship was the other way around. One does not possess one's values as one possesses one's toothbrush. One's values possess one; and they do so by virtue of something which to the naturalist was profoundly objectionable: They possess one by virtue of their requiredness. If value is the product of interest, in the last analysis the good is what a person wants. Make the account as complex as you need to because it is indeed not at all simple, it finally comes down to the fact that for the naturalist the good was what he truly wanted. In short, he made his values.

A way had to be found if this defect was to be avoided. Subjectivism had to be rooted out of value theory. If it was, there was a possibility that a way could be found to indicate how, in theory, radical moral conflicts could be resolved morally. This would be the answer to Thrasymachus and his tribe.

Alonzo was aware that he was asking a genuine question; and this meant that the answer to it might be that the nature of the world and of man were such that all that the term *right* meant, in the last analysis, was the claim of the strong to impose their will on the weak. Why not? The Athenians' speech to the inhabitants of the island of Melos might be right; Thrasymachus, the mad German, Nietzsche, McGilvary, and Charner Perry might be right. Why not? Morality might be no more than a clever camouflage that worked on the weak but which did not fool the strong; certainly at the international level it was obvious to anyone who cared to look at the facts that that was all that morality seemed to be; and anyone who was honestly outraged at a statement that a treaty was nothing but a piece of paper was a simpleton, an ostrich, a man who had not read history or had not digested the history he had read. To assert that this was the case would be called cynicism by simpletons who insisted in spite of the evidence that things were as they ought to be. Let the simpletons call it what they would; they would be right if they could point out that nations as a rule behaved with honor and honesty toward one another, suppressing their interests in favor of their pledges or the rights of others.

Alonzo did not forget that he had to face the possibility that for all the unseemly kerfuffle about right and justice and the conscience that the preachers and the philosophers had been making for at least three millennia, all there might be to morality was what the social Darwinians had once seriously said it was, nothing but the phony claims of the weak on the strong—claims that occasionally worked.

But before you accepted this appalling conclusion you had to make certain that it was irrefragable. One serious indictment one could bring up against naturalists—an *ad hominem*, but in view of their claims, not an irrelevant one—was that they had accepted a view of value the entailments of which they had not considered and accepted it because it followed from a view of the universe that they had accepted without qualification. Naturalists, as a group disdainful of a priorism and insisting they were empiricists, on questions of moral philosophy departed from an a priori basis—a priori to their moral philosophizing, namely the notion of a value-free universe they imported from classical physics.

XVII

The Moral Life
and the Ethical Life

1

ALONZO was now confronted with a technical problem, namely to show that the notion of a value-free universe, which was the basis of naturalistic moral philosophy, could be repudiated. How could that be done? The naturalist's view of the universe rested on the fundamental assumption of the primacy of science, in the narrow anglo-American sense of the term *science*. But not of the primacy of the science of today, but of classical mechanics. One could put one's finger on the very moment in the early history of physics when the assumption had been uncritically reintroduced into the modern world from sources that were originally Greek; it had happened when Galileo had defined *body* in terms of what later came to be called *primary qualities*, relegating what came to be called *secondary qualities* to the mind. Galileo had not worked out the theory; he had merely stated that he could conceive of body without color or odor or taste or any of the other secondary qualities but that he could not conceive it without length or breadth or depth, without mass and a position in time and space and whatever other primary qualities could be brought to his attention.

Descartes had completed the story: Physical body, material substance, is what mechanics define it to be; but there is also mind, a substance in which secondary qualities reside. Materialists held that there was nothing but physical body. The history of philosophy since Descartes had been generated in part by the disagreements regarding the question of the relation of mind to matter—not altogether, but to a large extent. Naturalists accepted the view that the real world was a stripped body, if not stripped of secondary qualities which some believed to reside in objects and not in the mind of their beholders, stripped of values, which Santayana had termed *tertiary qualities*.

That the consequences of this bold reduction did not present themselves immediately as absurd is the story of the folly of the lovers of wisdom, and their ability to pursue a chain of argument from false premises that commend themselves as valid. The lovers of wisdom, the philosophers, carried on their quarrels, and occasionally one of them arose and pushed them farther than those who did not altogether abandon their common sense cared to go. Such a man was Berkeley. But common sense, embodied in the foot of Samuel Johnson, asserted itself by a resounding kick at a stone—a kick whose echo had since then deservedly resounded through the halls of the learned, to the joy of intellectual Philistines.

For any number of reasons it was not difficult to accept the view that the natural world was a world of material substance and primary qualities. One was the success of science as compared with the perennial frustration of philosophical activity. The other was a kind of lingering Pythagorean faith—the faith that had glowed brightly in the minds of the early scientists—to the effect that geometry was the alphabet of God. Read numbers for geometry and you see what lies at the bottom of the naturalist's faith that the universe is value free.

But there is another reason: Galileo could think of body as devoid of secondary qualities because secondary qualities were irrelevant to his purpose. This is to say that his definition of body was functional—as indeed all definitions are. But this fact was not noticed. The lead ball that Galileo rolled down the inclined plane in order to measure its acceleration could be of any color, odor, or taste; this only meant that secondary qualities are irrelevant to the laws of motion. However, the body of the physicist, the lead ball that rolled down the inclined plane was the same as the ball that he could have used, had his fingers been strong enough, to play marbles with. Otherwise stated, Galileo had no need to distinguish the bodies of physics from physical bodies—the balls as objects of investigation from the balls that might be used to play marbles with; the lamp he observed swinging in the church was the pendulum, although many of the features of the lamp were of no relevance, since all he was interested in was the regularity of the swing.

It was not until much later that the bodies of physics and physical bodies had to be distinguished; the bodies of physics now were atoms and electrons, and these were physical bodies, if indeed they were bodies, but could not be handled as marbles and lamps had been handled; they could not even be seen; they had to be inferred. How much of the processes that produced their laws was a directly observed matter, how much was matter of perception, how much construction, was a question on which philosophers of science disagreed, as far as Alonzo could discover. That the objects of physics were different from physical objects—that atoms and electrons were different from marbles and lamps—was the reason Eddington, when he sat at his table, had before him two tables, one on which he did his writing and leaned his elbow and the other a swarm of electrons whose whirls he knew something about.

Galileo's confusion of physical body with the body of physics was thus perfectly natural; but it concealed the fact that in defining *body*, he had not qualified his definition. He or his followers had thus given the body of physics primacy in reality. He had not merely defined the objects in which he was interested, but those who had followed him had philosophized about them, and the mess they left is the history of modern philosophy, a mess that has troubled our intellectual nostrils until this very day. It was the con-fusion that had led Galileo to assert with full confidence that secondary qualities and *a fortiori* the values that were later to be called tertiary did not belong to body. They did not —but to which body? The universe might be value free, but value free for the scientist for whom values, when in the passage of time he came to notice them in the social sciences, were or at least were not supposed to be any more or less factual than the qualities measured by the physicist.

There was another way of putting the matter: One could say that the world of the scientist, the world from which he drew his laws and to which they applied and the world in which we live, were not identical; the former was a stripped world, it was only part of the world. The stripped world, whenever possible, was expressed in differential equations; this was the scientists' "nature," and it was something as regards which scientists, philosophers of science, and anyone else who was competent to take part in the discussion, differed greatly, some assuming that the scientist's "nature" was what science discovered it to be, while others argued that into the picture of nature entered, to some extent, the scientist's own creativeness. If the scientist said that his nature was the whole of reality one could answer, "Yes, for you, as scientist, it no doubt is; but not for me, who has different interests."

There was still another way of putting the matter: One could say that the world of science rested on metaphysical foundations which were not themselves the product of scientific inquiry. Why had not Alonzo seen this earlier? He had read E. A. Burtt's *The Metaphysical Foundations of Modern Physical Science* shortly after its publication some time before going to State. It was all in Burtt's book. But when he read Burtt, it had not taught him what it had to teach. Like a time bomb, it had lain in his mind, and it was only now that it had exploded—blowing to pieces the metaphysical foundations of his scientistic naturalism. He could now consider seriously the possibility that the universe was not value free as the naturalists had confidently held it to be. He could now entertain the idea that somehow or other, in a way that he had yet to discover, value had some sort of status in being independent of the interests, scientific or any other, of men.

This did not mean that the world was what Samuel Johnson took it to be. You could not disprove Berkeley by kicking a stone; "common sense," as it is referred to in the schools, is a tangle of problems. But it did mean that the naturalist's view that the universe was value free was not the irrefragable proposition that naturalists took it to be.

The distinction between the two worlds did not settle the question about which of these two worlds was more real than the other, or whether another world, a third, might be more real than these two. How could this question be answered? One could assume that there had to be one reality that was the most real; on this assumption the question could not be answered; or one could say, what we call "most real" is most real by virtue of a definition which was stipulative and of interests that were not chosen by the process by which the question itself was answered: There was no way, if we judge by the failure of philosophers to settle the matter, to choose between the pictures of the world of the scientists and of common sense; for the scientists the real world was the world to which their equations and constructions pointed; for common sense, the world in which we live; the assignation of superior reality depended on who made the assignation and in terms of what interests the assignation was made. But one thing was clear, and that was that the basic assumption of naturalists to the effect that the universe was value free was not a self-evident truth, but a metaphysical assumption that could be challenged.

2

Alonzo was now able to examine the problem of moral philosophy with a chance of success. If for him the fundamental task was to show, in general terms, how radical conflicts and perplexities could be resolved morally, naturalism with its value-free picture of the world could not do it. But belief in a value-free world, widely accepted as it might be, he now saw, was not infrangible; it was only infrangible for those who accepted as a base for their picture of the world Galileo's definition of real body. To accept this definition as basic was to assign primacy to the conditions for knowledge drawn not even from physics as known today, but from a narrow area of it, from classical mechanics.

Had this primacy been proved? No, it had been taken for granted. But why should the conditions for knowledge, even for a search for knowledge wider than that yielded by classical mechanics, be given primacy over the conditions for any other mode of human experience? It was not difficult to understand why men whose vocation was the pursuit of knowledge should assume that no activity could be properly carried on unless it subordinated itself to its exigencies. Surely the moral actor qua moral actor, making decisions in a world in rapid flux that confronts him with what are, or seem to be, utterly novel situations, cannot dispense with knowledge, and much less can the moral philosopher; but the moral man's activity has to satisfy conditions which, although they have to be cognitively acceptable, arise from within moral experience itself. Moral philosophy, examining its own data and using categories quite different from those of physics, surely could be assumed to have some sort of relative autonomy.

To assume the primacy of science was to prejudge a problem that was outside the jurisdiction of the philosophy of science, it was to deny in an a priori way, the autonomy of the various modalities of experience—whatever that autonomy inquiry might find it was. Alonzo had already begun to see that the modalities of human experience were distinct, even if they could not be separated, and had relative autonomies. The movement of the unity of science, in whose platform he had once believed, simply annexed, without proved justification, all human activity of whatever kind and declared scientific method to be the sole judge of any knowledge arising from the examination of any kind of activity.

What were the conditions of morality, given its central task as conceived by Alonzo? The first was to posit an alternative to a picture of the universe as value free; this alternative called for a universe in which value had status in being independent of human wills or interests or desires, to which men could subjugate themselves freely as in fact they did when they tried to act morally; it called for a picture of the world in which, as Alonzo thought of it, values had "ontic status." It is to ontic value or to the values that one takes to have ontic status, that one appeals when one seeks justice or tries to decide on the rightness or goodness of an act or on the holiness of a man or the beauty of a lyric. The moral man does not say, "My judgment about this action is right because it satisfies my desires, or because it harmonizes with my interests in some way or other." He sometimes has to say, "My judgment is right, although, alas, it commands me to go counter to my wishes, although it violates my will. It destroys my plans and wrecks my happiness; but if my intention to act morally is serious, I have to obey my judgment."

This goes also for the group to which he belongs. Social objectivity, which naturalism could provide, is not sufficient, since one could always challenge the validity of an operative social arrangement; what a valid judgment rests on is the discernment of the kind of objectivity which is not open to willful tampering either by an individual or a group. Such values are probably only discerned by men or by other beings—if there are any such—that have the equivalent of human faculties.

Of course the notion of ontic value brought with it a number of problems and Alonzo had to decide whether their solutions were not as faulty as those that were inherent in the various naturalistic notions of value with which he was acquainted. One problem is that value is discovered, but the tendency of men is to assume that one could apprehend it apodictically; the practical result of such belief is absolutism. Value is discovered, but in and through experience, and our perception of it remains as problematic, when discovered, its existence as hypothetical, as any object of experience.

This was one reason—but only one—moral experience was a search, a continuous process, instinct with the possibility of error. And this in turn was the reason that the confidence one could place in one's judgment of value was not like the confidence one could put on one's knowledge of the Pythagorean theorem. Although value has ontic status, our apprehension of it is conditioned by our frailties, it is reached within the context of prejudices that, in principle at least, could be examined thoroughly; our apprehension of it is corrupted by our interests and passions; we cannot get a clean picture of it because we get it with dirty tools.

It follows that we can only claim validity for our value judgments with the kind of hesitating confidence in human reason that Plato attributed to Socrates' belief in immortality. And this is the reason that the intolerance of the believer in absolute values, who usually believes that the values he apprehends are the true ones and who assumes that those who disagree with him are wrong, is not only wrong but abominably ugly. The absolutist's moral responses are not truly moral, they are the product of willful egoism and his incapacity to subjugate his passion to the requiredness of objective value.

But ontic objectivity is not the only condition of morality. There are other conditions and in order to find them one has to turn to a careful examination of the way a moral man goes about seeking the moral resolution of a practical perplexity. The logic of moral action and of the judgment it elicits must arise from moral experience, and not the other way around, as some thinkers, even though they consider themselves empiricists, seem to assume, if we judge by the way they go about philosophizing about morality.

One methodological problem that fortunately did not bedevil Alonzo at the outset—as it had bedeviled him when he had tried to give an account of the aesthetic transaction—was that of choosing among the many varieties of moral experience in order to define what constituted a moral act and not something else, and analyze the logic of the moral judgment. In aesthetics writers usually assume without examination that the way they respond to aesthetic objects is the proper way to respond, but since there are a large variety of responses to objects taken to be aesthetic—in the sense in which William James wrote of the varieties of religious experience—and since to accept them all as legitimately aesthetic is to remain in a chaotic relativism, it was necessary to decide which was the properly or legitimately aesthetic.

It was the failure to make this decision that led writers to believe they were discussing the same problems when they were not. This was no less true of moral philosophy: What was called a moral act or judgment by one thinker differed widely from what other thinkers called moral acts and judgments. If you took the objective of moral conduct to be to arrive at happiness, either for the individual or the group, you could not communicate with Kant unless you showed that Kant's radical distrust of happiness was in error.

Fortunately Alonzo did not have to face this complex methodological problem because he began explicitly with an objective: He sought the conditions that had to be met to arrive at a moral resolution of a practical perplexity or conflict. Moral philosophy is not exhausted by this inquiry as the many types of moral philosophy one finds show. He could legitimately restrict his own interest to his problem, so long as he kept in mind clearly the limitations of his approach and of its possible results.

One condition was recognized to apply to morality by all moral philosophers irrespective of the objective they posited as the end of moral action. To judge morally one had to place all claims, those made against oneself as well as one's own, on the same plane, giving each and every one a chance to be heard, not prejudging one over the others, and always keeping an eye on the cloud of prejudice in his own favor. This was very difficult to do in practice, since one is not always aware of the way in which prejudices lead to the misinterpretation of claims against oneself. It was furthermore incapacitating, if life was struggle, if it was the sort of thing one finds politics or competitive commerce or war to be, if it was what William James took it to be in his review of Herbert Spencer's work on ethics, in which James glorified the struggle and came close to proclaiming that the moral life was the Darwinian warfare for survival. But although in practice it was difficult, it is not impossible, and it is sometimes actually accomplished by men.

Another condition generally recognized by thinkers was the universal validity of the maxim that rules the judgment. The maxim or criterion or standard that leads to a specific judgment is not a privilege of the situation or the man who judges but is applicable to similar situations or conflicts or perplexities. If it is wrong to steal under certain circumstances it is always wrong under similar circumstances— not absolutely, since circumstances may subtly but substantially alter the case. But when a person is hungry, has made the effort to obtain food honestly, and has utterly failed to do so, is it wrong to steal a loaf of bread?

3

These two conditions were generally known—in theory at least—by thinkers. But how did one arrive at a moral decision, when confronted with a radical perplexity or when confronted with a conflict the moral resolution of which one feared would destroy one's plans or mode of living or the possibilities of one's own happiness? The answer is that the aim of moral activity is the resolution of a perplexity within a moral scheme that has been accepted prior to the need to resolve any problems; this is what is meant when it is said that one seeks to resolve a conflict or perplexity morally.

This seems obvious and would not have to be made explicit were it not for the fact that Deweyians sometimes gave the impression that problematic situations could be resolved without reference to a context that was in being before the problem arose and was operative and had authority to which the problematic situation was referred. The Deweyian abhorrence of rules, his distrust of customary ways of doing things, his orientation towards the future, made him often overlook the context in which decisions are made, made him inimical to habit and to fully formed character; he had little use for tradition, which he assumed to be a restrictive Nessus shirt. This was true, at least, for some Deweyians Alonzo was acquainted with.

A moral scheme is a constellation of values, which is to say of qualities that are taken to be values because they are endowed with a requiredness, although not necessarily a requiredness upon us, that elicits from us the obligation to maintain them in being or to bring them into being. The constellation is arranged in an order of rank; at its core there are a number of values Alonzo called espoused, because they are the object of special loyalty and devotion and because the moral man who espouses them feels, and rightly, that their impairment constitutes a threat to the whole scheme.

Sometimes these espoused values are tyrannical and restrict living, forbidding and excluding, ordering life rigorously and narrowly. One thinks of the early New England Puritans or of Pulcheria, the older sister of Theodosius II of the Eastern Empire, who was regent during her younger brother's childhood in the early decades of the fifth century. At an early age she pledged herself to virginity and induced two younger sisters to do the same. Incidentally she was not loath to proclaim her superiority over her fellow beings and her pledge led her to claim and obtain considerable prestige and power.

Besides the espoused values there are those we merely recognize as values, to whose requiredness we do not respond. Taken together Alonzo thought of them as the acknowledged values. The two do not divide into separable classes, nor are our values fully formed or crystallized. Pulcheria married sometime after her brother had come of age, but whether she lost her precious maidenhead Alonzo could not remember. This is to say that the requiredness of value is not exercised upon us with a constant strength. The pattern of our values is subject to changes; their order of rank shifts; their urgency varies according to circumstances; the conformation of the pattern varies like Pulcheria's, although she seems to have been the victim of a tyrannous will to hang on to what she thought was good at the cost of what ordinary people think worthwhile.

Within the world of moral actors we must distinguish two polar or extreme types: the fanatic and absolutist on the one hand and on the other the man whom we believe to be amoral. The values of the absolutist and fanatic are frozen, unyielding, sustained by obdurate will, and make him a domineering person, often a bully, for he not only guards zealously the pattern of values he espouses but, convinced they are the only true values, he attempts to make others espouse them—for their own good. The existence of other values espoused honestly by other men he finds difficult to believe: They are in error and constitute a threat to him. He fears tolerance, generosity, diversity; and rightly so, from his standpoint, since these qualities reveal to him other schemes and cast doubt on the belief in the exclusive validity of his own scheme. Hence he is incapable of turning his mind irenically on a conflict to examine it objectively. When a conflict arises he already has the answer: He is right and the other party is in error and as a body of religious believers used to say—and for all Alonzo knew, some of them may still be saying under their breath—error has no rights.

The other extreme type does not exist but is only a notion of the imagination, for there are no completely amoral men; by amoral men we usually mean men whose morality—whose values—we are not able to acknowledge. But Alonzo had found out a great deal about amorality from Maxie Waxie. Maxie was not merely a pragmatist from theory but one, so to speak, from instinct. He hated principles, ridiculed the decalogue, was absolutely horrified by the word *absolute*, and thought of William James as he thought of Dewey, as men who, in their moral theories, took each case on its own merits. But how can you take a case on its merits if you do not believe that there are principles that make one case more meritorious than another.?

Before Alonzo became well acquainted with Maxie Waxie he had thought of him as a genuinely tolerant person. Alonzo was then under the delusion that *liberalism* and *tolerance* are almost congruous terms. He subsequently decided that Maxie was an utterly amoral person. Again he was wrong. On a better acquaintance Alonzo discovered that under the liar, the dishonest man, the envious and resentful man embodying the qualities Nietzsche had attributed to the slave, under the constant claim to be humane and be concerned with equity and social justice, there was an ill-concealed racist who was, nevertheless, a rigorously principled man, one of the most rigorously principled men Alonzo had ever encountered. Maxie Waxie's morality was as simple as it was elegant: The one moral principle he espoused and espoused with a fierce devotion that almost went beyond belief, was that Maxie Waxie and what he wanted came first; what he wanted was good and right, and the many things he despised were beyond contempt.

What Alonzo learned from Maxie Waxie of relevance to moral theory was that one possible polar opposite of the fanatic and the absolutist was not a man without principles but a man who did not take seriously the principles and criteria that are generally accepted, since acting on them constrained or inhibited his willfulness. Of course, an amoral man may also be one who, morally speaking, travels lightly, who disregards the moral patterns that others try to live by, who ignores honesty and truthfulness and reliability and decency or does not take these and the other generally recognized values of our society seriously. But what was important, as Alonzo thought, was to recognize that while there were monstrously fanatical men and rigid absolutists, a man without some values, however loose, however fluid, however lightly acknowledged, did not exist.

In general, men are concerned with the maintenance of values; they are much more concerned, of course, with those they espouse than with those they merely recognize; but they are concerned for the values they acknowledge, concerned for their maintenance. Alonzo thought of a trivial example. A little boy likes to go along the road decapitating wild flowers with a stick; but a mature man cannot accept the boy's actions as desirable, although the boy is not doing great harm. To the extent we value anything we wish to see it prosper or, at the very least, remain in existence.

It is not difficult to see, therefore, how we go about resolving a practical perplexity or conflict. We seek to solve it in such a way that, preferably, we strengthen our value scheme, but if this is impossible we try to maintain it unimpaired, and at the very least we cause it the least damage possible. When we act morally we weigh alternative courses of action to see which is more congruous with our scheme or in harmony with it and which threatens its destruction. The right action is·that which fits—which fits a scheme already operative and for whose maintenance we are concerned.

The conscience is our awareness of our values exercising requiredness upon us. But the values for which we are concerned, while they are our values, are not ours in the sense that we can do with them what we wish or desire: They have requiredness, they have authority; indeed it is more exact to say that we are theirs, when we truly espouse them. And thus we have the rather common case of the overanxious conscience, a conscience that is a slave even to trivial values that are not worth the sacrifice in happiness they demand for their maintenance.

Alonzo did not believe that the moral life was a matter for the individual and solely for him. Societies had a great deal to do with the shaping of the individual and the maintenance of values; they seem to make it impossible for the individual to act in ways contrary to its mores or accepted code of conduct. They seek to close out genuinely problematic situations. But no social group is to be found that is as rigidly custom bound as Dewey and Tufts had taken early man to be in the first edition of their *Ethics*. Malinowski had shown that the savages he had studied in *Crime and Custom in Savage Society* were not custom bound, although custom might have greater force among them than it would have among us.

This holds for all societies. While societies establish regulations commanding and forbidding actions, they usually allow areas of discretionary activity in which the individual is free to act without externally dictated commands and without praise or blame. And of course no society could possibly undertake to rule the life of its members in every sphere of activity—not even the city sketched in Plato's *Laws*.

Societies are more or less closed, more or less open, and no society reaches either extreme even in the most successfully rigid dictatorship or the greatest chaos.

But while a society is never hermetically closed or totally open, the resolution of a radical perplexity is always novel for the individual confronted by one, however run-of-the-mill such a perplexity may be for other members of his society. A man's knowledge of the ways of his world may incline him one way or another when he makes a decision to act, but the inwardness of the perplexity has its own immediately felt character, its own specific feel which give it its novelty and must be encountered directly and cannot, so to speak, be communicated by another man. Fiction gives one a feel of the quality of life lived by imaginary characters and an almost immediate sense of the grounds on which decisions are made and acts performed; but there is no substitute for direct, immediate, private experience of a perplexity; and one who has not ever been confronted by a radical perplexity will not learn from others what it is like to arrive at a decision, or more precisely what he is in for when he is confronted by a radical choice.

When a perplexity arises, the resolution achieved is moral when the values involved in the conflict are, as stated, preferably strengthened or at least not destroyed by the decision. To the extent that values are sacrificed the decision is morally unsatisfactory; but some destruction or at least modification of one's value scheme is inevitable, since that scheme can never be perfect and therefore beyond the reach of an outside claim.

In the sketch so far presented it is still possible that no resolution of a radical conflict can be reached, since the demands made by the parties in conflict, each of the other, may threaten the total destruction of the scheme of espoused values one is seeking to preserve. So far then the sketch does not provide a means of avoiding the warfare of moral ideals of which McGilvary used to speak. Is it possible to avoid such a conflict? Rarely, but sometimes, and only when each of the conflicting parties posits at the very heart of the scheme of espoused values the value of the personality of the other. When one espouses the value of the personality of one's claimant and gives that value primacy without qualification, all adjustments called upon by the conflict must be achieved without threat to the value of the person of the other.

This view called for the distinction Alonzo made between what he arbitrarily called the moral life and the ethical life. The latter is ruled not by loyalty to one's values but by loyalty to one's values when they recognize the primacy of the person. Is this too ideal? Is it quixotic? It is, almost always, but not always, for in their intercourse with one another men occasionally respect the claims of others—certainly rare as a mode of group action and never between nations or such aggregates. But occasionally among individuals.

The espousal of the primacy of the other person in conflict that is at the heart of the ethical life, Alonzo recognized, was no discovery or invention of his; it was merely the formulation in his own terms of Kant's Kingdom of Ends, which was in turn a formulation in his terms of the heart of Christian ethics.

But why should you respect the person of the other when he is making claims on you that threaten your values? Why should you give the value of his person primacy above all your values and consider it inviolable? Because he is a person. To be a person is to be a psyche that exercises a congenital capacity to espouse values throughout the whole of his conscious life. This capacity endows each person with a higher value than any of the values any one espouses and he ought to espouse it in preference to all other values. Thus the term *person* is not a psychological category, it is an axiological category; there is nothing like it anywhere in the animal kingdom, for while other animals than man may be endowed with the capacities and powers of man, more or less —may be capable of some abstract thought and the kind of problem solving we involve ourselves in—no other animal seems to be able to espouse values; *seems*, because on matters of this sort that is all we can claim.

I reminded Alonzo of the objection frequently made to the effect that human beings never act ethically, that they never place above their own values the value of the person of the other. A few words on this point should be added, I said. You know, he replied, that I have insisted that they sometimes do, when they act through love in the fullest sense of the term. But allow for the sake of the argument that they never do. The answer to the objection is that the solution I offer is theoretical, not practical. There is a difference, even in classical mechanics, between the theoretical behavior of physical bodies and the actual behavior of things. Bodies accelerate towards the center of the earth at the rate of 32 feet per second per second. In actuality they obey the law approximately, and then only under strictly controlled conditions. Even if men never acted practically as the theory counsels they do, this is the way they ought to act in order to act ethically. That men seldom do is to be regretted. That they sometimes try and come more or less close to the ideal is not utopian to suggest.

XVIII

Politics or Idiocy?

1

ALONZO had given up his philosophical views because they were inadequate to basic human exigencies and he had seen through the inadequacies of his liberalism. Where did he stand now politically? There was no question in his mind: Liberalism was wrong; not altogether wrong, but wrong enough for Alonzo to feel that he had to give up the label. The views that he had held until recently had been shown up in a few days on the Western Front. A social philosophy—if such a mixture of errors, half or whole truths could be called a love of wisdom about society—that robbed men of the will to defend their civilization could not be espoused wittingly, for any reason, whatever the cost of repudiating it might be.

The erosion of values that his liberal doctrines had brought about had done in France what he and his friends had done in the United States. He had to leave these people. But didn't that mean moving to the Right? The thought was deeply repugnant, brutally shocking. And yet it was the only choice, for the other choice, that of remaining apolitical, was not to be entertained; while sane, one could not decide to become "a man who made his own"; this would be to turn from a Greek idiot, from an apolitical animal, to a modern one, a man devoid of intelligence. There was no choice; one had to move—but to the Right? How was that possible?

But why was it impossible? There were two reasons. One was that the goals of the liberals and the socialists were not altogether wrong. The desire to build a better world was beyond reproach; it could not be repudiated. Evil that was remediable ought to be remedied. Nothing that Alonzo had come across after the traumatic realization that his philosophy and his political beliefs were a pack of errors had in any way put into question the validity of the goals of liberals and socialists: Evil had to be controlled, somehow, as far as possible. But the qualification, "as far as possible," was essential, for it was utopian to believe, as the Communists professed to believe, that evil could be done away with altogether. This was nonsense and whether the Communists really believed that the dictatorship of the proletariat would finally bring about the classless state, the result of their rule, wherever they had taken power, had been to bring about much worse social and political conditions than those that had existed previously.

No doubt there must be some Communists who honestly want to do away with exploitation. Alonzo could not judge by those with whom he had collaborated because the control they exerted among themselves was rigid and restricted their freedom, but they might not be typical; there might be honest Communists in Russia who believed in freedom and did want to do away with exploitation and liberate the masses. Indeed there were. Some of these people might have survived somehow the dog-eat-dog struggle for power that takes place among them wherever they rule.

An acknowledgment, however, of his differences with his former friends was of no help in answering his question; it did not tell him whether he could or could not move to the Right. Perhaps the strongest reason he could not see himself moving to the Right was his belief that the men of the Right were thugs. This belief he had carried with him for so long and it was so deeply rooted that it was not easy to uproot it. The conviction that the men of the Right were evil, selfish, indifferent to the well-being of their fellowmen, interested solely in themselves and their relatives and friends—this deeply rooted conviction had carried for Alonzo, since his teens, the certainty of an apodictic proposition, and it could not be thrown off as a hat or a shirt. Since beliefs and value espousals made up the core of one's moral constitution, one could not throw off one's beliefs except at the risk of destroying oneself. Alonzo had long known that the men of the Right were evil. That he had known some who were not made no difference to his conviction. It takes a great deal of evidence and profound psychological traumas to destroy one's faith.

2

The disappearance of what seemed to be a genuine dilemma for which he could not find a satisfactory solution came quite suddenly and when it did come it turned out to be utterly obvious. There was no dilemma; Alonzo had been using a false dichotomy: He had been posing the problem as if one had to be either a liberal—with no enemies to the Left, of course—or a Fascist or Nazi. But were all liberals good men and were all men of the Right evil? If the Left was not made up of a flock of angels (or do angels come in exaltations or in nides?) why should the Right be made up of a drove (or perhaps pack) of thugs?

When this utterly obvious truth forced itself on him, he had to acknowledge that on either side he had known good and evil men; on the Left and not only among the Communists, there were to be found men who were as morally ugly, odious, dishonest, unreliable, authoritarian, as one could find on the Right. Enslavers were to be found everywhere. On the other side one could find men who were as honest, kind, generous, decent, concerned for human unhappiness as on the Left. Mr. Sharp, for instance, was a morally admirable man; and the business man who was the husband of a poet whom he had met in the Village, was as thoroughly decent a man as a human being could be. These men were not perfect, but then perfect men existed only in the chiliastic imagination of dreamers.

Utterly obvious as all this was, Alonzo simply had not thought about it. It had to be acknowledged that the quality of a man's character and the quality of his opinions were not to be defined by his professions or by what he called himself. He had really known this obvious fact all along, long before he had run into Maxie Waxie; but this odious man had rammed the lesson down Alonzo's throat. And yet, at crucial points, Alonzo had failed to apply his knowledge that labels often designate something altogether different from the content of the bottle on which they are pasted. This was a truth that Alonzo frequently forgot and had utterly forgotten when he faced the perplexity about what direction to turn to politically. The Manichaean habit of mind was natural to human beings since it made it easy to arrive at judgments that were satisfyingly free from qualifications. It was this habit that made it possible for the Left or the Right to think of itself as having a complete corner on virtue while the other side was altogether vicious and instinct with error.

It was necessary, therefore, to discriminate; it was necessary to analyze the various kinds of people who made up the Right, although analysis and classification of this kind of subject matter were condemned to be rough and essentially inaccurate. It was necessary while proceeding with the analysis to bear constantly in mind that membership in a political party did not commit one, so to speak, to an ontological judgment; one was not a liberal or a man of the Right because one responded to the immutable nature of things; there was nothing immutable about society and its needs; one was not a liberal or a man of the Right forever, under all circumstances, irrespective of external conditions; one's loyalties were aroused by circumstances that were constantly changing; membership in a political party was relative to factors as variable as the weather.

Alonzo kept on reminding himself that he had known this all along, since he had often thought that if he had been living in Boston in 1850 he would have been sympathetic with the abolitionists, as repugnant as he would have found some of these people and their activities to be, and had he been living in Russia in 1915 or 1916 he would have been against the czar, although siding with those who overthrew the monarchy would have led him sooner or later to regret it if he had not been prevented from regretting it by being liquidated by the Bolsheviks, for he would have found Lenin's despotism considerably more objectionable than the corruption, the incompetence, and the absurd absolutistic claims of the monarchy. This held for his attitude to South America: It would have been impossible—or so he hoped—had he been living in Venezuela, even after the death of Gomez, to side with the ruling classes.

There was no reason, therefore, for not calling himself a man of the Right, since by doing so he was not siding with the Nazis or the Fascists, who were not men of the Right, anyhow, but thugs bent on wrecking the world in which they lived; these thugs were no different in their techniques and goals from Communists.

Not easily distinguished from these men there was a type of men whom Alonzo called "dollar conservatives." Alonzo knew some of them. They were conservatives, no doubt, but what they wanted to conserve was their wealth, their privileges, their positions, their advantages, irrespective of the iniquities that that conservation entailed. There is, of course, nothing wrong in itself with wanting to conserve one's wealth, one's privileges, one's position and advantages if they were legitimately come by and if they did not entail the misery of others. What was wrong with the dollar conservatives was the means they were prepared to use to achieve their ends; these people were often to be found on the side of iniquity, oppression, inhumanity, indifference to the undeserved misfortune of others. They did not hesitate to lie to defend institutions that could not be defended in good faith; their objection to socialism was almost solely that it threatened their wealth. They had no objection to a state, however constituted, that would allow them to behave as their robber-baron ancestors had behaved before and for too long after the Civil War. They would gladly return to the time when the pirates in striped trousers, cutaway coats, and high hats, so to speak, had proclaimed their attitude in pithy phrases like "the public be damned."

Alonzo knew some of them. He had once heard the president of a steel company defend the destruction of the North American Indians after the Civil War. They were worse than dirt, these crummy savages, they were nothing. Obviously this man had no sense of the respect a man owes other men, no sense whatever of the intrinsic dignity of man. Only once had Alonzo heard human beings disposed of with the profound contempt expressed by the president of the steel company; in Germany a university girl, speaking of Poles, had dismissed them as swine, with a hatred that seemed to erupt from a source beyond herself. There was only one thing one could say in favor of dollar conservatives, and that was that they did not pretend to be other than what they were, highwaymen in well-tailored suits. This was something that could not be said for liberals, among whom one encountered a large number of fakes.

Another group with which Alonzo would not want to be identified was one that could legitimately be called rightist but was made up of men who were literally reactionary, men who believed that "the clock could be turned back." This was impossible. Such a dream, Alonzo knew, was utter nonsense. It was not possible to return to a previous historical period. Alonzo thought of at least two reasons for the impossibility of reviving a past period. The first was that we know much today that the period to which we would return did not know, and part of what we know is how it changed and what has happened between then and now. Our knowledge has more or less consciously transformed our sensibility and altered our values; and we cannot by an act of conscious will go back to the relative state of nescience of the past.

The second reason was that our understanding of the past and of the present is at best limited and we cannot very well give up a complex condition and go back to another, when we do not fully understand what makes ours what it is and the other what it was. This limits our powers. The rearing of a society cannot be accomplished at will. What can be done at will is to wreck one. The erecting of an utterly new society is not one within the deliberate powers of men.

Alonzo knew that the man who wants to restore the past would argue that he is not interested in the restoration or recreation of the whole of the past; what he wants is to revive an old institution that he considers desirable and that flourished satisfactorily once upon a time. Not the whole of industrial England in the nineteenth century or pre–World War I America, but only a selected aspect of it is what he is interested in reviving. Why should this not be possible? It isn't possible because a society is not a machine whose parts are standardized and replaceable. If the carburetor of a car goes wrong, a new one from the stockroom can be installed, and this is true for any part of it and holds for any machine. This is obvious; what does not seem obvious but should be— at least to conservatives—is that society is not a machine. It is more like an organism than a machine; it is not an organism in a literal sense, but it is more like one than a machine.

A successful transplantation of parts or organs is not any easier for society than for an animal. So far as Alonzo's reading went the experts knew very little about the possibility of borrowing institutions from one culture to another. That diffusion goes on is obviously old hat. But what "laws" control the borrowing? And what happens when an institution is transplanted from one society to another? Japan copied Western ways and in a short time transformed itself from a feudal, preindustrial, society into a hybrid one in which industrialism somehow managed to live with feudalism apparently in a more or less successful way. But Alonzo did not believe that one could generalize from a single instance. He concluded that the reactionary bases his case on hope and he knew that against hope there is no argument.

Another type of conservative with whom Alonzo did not want to identify himself was the standpatter. He is a man who does not want to revive dead institutions; he just does not want any change whatever; he is happy with things as they are; he is used to them and dreads having to face new conditions. All change is painful to him. If men had achieved perfection this attitude would be understandable although impracticable, since living men, men in history, would not be likely to remain perfect for long. But our contemporary world is not perfect and it is not possible to freeze it. There may have been civilizations that were relatively static, although Alonzo was quite clear that what made a civilization like the Egyptian seem to be relatively static was his own ignorance of its history. But whether there had been or not, ours was essentially dynamic, and it would be fatal to freeze it even if it could be done, which of course it could not be. To freeze it we would have to put a moratorium on science and technology and that was not only impossible but it would be fatal, since the Russians wouldn't go along with us in our plans.

We have a wildcat by the tail that we can't let go. We are not likely to win our struggle with technology, but that was no reason for surrendering. We must fight on. Contemporary man—all men now living, except for a few tribes in far-off valleys and deserts—is condemned to endless change. Alonzo did not believe that one could make sociological predictions about the future; as a rule such predictions were silly. But it was fairly clear to him that our civilization is condemned to endless change until we wreck ourselves—or, accidentally, become angels. The reactionary proposes reforms the possible succsss of which is doubtful but is not in principle impossible, since something like a dead institution could be revived. The standpatter, Alonzo was sure, desires a condition of affairs that is clearly impossible.

Alonzo concluded that what was possible and seemed eminently desirable was to retard the furious rate of change in our society and to guide that change more wisely than is done today. Socialists and liberals were for speeding up the change and were slowly wrecking our society. They not only claimed to know what was wrong—we all do, Alonzo realized—they also were quite sure that they knew how to correct it. Many of them seemed to believe in change for the sake of change.

He concluded that there could be no objection to thinking of himself as a man of the Right if what the label stood for was that he was in favor of slowing up the present rate of change and of directing it towards the conservation of our civilization. That the directing of the change was necessary he inclined to believe. He could not quite accept von Mises and Milton Friedman's idea—if that was what they believed —that all contemporary society required was a free market and minimum regulation. Joan Krieger—Murray's superbly intelligent wife—

had once said to Alonzo that all his conservatism added up to was rear-guard action. True. But there were times when that was all one could do and not wreck the joint. Frank Meyer had once told Alonzo that all society needed was internal police and courts to keep crime from flourishing and an army to keep American shores from invasion. This was one of those statements Frank Meyer often made, more to start an argument than to state a position. Some regulation was necessary, but how much and of what kind, Alonzo did not know. Those were not questions he had the competence to answer and he suspected very few men had it and what they had was very exiguous.

3

Alonzo had to acknowledge to himself that he had moved to the Right. But by the label he did not mean that he was in favor of reaction or of standing still. What he was in favor of was slowing up some the change that was taking place. There were some conditions, Alonzo was clearly aware, the change of which ought not to be slowed up. And there were some that it was desirable to speed up. For instance, in a technological society, progress toward functional literacy is desirable, is largely possible, and its realization ought to be speeded up as fast as possible. But functional literacy did not mean that those who could read, would or should be interested in reading Milton or Ruskin or George Eliot. Alonzo once read about a man who could not read; pathetically, he always carried a newspaper in his pocket to give the impression that he could read. He had to be taken where he needed to go for the first time, since he could not read street signs and house numbers. This was a pathetic story and the newspaper article went on to point out that in large cities in the United States there were large numbers of people who were in the same boat. Literacy, the literacy that was possible and indispensable, was minimal literacy, which involved the ability to get along in a society in which it was indispensable to read road signs, so to speak, in order to get anywhere. Of course, the more literacy the better.

Another instance of a desirable change that was to a large extent possible and ought to be speeded up and enlarged was the recognition of the supreme value of the person. What it meant to be a person, Alonzo knew, was not generally understood. But the increasing recognition of the primacy of the person and the dignity that attached to it Alonzo thought was an inestimable moral advance that was taking place and was desirable to accelerate. Achieve a full and adequate recognition of the primacy of the person, however, and you brought about other radical changes of a practical nature, which would in turn bring others and others, endlessly, although the desirability of some of these could not be foreseen. But what else was there to do? Alonzo had no doubt that change could not be stopped and that it was not desirable to stop all change even if it were possible to do it.

Why should the man of the Right want to slow up the rate of change? The liberal answers this question by psychoanalyzing his opponent. The man of the Right, according to the liberal, is stupid and hardhearted. But the judgment is utter nonsense. Conservatives are no more stupid today than they were in John Stuart Mill's day. To call them the stupid party is a piece of stupidity, even if it was John Stuart Mill who made the statement, unless you equate arbitrarily intelligence with commitment to liberal goals. Neither stupidity nor hardness of heart is the monopoly of one group—not in our society. There are plenty of hardhearted men on the Right and plenty of stupid ones; but Alonzo also knew that once you went beyond the liberal's professions and tried to find out how he acted you discovered that cruelty and indifference to human suffering, selfishness and arrogance, were as much part of the character of many liberals as concern for the well-being of others was part of the character of many men of the Right. This was a lesson he had learned from Maxie Waxie. Indeed it was in part the realization, among other things, that the equation liberal = good, conservative = evil, was as often false as it was correct that had led Alonzo to see the need to change sides.

The error of the equation was rooted on the assumption that men were wholly good or wholly evil in a homogeneous way; but they are no more homogeneously good or evil than a political party is made up entirely of one kind of men, good or evil. There are pretty stupid people, but they are not easily to be found at the controls of society. This does not hold for evil men; but usually what is to be found at the controls are men who are a mixture of good and evil qualities difficult to analyze and impossible to separate: intelligence and stupidity, blindness and acuity, creativity and habitual behavior.

Moreover, if we are to judge groups by their intelligence, Alonzo said to himself, one had to begin by remembering that his liberal friends did not exercise their intelligence on important matters on which they claimed the right to judge. Alonzo had not done any independent thinking about social and political matters when he was a liberal; he simply had accepted the convictions of his group. Uncritically he had swallowed its views.

4

There were a number of questions I wanted to ask; I was confident that I knew the answers to them, but I wanted to be certain that I had them straight. I have known for some time, I said to Alonzo, what you meant by calling yourself a conservative. You use the term in a rather idiosyncratic way, but there can be no logical objection to it; the only possible objection is practical: Your use is certain to lead to misunderstandings. But I know, I continued, that you believe that there is nothing that can be done to avoid misunderstandings in matters of this sort, even if you invented a term for what you had in mind. What I wanted to know was how he was going to go about conserving our institutions and values, what sort of activity he was ready to undertake to achieve his purposes.

Alonzo replied, as I had expected him to, that he was not going to become politically active as he had been when he cooperated with the Left; he was not going to join a political party; he would vote and would write as many checks as he felt he could afford for causes that he sympathized with, or candidates he trusted. But that was all. One of the things he had found out about himself as he moved away from the Left was that he no longer had any faith in parties or in candidates. Many of the men who were interested in politics were conventionally honest in the sense that few of them ever landed in jail because of their peculations; but one of the things he had found out about himself was that for him the kind of activity demanded of a man in politics was repugnant; to be effective a man in politics must deny the validity and effectiveness of the claims and programs of the opposition and must assert a half-truth, but since truth is systemic, a half-truth is probably a whole lie.

Alonzo had found out in his long and painful ordeal as he moved away from the Left that while he had cooperated with his former friends he had deprived himself of what little understanding was possible to arrive at on social problems on which he had then entertained firm opinions. This had meant that while he was engaged in political activity on the Left he had effectively frustrated his primary interests. Political man was an activist who denied the truth of the opposition and thus tended to deprive himself of a full understanding of social and political problems. It took no great acuity to see, once he renounced liberalism, that opposing political sides sought to impose their wills. There may have been a time when statesmen sought the good of the nation as a whole; Alonzo did not know enough history to be able to name such a time, but he could not let his ignorance decide such an important question. What he had discovered from the little history he knew was that parties identified their own good with the good of the nation.

This, at any rate, was true of contemporary politics in which the stronger, not necessarily the best, wins out. And he had had enough of that kind of struggle. "Basta, basta, basta!" he cried inwardly, as he considered the prevarications, the willful misunderstandings, the self deceptions, the outright dishonesty of men engaged in political struggle. Enough! Not for him, not any longer; he had had enough of that. One could not be an apolitical animal; one could not seek voluntarily to play the part of an idiot; about that Alonzo had no doubt whatever. But one could not let oneself get involved in the kind of "game" that political activists enjoyed playing. If what he sought was a true understanding of whatever came within the range of his aroused awareness, he could not get down to the political arena, where what was true was what was useful to the party that advanced it.

That was not a very satisfactory position to be in, I pointed out. It was not, Alonzo agreed; but it seemed to be the best possible, unless he was to imperil his primary interest, which was to achieve true understanding of whatever came within the range of his curiosity.

I was interested in another question. Alonzo had said that there was no formal difference between the goals of liberals and socialists on the one hand and his own on the other; both wanted to remove anything that deprived men of a decent life; both wanted a world in which there were no obstructions to human fulfillment that could be removed. But he had indicated that when the nature of the goals was stated in concrete terms there appeared irreconcilable differences between them. What did the differences consist in?

I guess I put it wrongly, he replied, I should have said that there was a purely verbal similarity between their goals but that when you began to specify their nature, a substantial difference appeared. Concretely, the difference, he continued, was irreconcilable and it arose from two incompatible conceptions of human destiny, each based on its own conception of the nature of the human person; beyond that, what was involved were two different theories about the nature of the world. One recognized, while the other denied, a metaphysical component to man; one took the term *person* to be merely a psychological category, while the other took it to be a metaphysical or an ethical-metaphysical one; one defined value in terms of interest (or desire or wish or drive or appetition) while the other asserted that values have status in being independently of human interest; one, in short, conceived human destiny in naturalistic terms, while the other asserted that human realization demands of men that they recognize that the end of man, and therefore of history, is not to be found in the anthropocentric conception that "scientific humanism" advances.

I saw that Alonzo was hesitant to go further into the matter and I asked him why the hesitation. He answered that the problem was too abstruse for a summary discussion. If such a summary was insisted on, it would have to be borne in mind that neither liberals nor conservatives—unless they were professional philosophers—base their convictions about man on a carefully worked out system of beliefs. Educated men today, even church-going people, accept whole chunks of naturalistic philosophy unaware of what it entails; they are as inconsistent as men have always been. If professional philosophers fail to achieve consistency even when they seek it by reducing the range of their speculations, we cannot expect ordinary individuals whose beliefs are picked up while they run about their business to be fully aware of what their convictions commit them to.

If a summary is nevertheless insisted on it would run something like this: If men are merely animals, the only notion of destiny that is consistent with this belief is that which they happen to propose to themselves—when they propose any; a man's end is what he works to achieve. Men's destinies are what they set out to accomplish, whatever that may be. If you assume that the accomplishment of their ends is happiness, then, in general terms, the destiny of man is happiness. But what in the last analysis *happiness* means is the pleasure that the achievement of their purposes brings with it. For the naturalist, the rational meaning of destiny is pleasure. Some scientific humanists do not agree with this assertion; Alonzo remembered that John Dewey had written an early paper against hedonism. But if value is that character in an object that satisfies desire—or whatever other term one may put in the place of *desire*—one cannot speak of value if one is not aware of the satisfaction the object produces, which is registered in consciousness as pleasure.

Of course, we speak of value when something brings about a condition that furthers, mediately, conscious ends, thus vitamins and iodine are said to be valuable although we are not conscious of a desire for them, because they are means to something we desire, namely health. But value involves, mediately or immediately, consciousness of satisfaction.

Satisfaction and pleasure are not identical, although they are often taken to be—by Freud, for instance. But if satisfaction is not registered in consciousness, how can one speak of the character of an object that brings about satisfaction? One can say that whatever satisfies a need or wish is valuable; but the term *value* has now changed its meaning. One can say that parched corn is thirsty and water is valuable to it, but water is not valuable to parched corn in the way in which water is valuable to a man who is thirsty. If a man believes that parched corn desires water, in a literal sense, as a thirsty man does, and that rain brings about satisfaction that is registered as pleasure by the corn, then of course water has value for corn. But the evidence that plants feel is not the same kind of evidence we advance when we say conscious men feel. The true value of an object is registered by, although it is not identical with, the pleasure that satisfaction brings about.

Alonzo did not need to be reminded that a large number of hedonistic philosophers distinguished higher from lower pleasures; and they seemed to think that the distinction robbed hedonism of the ready identification between the pleasure of a pig and that of a man of parts. The distinction between higher and lower pleasures is valid but the place of a pleasure in an order of rank does not depend on the pleasure qua pleasure, but on the object that elicits it; pleasure qua pleasure varies only in terms of duration and intensity; by pleasure qua pleasure is meant pleasure considered independently of the object that elicits it. If reading Shakespeare is a higher pleasure than reading the comics, it is because the plays of Shakespeare are better than the comics. Leave the plays and the comics out of the reckoning and consider the pleasures independently of their stimuli and the pleasures are identical in kind. But if value is constituted by the character of an object that satisfies desire, Shakespeare can have no value for a person who prefers the comics and finds the reading of Shakespeare's plays boring or irritating or just uninteresting.

This holds for the notion of a person, when the term is used by the naturalist for whom *person* is a psychological category. For him men are, in the last analysis, merely animals; they are superior in intelligence to other animals, but this is only a difference in degree, not in kind. But if men are not merely animals, if they are endowed with a metaphysical component, human destiny cannot be interpreted in terms of happiness—or if it is, the term *happiness* refers to something other than pleasure. On this view, value has status in being independently of desire and men respond to it because it possesses a requiredness that elicits their interest. This is an oversimplification, for not all values elicit interest in all men equally; requiredness is modified by cultural and idiosyncratic factors. But on this view, in the last analysis, the need to realize a value and to maintain it is basic to men, and the term *person* refers to the capacity all men have to respond to some values. The values men respond to differ considerably, but all men have the capacity and it is this capacity that makes all persons equal.

Of course we respect some men more than others. The reason is that the values those we respect espouse are taken by us to be higher. But to all persons, to the most vile of men even, we owe respect as clearly as we owe it to the saint and the hero. On this view of man human destiny is conceived as the realization and maintenance of values, irrespective of the pleasure their realization yields.

Alonzo knew this was hard doctrine and not likely ever to gain general acceptance, but he held it because the alternative, the naturalistic view of man and of value as the function of desire, offered no ground for the respect men owe one another. But without such a ground there is no obstacle to treating other men instrumentally, unless you happen actually to love them. And once you felt free to treat other men instrumentally, you could offer no other reason than the utilitarian for not eliminating those men whom you believed stood in your way. But Alonzo was not only deeply convinced that utilitarian moral philosophy was intellectually in error, but he readily acknowledged that utilitarianism called forth from him a reaction that could not be accounted for by its intellectual defects. He found it profoundly repugnant. But of course he would not confuse the philosophy with the men who espoused it. Utilitarians were like other men, some decent, some sensitive, some generous, and some evil.

XIX
Art and Knowledge

1

WHEN I finished the last chapter I asked Alonzo whether it would not be desirable to report on a number of subjects we had not yet discussed. I had in mind, first, I said, his views on aesthetics, criticism, and art. In view of the fact that he had done a great deal of work on aesthetics, had written a book on D. H. Lawrence, and had written a number of essays on literary criticism, some of which he had told me he was not ashamed of, and some of which had been well thought of by readers he respected, I thought that at least a brief account of his opinions on these subjects—I was careful to speak of his opinions, for I was well aware of his attitude toward views on these matters—should be included in my report. I also wondered, I added, whether it would not be desirable to report on his attitude to philosophy which I more than suspected, I knew, had undergone a profound change in recent years.

My opinions on art, criticism, and aesthetics—and remember that I speak of "my" opinions for short, since you know I am an intellectual shoplifter—he replied, were no part of my baggage on my trip East and my U-turn at Moscow's city limits. The aesthetics I have borrowed, which is to say, the opinions I hold on the nature of art, the proper response to an object to turn it into an aesthetic object, the residential function of art, the place the arts occupy in the human economy, and my views on criticism—these opinions may have undergone some change through the years, but as far as I know the change has not been as radical as the change in my other philosophical opinions.

Before you go ahead, I interrupted, let me remind you that while I may be well acquainted with your technical patois my readers are not likely to be. I think I ought to tell them, before I go into your views, what you mean by the residential function of art.

You know, he replied, that I borrowed the term *residential* from De Witt Parker, but do not accept his notion of what this function is. By the *residential function* I mean the function an object—almost any object—performs, as art and not as something else. For this reason the widespread belief that those who insist that art has a residential function are "formalists" is utterly false. Some may be, but not others. I, at least, argue that art can only perform nonresidential functions well when it first performs its residential function fully. Without functioning residentially first it may function nonresidentially well, but does so only by accident. Remember that I showed about Dostoevski in as irrefutable way as one can in such matters, that those who read him as if he were a philosopher and overlook the fact that he was first a novelist, fail to see what the writer—not the opinionated citizen—put into his novels. But to get back, the reason there's been no radical change in my views on art, I believe, is that my attitude to these questions has always been, from the beginning of my interest in them, phenomenal. From the beginning I have tried to report accurately the part art actually plays in human life, as distinct from the part it is said to play or that moralists or legislators decide that it ought to play. Such a report should be compatible with different philosophical assumptions about the nature of the universe.

In one respect, however, there has been an important change; but I believe it is more accurately called a deepening: Before I saw the inadequacies of naturalism I could not have seen that art contains an ontological element. But I do not use this awesome term as Pappy Ransom did. I mean that in the in-formed substance of art is to be found cultural expressions of value components that have ontic status. My naturalism, therefore, prevented me from seeing clearly the implications of this fact for the theory of imitation and the way in which, in order to enter into an aesthetic transaction with an object—something we seldom try to do and when we try, seldom succeed at—we have to treat it as self-sufficient. I had to do a three-year stretch at the University of Chicago to find out what a catastrophic heritage Aristotle bequeathed to the West in his *Poetics*. This is not to deny, let it be emphatically clear, the towering stature of the man, one of the Himalayas of Western thought, or the permanent importance of his contribution to logic and to one style—but only one—of philosophizing.

Anyhow, my rejection of naturalism did not involve discarding my old views on art. By the way, he continued talking, it seemed, more to himself than to me, my discovery—and for me it was a startling discovery—of the ontological content of art has been interesting objectively because of the way that those who have come across my exposition of it have reacted to it. No one, he went on, not even those students of mine who had traveled along the trail I had a hand in cutting, would even consider the possibility that there might be an ontological component to art. This is interesting because the sight-unseen rejection of it was an almost automatic—you could say, "instinctive" —expression of the nominalism of the age. People who have no right to opinions on this question because they are not acquainted with the arguments for and against nominalism, react without thought, often in anger, against those who question nominalism. And this, in turn, is of interest, because it throws light on the way in which even in the realm of scholarship, the idols of the theater reign supreme.

I agreed with Alonzo about the regnant nominalism but suspected that he was not fully aware of the signs that its grip was beginning to relax; however, I said nothing about it because I wanted to return to my question: Shouldn't I say something about his aesthetics and criticism? You were once called the aesthetician of the New Critics, I pressed, isn't that of significance to your U-turn? After all, one of the earlier and totally false objections to the New Criticism was that it was conservative. Yes, I was called their aesthetician by a stupid critic who meant it in disparagement. He added that his relationship to it was more complex than the stupid critic suspected. What had happened was that the moment he saw what the New Criticism was after, he discovered a strong sympathy for it that came out quite spontaneously from somewhere inside him. The reason for his sympathy for the New Critics was that they had genuine respect for literature whereas other critics had little or none at all; indeed the others not only did not know but they did not want to learn what literature is and what its primary or residential function is, and what its relation is to the other functions it can perform and how it can and does do it. More or less consciously, they turn literature into an instrument of partisan causes, some of which can be better served by other means and some of which cannot be served by literature at all. These people never face the pertinent problems as they ought to be faced; but their ignorance is more than made up by their confident prejudices—prejudices, because they have prejudged an extremely complex set of empirical and normative problems of a highly technical nature. Their confidence and their intolerance are directly proportional to their ignorance.

2

I did not know how to put the next question. I thought I had noticed a change in Alonzo's attitude toward philosophy in recent years. The work he had done in the last few years had been chiefly in literature and aesthetics. The change, I thought, had gone along with a feeling that it was not worth putting his time and effort into philosophizing. Was I right?

Before I answer, Alonzo replied, let me remind you that while I studied philosophy as seriously as I could, I never called myself a philosopher—except under circumstances where to have denied I was one would have caused trouble. My feeling about men who called themselves philosophers is that they lack modesty and as Ishmael put it in *Moby Dick*, "So soon as I hear that such or such a man gives himself out for a philosopher, I conclude that, like a dyspeptic old woman, he must have 'broken his digester.'" But you are right, I lost all faith that what I once took to be philosophy can yield solid, genuine knowledge —yield, to me, and of course to anyone else. The need for philosophy is there—for some people and for a culture, if it is to attain high civilization. I doubt whether those who feel the need can do away with it. But the trust most so-called philosophers put on their speculations astonishes me now. Alonzo continued in a vein I was well acquainted with: Initially he had gone to philosophy driven forcefully by the urgent need to find answers to a number of fundamental questions about first and last things: the whence? where to? why? of "it all." But for these questions, he could now see, there were no validly cognitive answers—putting emphasis on the term *cognitive* and using it in its most demanding sense. The mystery of existence remains forever. How had "it all" come about? Where was "it all" going to? What was the relation between man and other living things and the vast ranges beyond the reach of human knowledge? The mystery hurts because it does not yield, because it remains impenetrable. The confidence of each philosopher in his answers about these questions means nothing, since no philosopher worth his salt lacked confidence in his own opinions, yet the chaos of mutually exclusive views and systems remained, and the effort to reduce it created greater chaos.

But that was not all, because somehow a feeling remained, incapable of clear expression, an inchoate distrust, that if all the philosophers were to find all of a sudden some satisfactory way of resolving their differences about the ultimate mystery, the mystery about the beginning of "it all" and its possible end, would not yield. Like fish in the depths of deep, dark seas, men swam in darkness, throwing a weak ray of light ahead of them, barely capable of guiding them practically. The ultimate mystery remained.

It was easy to see that there was no way of settling the quarrels among philosophers. But until you could settle them you could make no claim to solid philosophic knowledge about these matters. Scientists had solid knowledge; even if you took Thomas Kuhn and Michael Polanyi into account, scientists have means of eliminating their conflicts. But science did not answer, it could not even ask, the questions that had driven Alonzo originally to philosophy. So long as these quarrels remain unsettled there is no knowledge, for knowledge is systemic. This is the important point, knowledge is systemic, and so long as mutually conflicting systems remain, there is no solid knowledge.

3

The possibility of arriving at something that could be called genuine knowledge encountered, first, a psychological obstacle which in principle was removable but in fact, unless human nature was to change radically, was not. In their pursuit of philosophic truth men could not eliminate subjective factors that deflected them from the truth they claimed to seek. Like surgeons in the nineteenth century, they—we all, rather—sought the truth with unclean hands and dirty tools; vanity, envy, pure prejudice, were operative in the pursuit of truth, not to mention the factors of time and place and cultural habits of thought difficult to flush out, all making for the uproar of the schools. Sometimes the prejudice could be spotted on the surface, unashamed, although its cause was not always easy to detect.

Let me give you an instance. You know Professor Disney Haten, and the high offices he occupies. He is Prime Minister of King John The First of Instrumentalia as well as Primate of The True Church; he is also Grand Inquisitor, heresy hunter, and preserver and enforcer of the true faith—which he objects to being called faith, since it is verifiable and corrigible knowledge, although I have yet to hear that he has ever corrected any of his philosophical opinions which, he claims, enjoy cognitive status. He is of course committed to scientific method— beg your parden, *the* scientific method, in the singular—which he sometimes calls by the value-free term of *creative intelligence*; and you also know that *the* scientific method is peddled by him as a panacea that cures all diseases, moral and political, private and public; since he believes in *the* scientific method, he holds that knowledge is open and truth corrigible. Well, I once had the good fortune to hear His *Alteza* read a paper on the betrayers of John Dewey—so help me, cross my heart, the betrayers of John Dewey. I may not have the title exactly to the third decimal point, but it made such a deep impression on me that I remember vividly that the notion of betrayal was part of it. Some of Dewey's disciples had betrayed him: No, they had not cuckolded him, they betrayed his truth by misinterpreting it. I do not need to tell you that the notion of betraying a philosophical doctrine is utter nonsense. If criticism of a view is a betrayal, the view is not open or corrigible, nor is it even philosophy, and the man who puts it forth is not a philosopher but a prophet.

All of this is troublesome enough, but there is more: Each philosopher worth his salt tries to start from scratch, some claiming that they have at long last discovered the true method—for instance, the application of the method that has produced good results in science or mathematics; once they have their method, they are in a position to assert with the aplomb of an Eastern potentate that they are right and everybody else is wrong, while giving solid evidence, unbeknown to themselves, of bigotry, intransigence, indifference to contradictory evidence, and all sorts of ugly little and large intellectual sores that disfigure them and inject error into what they produce. What philosophers do if you step back to look critically, is to claim that their own idiosyncratic vision, their own partial perspectives, the product in part of their prejudices and limitations are adequate accounts of all there is. Arguments are seldom examined for what there is to them; the assumptions on which they are reared are disregarded or misinterpreted; the sight-unseen dismissal of whole areas of human experience that are presented honestly is denied almost systematically, and the acceptance of views that were merely agreeable to the thinker is common practice.

Where or how can truth be found in that kind of activity? This isn't all, there is much more. Had I the time I would go into some of it. But this is enough, I believe, to show that the claims of the so-called philosophers are not worth much. They are what Medawar calls intellectual analgesics. If after a lifetime of running into this sort of thing one can retain faith in philosophy, it merely shows that one is not competent to philosophize.

4

These and other psychological factors preventing philosophers from arriving at agreement can be done away with, in principle at least. What can't be done away with are the logical—or if you prefer, the epistemological—factors that enter into the production of knowledge. They are irreducible because they arise from the aesthetic basis of experience. All thinking, whether commonsensical, philosophic, or scientific—the latter at the beginning of a science—starts from a world of which the thinker is in conscious possession and which he can examine but which he can't altogether abandon. The belief put forth by some philosophers that they can do away with all presuppositions is a delusion. (Remember Gilson's examination of the medieval ingredients in Descartes's philosophy.) Why? Because the initial picture from which thought starts is an aesthetic construction in the two senses of the term, and neither gives us a rational choice. The two senses are: the primitive sense, a picture that results from an act of aesthesis, a product of perception, but a perception that is not passive but constitutive; and the current sense, the product of the employment of the arts as categorial means of perception. Simplifying considerably, it is with the aid of the arts, particularly of literature and the graphic arts, that we arrive at a picture, such as it is, of what the world is like.

In one way or another many thinkers had come around to accept this idea, although of course epistemological realists of one variety or another will never surrender. Men who begin more or less clearly with the conviction that myth is basic to thought and is a sort of dramatic organization of the world, and not a false physics, or a primitive religion, or a protophilosophy, men who insist that the mind plays some sort of constitutive role in the grasp of the world it finds before it, ethnolinguists who think that different languages give us different worlds —these and other thinkers from other disciplines have concluded that the world before them is not a pure given, a reflection in a mirror-mind whose distortions are caused by faults in the mirror. This is old doctrine which you can think of as the idealistic minimum component of a true epistemology, and it is gaining increasingly wide acceptance for many reasons I cannot go into here.

What is important about this doctrine as regards philosophy is that different philosophical systems are rooted in different aesthetic acts, on different perceptions of reality arrived at by different categorial schemes furnished to the philosopher by his aesthetic vision, his act of perception. This leads to a relativism that is as inadmissible as it is inevitable, if you insist that truth is systemic. It leads in short to a mess.

I do not quite see it, I said, try again. There are two reasons, he replied. The first is that since all thinking starts from presentations, from constituted pictures, among these presentations there can be no choosing one that is cognitively superior to the others; since each is the basis or starting point of knowledge, the starting point is not itself, cannot be, an object of knowledge—self-evidently, but if you do not take it to be self-evident, remember Aristotle's *Posterior Analytics*. The product of an act of aesthesis, therefore, is not itself open to cognitive choice; the presentational is beyond criticism. One can supplant one picture by another, as Dewey did when he abandoned idealism and embraced instrumentalism, and as I did several times; and in a very limited way, within the picture itself, one can discover inadequacies and lacunae, such as the indifference of Dewey to tragedy and heroism which was one of the first reasons that led me to abandon naturalism. But the belief that knowledge, based on one presentation, is more true than another, because the presentation is more true, is an inexcusable and egregious delusion.

But if so, I interrupted, what about the criticisms of the partisans of one school against another school? Those, he replied, when they are not addressed to internal contradictions and lacunae have only a limited value, since they cannot totally depersonalize—if you permit me the barbarism—the knowledge claimed by the system builders.

Consider next the second usage of the term *aesthetic*. If the act of ordinary perception, when it is not habitual, is the ground or the initial source of our picture of the world, this holds all the more for the second usage of *aesthetic*, its honorific meaning, that which is applied to the arts. The activity of the artist is creative. His products are profoundly constitutive of our picture of the world. Put simply, our idea of what the world is like depends on the artist who is dominantly constitutive of the vision of the world of each of us. If you live in the world dominantly formed by Aeschylus, your world is significantly different from the world you live in that is formed by the soap operas offered on our television screens. The matter is considerably more complicated, since in our world we live under the influence of diverse artists whose visions of the world presented in their work is more or less mutually inconsistent. But essentially what I have stated holds. The result is catastrophic, since there is no cognitive basis for choosing one picture of the world over another.

If you are in a mess, I asked, why don't you give up the assumption that leads to such unsatisfactory conclusions? All you have to do to avoid the mess is to give up the notion that knowledge varies as the aesthetic grasp of the world varies. Return to some sort of epistemological realism and you avoid a cognitive relativism that is obviously self-contradictory. Unless you do, you are open to the very same criticism I have heard you make of Hume, who acknowledged that his philosophy was in total disharmony with the world outside his study.

That, said Alonzo smiling, is what I ought to do and what I wish I could do. But I am so deeply convinced of the view that our picture of the world is the product of the aesthetic activity—which is to say, that our world is phenomenal—that even if the conviction leads me straight to a contradiction, I do not see how I can give it up. I would rather accept, he continued, the contradiction, unpleasant as it is. The evidence in favor of this view increases, one might say, day by day. I do not believe that it can be rejected. Our picture of the world is phenomenal.

I was about to speak when he held me silent with a wave of his hand. Let me add, he said, two important considerations with which you, I know, are well acquainted, but with which I hope you acquaint the readers of your report. The first is that philosophy is essential, indispensable, inevitable. You can't repudiate it, you can't avoid it. There are men who dismiss philosophy, learned, intelligent, responsible individuals; these men are, nevertheless, blind about the part that philosophy plays in their lives. They are unaware of the fact that avoiding an explicitly espoused philosophy they either accept the views of their class or culture or some organization which they take to be important, or they smuggle into their minds many philosophical scraps and suffer from the incoherences of which they are not aware, generated by these warring scraps. Views, whether mystical or cognitively valid—views the Germans call "scientific"—or mixtures of these two types, are found present in human activity at the individual and the social level. This is unavoidable, and hence philosophy is unavoidable. It is better, it seems to me, to have one, with all the limitations it carries with it, and they are great, than many, with all the errors and incoherences that they produce. The military say that it is better to have a second-rate general than two first-rate ones. This holds for philosophy, because the errors of one are detectable—in principle at least —while the unconsciously held errors of several do not show themselves in theory but in practice.

The second consideration is this: I lost faith in the capacity of philosophy to answer first and last questions in a satisfactory way. Such answers as I once entertained with confidence have no cognitive value in the sense in which I once thought they had. But my views on ethics —the value of the person and the respect we owe him, which I take to be the foundation of a truly ethical life—the nature of art and the part it plays in human society, the ontic status of values, and even my social and political views, all of these views are, I believe, valid, with appropriate qualifications, as against the views of men like Professor Disney Haten. But these opinions of mine—and you know I use the term *opinion* in the Platonic sense—are not first-class citizens in the Republic of Knowledge. In the Republic of Knowledge *apartheid* is morally obligatory. Truths are not all born equal, some have better methodological ancestry than others. My opinions on questions of aesthetics, although I hold them seriously, are mere opinions, with emphasis on the *mere*. They cannot claim the same status as hypotheses in the physical sciences. What I am trying to say is that it is not a matter of either/ or. Although mere opinions, my views on ethics, aesthetics, the nature of value, the conditions of knowledge, can be shown to be superior to those I abandoned when I gave up naturalism. If I have given the impression that I have rejected all philosophy I have given the wrong impression.

5

I saw there was no point in continuing to press this subject. I went on to the next, reminding Alonzo of a long discussion we had had quite some time ago. I had initiated the discussion by calling his attention to a statement of Theodore Dreiser that had distressed me, to the effect that he passed quite as he came, confused and dismayed. What do you think of that? I had then asked. That, I remembered vividly he had replied derisively and without hesitation, is inexcusable. Here was a man who had spent his life brooding about human existence; who had brought to that activity a number of preeminent gifts—profound sympathy for human beings, undimmed vision, superior honesty, unsurpassed dramatic gifts—in short, here was not at all an ordinary man, here was a man who had great talents and had spent his whole life in the mastering of the human riddle and who had bent his efforts toward doing what very few novelists did, for he had considered man against the framework of the cosmos. This great writer—great in spite of the total eclipse under which the rotation of fashion had thrust him at the moment—had run into the mud, if you could do that in an eclipse, and could not get out no matter how fast or how slowly he spun his wheels. This great man, he went on, about whom Alonzo had written one of his successful literary essays, was, when it came down to it, for all his superiority as a novelist, a philosophical chump, a nitwit. No man of that stature had a right to honorable defeat in that respect. He should have spent his time finding out why he was confused and dismayed. If he had tried, he would have easily found out that what confused and dismayed him was that, believing as he did, he had no business asking the questions he was asking.

It turned out, however, Alonzo added, now in bitter self-derision, that it was he who was the chump, not Dreiser. He, Alonzo, was not passing as he came, for he had not come confused and dismayed. He had come as full of certainty as any cocky punk could ever come. It now turned out that these hard earned convictions did not have the quality of truth he had once sought and was certain that he could obtain.

I wanted elucidation on three points. Wasn't he now turning to a kind of frankly anthropomorphic way of thinking? Yes, in a way he was, he acknowledged, for the abandonment of naturalism was the giving up of the view that the universe was value free or that value was a purely human concoction and that the term *God* or *the gods* was meaningless. But the fear of anthropomorphic thinking was one of the tribal fears that went with the illusion that you could get out of your own skin, transcend your senses, leave behind the physiological equipment that made knowledge possible, and arrive at a knowledge of things as they are by themselves and in themselves when you were not there to look at them. This was one of the permanent illusions of a large number of philosophers, but it was, nevertheless, about as false as any nonsense they could believe in.

The other point on which I wanted light was this: Wasn't he returning to a kind of cryptic and diluted positivism? He rejected philosophical knowledge because it could not be subjected to the process that made it systemic—although his rejection was not as drastic as the positivists, since he believed the questions he asked were meaningful. He held that philosophers could not get together but continued arguing from the very day when Thales, falling into a well, managed to climb out and exclaim, "The All is water," when what he should have said was "I am all wet."

Yes, that was indeed the case, he replied, it was a diluted kind of positivism, but cryptic it was not. It was more like quasi positivism. But what was wrong with that? The positivists had not been completely and altogether wrong; they had had something very valuable to teach, although contemporary philosophers, in spite of their claims to open minds, had been pretty impervious to the lessons these narrow men should have taught them. What they had to teach students of philosophy could be put simply: Regard for evidence, scrupulous distrust of pure speculation about matters of fact, repugnance of verbiage.

What then, I asked, did he take philosophy to be? It should be—because at present there is no such thing, there are only systems of fideistic convictions—a systemic picture of the world based as far as possible on empirical fact. But such a picture, since it claims to report telic as well as efficient causes is neither true nor false. To call it true would be pragmatism. To the degree that it allows us to organize our experience it is indispensable. But there is a large margin of free play within which quasi facts, and myths, and hopes so vivid that they look like facts obtain. Much else enters our picture of the world without causing disruption to the established ways of life. Let me iterate: These pictures are not true, they are useful. But they are more than useful, they are indispensable to the ordering of life, and it is in this sense— and in this sense only—that they work. No man can do without a picture of the world; if he thinks he can what he is actually doing is accepting unconsciously the regnant picture or several pictures available at the time, unaware of the incoherences he entertains because of his lack of critical alertness, since a picture that is not explicitly held is not open to criticism.

We live wrapped in a little light as in a luminous but narrow and tight cocoon, and beyond it there lies impenetrable darkness about beginnings, ends, designs, about the ultimate mystery. In that Dreiser was right, although he claimed he did not know while assuming that he did know that it was all matter and motion and nothing more. The mystery, infinite, desolate, was far more frightening than Pascal's atheist took it to be.

Let me reiterate: Please, please do not confuse this view of the nature of philosophy with pragmatism. In spite of the superficial similarities with pragmatism, it is not pragmatism. Early in my philosophical studies I was inoculated against that virus, and the inoculation seems to have taken permanently. A very important reason—one only—for my aversion to calling myself a Deweyian even when I accepted whole chunks of his naturalism was the hybrid pragmatic block in Dewey's thought. What is more, he added, although the joke was on him, he had to confess that his repugnance to pragmatism goes way beyond argument. It is something deep, congenital, I would say "somatic." It is as profound as my repugnance toward utilitarianism. There are many points at which a man's philosophy is grounded in what in Spanish is called his *genio*, his character.

Although I had known for some time that Alonzo had given up reading philosophy and that he put most of his time and energy into literary criticism and aesthetics, I had not known until now with clarity why philosophy had disappointed him. Nor had I known how deep the disappointment went and how appalling and painful it was for him to contemplate the mess he found himself in. I didn't know what to say and to cover the embarrassment I asked him after a long pause, Where does that leave you?

Alonzo seemed about to begin to speak but kept silent; he was obviously in pain. Finally he said that it left him in a mess, in a very messy mess, with two unpleasant feelings. One was the feeling of hopelessness at the dogmatism that prevailed among men that caused a great deal of harm. People were dogmatic and cocksure, utterly certain that they were right and that those who disagreed with them were wrong. People do not get burned for heresy any longer—not at least in democratic countries where freedom of thought and speech are still realities; nor do dissenters get sent to labor camps or clapped in insane asylums—but there is no genuine tolerance, minds are not open, opposing views are not examined for their validity. This is true of all groups, of each and every group and each and every member, or nearly so. Liberals are as dogmatic as conservatives. Radicals, of course, need not be mentioned, the majority are granitic in their convictions. And this seems also to be true of all fields of human interest outside of the positive sciences, in philosophy no less than in the other humanistic disciplines. It is needless to mention politics, where dogmatism cooperates with self-interest to make the truth a matter of assertion. This is true of all of us, of myself no less than of others. All of us are like that. However, one did not expect to find dogmatism in the universities where men were concerned with the discovery of the truth about things. But were they?

Let me ask again whether you know anyone outside the so-called hard sciences, who seeks true knowledge, anyone who is genuinely devoted to the search for true knowledge? Among the men who call themselves philosophers whom I have known, I can't think offhand of any. Many parade their pretensions as truthseekers, but when you examine their activity you soon find out that they are as controlled by their prejudices as the ordinary mortal. I often have in mind a distinguished thinker who has made a very solid and deserved reputation in philosophy of science—Haten's friend, Shimata Legan: This man is certain that belief in natural law is an abominable error. He is viciously intolerant of anyone who considers the question of natural law even if the consideration is historical, undertaking to present what those who have believed in natural law have maintained. Why has not this man asked himself, if he believes in inquiry, as he maintains he does, what small grain of confused and blundering truth there may be in such a silly belief? What basic need did the belief try to meet? No, he is certain, he is as certain as any religious believer or political bigot could ever be, that the notion of natural law is utter, complete, flagitious nonsense. And remember, Alonzo added in earnest, that I myself do not believe in natural law and have written against the belief. But whether I believe in natural law or not is completely beside the point; the point is that a man who claims to be dedicated to the search for truth, in whose mouth the term *inquiry* is always pronounced with a slight tremor expressive of his reverence for it, is as apt to be as intolerant, as bigoted, as closed-minded in some important respects, as the rest of us sinners.

This was the second mess and it was not at all pleasant. What was the first? I asked. Oh, that one he had already spoken about. It added up to the fact that he had originally gone to philosophy for solid truths about first and last things and had found out that philosophic systems were not much better than the stories told by primitives or the fairy tales told by nurses to their babies. Philosophic systems were elaborate, the language recondite, the apparatus of argument complex while myths had none of these traits. But in respect to truth they were no better. The darkness within himself and the cosmic explosions beyond the reaches of astronomers, like Pascal's infinite spaces, that terrified the atheist, also terrified him and urged him to seek a key to their mysteries. The terror, the anxiety that this wonder elicited created a sense of failure. This was the first mess, and it was not an easy mess to live with.

6

I wanted to get back to another important question on which I wanted more light. Discussing Dreiser and stating that he had abandoned Dewey *cum* Carnap because of the errors, limitations, and important lacunae they contained, Alonzo had mentioned in passing that he believed in God in a most serious way. This was something of which I had been aware for some time, but I could not see how his belief in God was consistent with what I took to be the radical philosophical skepticism at which he had arrived. I was curious whether he was aware of what seemed to be a serious inconsistency.

I believe in God seriously, Alonzo answered, but you should know that I do not use the term in an orthodox sense—if one can, today, speak of any such sense. Theologians have always defined the term to suit their data and I don't see why I can't use the same freedom they enjoy. By *God* I mean the impenetrable and creative mystery that lies outside and within us. But strong emphasis must be put on both terms, *impenetrable* and *creative mystery*. The depths of the psyche no less than the outward reaches of the universe are creative and their power is beyond knowledge; inside us there surges, at the bottom, currents of creative energy over which we have no control, they respond to no rule, they appear unexpectedly and laugh at our efforts to rein them in; the outward reaches that astronomers can explore are not the limits of the whole and even those ranges into which they can peer are ultimately closed to knowledge, for they throw no light on first and last questions. But we do know, or think we know, one thing, and that is that from the impenetrable inward darkness and the ranges beyond the reach of astronomers, and within these ranges as well as within us, creative energy flows.

This creativity is, in the last analysis, unintelligible; it is also mysterious, but not in the original sense of the word, for mysteries can be divulged, but in the sense that they are impenetrable to our understanding. The mystery is self-evident, but the creativity that flows from it seems to be beyond dispute. It is this creativity that men call *God* or *the gods*. Men have always thought of this factor in naïvely anthropomorphic terms; sophisticated philosophical and theological minds avoid naïve figurative and poetic terms and when forced to use them, as they often are, acknowledge them for what they are. But anthropomorphic thought cannot be avoided. In whatever terms you think of this mystery, when you think of it you are turning your mind to the source of creativity of all there is, or has been, or will ever be. And when you turn to it, if you are not altogether devoid of imagination and chained to the cave, or if you have not been brainwashed by scientism, you must acknowledge that it elicits a complex response made up of gratitude or piety, of fear and reverence, of awe and self-abasement at your finitude and impotence, and on occasion, when you are visited by catastrophe or by iniquity, anger, hatred, blasphemy, despair, anguish, depending on the circumstances.

Was the object that aroused the religious response an empirical object? Not a simple question. Alonzo thought that Rudolph Otto had come close to discovering its true nature. In *The Idea of the Holy* he has stated that the religious experience reveals a nonnatural object. But Alonzo thought that experience cannot go beyond itself. But the object was, as Otto argued, numinous and nonrational. All Otto had to do was to make the statement for Alonzo to recognize it, when he read it, as important. Alonzo's naturalism had made him miss in his own experience his awareness of a response that he had always been capable of.

Two vivid memories of his childhood now came back, disclosing their significance. He had once planted a bean, and seen the pale green break the black soil and shoot up. A marvelous event that he had often remembered, but which now took its place in a scheme of understanding that until then it had lacked. And he also remembers frequently gazing at the sky at night. He had already done so before Halley's comet made its appearance. He would do so again. He knew nothing whatever about astronomy, he could not distinguish one star or constellation from another. But he could and did respond to the mystery of the stars, the immensity and seeming power of the skies. To that complex source of power one turned in piety, in gratitude, and on occasion, in blasphemy.

Piety and blasphemy. Blasphemy, for Alonzo was no Job. The history he had read, the age in which he had lived, his own experience, all disclosed wanton cruelty, iniquity, ruthless brutality inflicted gratuitously on men by one another. But they also shone with spots of sheer decency, selflessness, kindness, generosity, fellow-feeling. There was reason for blasphemy; but there was also reason for gratitude, for piety, for reverence towards the source of one's being. There had been moments he would have stayed, had he been able to. These moments led beyond their immediate cause to the ultimate source of all creativity in the universe; they led beyond the reach of reason to what men call *God* or *the gods*.

These reflections led Alonzo to decide that he was a theist. But, please, he pleaded, do not forget to emphasize that I am a theist, not a deist. Someone who did not know the difference had once assured a mutual friend that he was a deist. To say one is a theist means that one takes God to be a Person and not merely a first cause, that He is an object of religious devotion and not merely a term in a philosophical argument. Does this naïve pseudotheology make sense? If it does, how could Alonzo, an empiricist, know anything about it besides the fact that He was the mysterious and unknowable source of creativity in the universe? Alonzo answered that to call It a *Person* was merely a way to honor It with the highest term in his vocabulary. Men had called It *God*, and he called It *Person* as the medievals had called Him *King* or *Lord*. One knew It was the source, since one thought in terms of causes. But that was as far as one could go, and even then that was going perhaps too far, for in his nescience, all Alonzo could do was respond to It, whatever It was, with dread, awe, piety, and sometimes hatred. But if it is not meant literally there can be no objection.

Alonzo had once seen with compelling lucidity that for purely pragmatic reasons we of the Christian West had had to think, from the beginning of our civilization, that God was both transcendent and immanent. This was a demand that could not be rejected if our civilization was to develop as it did—or so it seemed on hindsight. Again, on a rigorously monistic metaphysics such as that of Spinoza, the glory of the West could not have been reared. Nor could it have been reared on an unmitigated dualism, such as that in which the Albigenses or Cathars believed. Nor could it have been reared on an all-out hedonism, such as was preached by that energumen sputtering hatred of our world, Herbert Marcuse. The glories of our world—its conquest of nature, its science, its art, its developing concern for the dignity and well-being of human beings, its technology, all its victories and all its claims to pride of achievement beyond the merely animal and the purely ascetic—were possible because our world's operative philosophy, and not merely its professed beliefs, fell halfway between Catharist asceticism and an all-out hedonism and were rooted deeply, at least until very recently, in a transcendent-immanent notion of God that was effectively operative. The discipline, the self-denial, the capacity to take pains for the sake of distant goals—all the aspects of life in our world in which we rightly take pride—are based on both the acceptance of self-denial and the joy of life. Pragmatically, then, the complex set of beliefs that make up the orthodoxy of our world, are the source of its success. Oh, no, I do not forget, he asserted with emphasis, that our history is, even in our own day, a tale of continuous butcheries and gratuitous cruelty. But this is not the whole story. Pragmatically then the religious orthodoxy of the West was, until recently at least, successful.

But these speculations, highly debatable as Alonzo knew them to be, were distinctly secondary. What Alonzo took to be primary was that the religious response was to the creative mystery that surrounds us. To address it as *God* and call Him *King* or *Lord*, or *Person*, diffidently, with an awareness that the expression, in sentences that claimed to be propositions, were more like a cry, a dirge and a song, than a judgment —surely there could be no error in such a response. If error were to be found, the notion of truth and error would have to be liberalized.

But this belief, was it not inconsistent with his belief that philosophical systems cannot claim truth until they settled their quarrels? It was not, since his belief in God was not a part of a philosophical system but a response to a datum—and of course, an interpretation of it—as might be his response to a storm, to a sunset, a mountain, or a herd of wild animals moving in the distance. When the Inca priest rose early before sunrise, chilled to the marrow by the frost of the night in the high sierras, and looked anxiously to the eastern darkness hoping in fear till, in the faint, dim colors he saw the dark silhouettes of the peaks, his heart leaped in joy and to his lips came a prayer of thanks because the Life-Giver had deigned to rise again and give his people and himself another day. One gives thanks to the woman who brings him profound joy. One gives thanks to the creativity that is the source of one's being; one has piety toward it—again in the Roman sense of gratitude and reverence. If this is rationally inadmissible all the worse for that kind of purblind reason.

Your theology, I commented, is a sort of hybrid, apophatic view that is not going to satisfy many people. Alonzo interrupted. Call it anything you like, you should know that I have never done any thinking in order to satisfy people. My thought may be all wrong, but you know I have always been honest, and what I have tried to satisfy, if I must use your term, is my sense of the truth when I seek it. You are, I retorted, intentionally misinterpreting me. I meant that your theology will be rejected as inadequate because it is negative. Naturalists will say that you are playing with words and that they too recognize the creative forces of the universe; religious liberals will say you are a half-baked humanist; and truly religious persons—let's call them orthodox people —will say that you are a linear descendant of those eighteenth-century gents I have often heard you jeer at, the deists. The only people who may agree with you are mild atheists, who will nevertheless be amused by your fondness for ancient terms you have emptied nearly altogether of religious content.

I could see that Alonzo had been piqued by my comments. Let's take each item in order, he replied warmly. As for the naturalists, they will play the same game that Haten played when I pointed out that Dewey had nothing to say on tragedy. Caught with their pants down they'll sputter with rage asserting that they recognize the mystery; but in fact what they acknowledge are secrets which, when they are not defending themselves, they'll insist are in principle open to scientific investigation and will add smugly that they are being steadily reduced in number by the progress of science. But a response to the ultimate mystery they are incapable of, since they are totally terrestrial, altogether political animals. Morality—their kind of morality, that is— they are interested in. They are also interested in social welfare, and their paltry "happiness." Metaphysics is beyond them, although of course if you point it out they'll play the same game they play when you criticize their insensitivity to mystery. When they lift their eyes to the heavens all they see are the same sort of objects the astronomer sees, but what some astronomers feel beyond the range of their scientific purview, the naturalists are totally and completely indifferent to.

As for the religious liberals, they miss the fact that the center of gravity of their concern is through and through moral, and that like the naturalists, they are incapable of a depth of response that the religious man is capable of. As for the orthodox religious men, the best of them are equipped with compartmentalized minds, in one of whose compartments they keep, imperviously wrapped in faith, to keep them out of reach of what Walter Lippmann called the acids of modernity, their beautiful old fables. As for my being a descendant of the eighteenth-century deists, gents you rightly believe I do not like, that point hurts because you are not altogether wrong, but then neither were they. But their amorphous recognition that there is a God or there are gods was more political than metaphysical, and their rationalism . . . well, what can I say about it except that it was of a piece with the rationalism of the theologians with whom they disagreed, the old orthodox ones? But you are not altogether wrong. My theology, as you call it, which is hardly a theology since it is hardly knowledge, is, I admit, restricted; and it is restricted because it is tethered by the short rope of my empiricism—a tether that keeps it from galloping off to the wilderness of metaphysics. It is, I must admit, apophatic, which is to say, mostly a collection of negations or denials.

7

I suggested that we go back to his relatively new interest in literature. Wasn't it a reaction to his disappointment with philosophy—like taking up with a new girl on the rebound because your old love turned out to be a tramp? Not quite, Alonzo replied. Remember, if you are going to use that image, that initially I was a bigamist. No, more exactly, I started out with literature, that was my first love. I did abandon literature for philosophy, but never altogether, and I abandoned it because I had the hope that I could find true answers about the first and last things in philosophy. I came back to literature when I saw clearly that I could not get from philosophy answers to the questions that I could not shake off, and at the same time I stumbled somehow on the nature and function of literature, something I did not come upon until very, very late. I found that literature did not lie because it did not attempt to tell the truth; truth and lies are possible only when judgments are put forth, and literature merely presents objects for contemplation. It was natural that men should want to find morality, and knowledge, and wisdom in literature, since the need for these goods is deep in man. But literature did something more basic than to supply these goods; it supplied—as he had often pointed out—the means to perceive the world. It exhibited, it did not judge—if one is interested in using it as literature, or as what I call *poetry*, and not as something else. In philosophy, besides the factors that prevent the resolution of conflicts, there was an inherent tendency to falsehood, since the exigencies of system lead it to ignore or belittle what does not fit snugly into its framework.

In two cases Alonzo had shown in detail the lies of philosophy. Santayana's philosophic system was riddled with incoherences and contradictions which could not be resolved within the system. But in his so-called novel, *The Last Puritan*, these are presented dramatized in characters, and the question of systemic contradictions and errors is thus eliminated. The second case was that of Dostoevski that I already mentioned. Sometime during his stay in Siberia Dostoevski made up his mind to repudiate the views that sent him into exile and to become an archconservative. But his novels, carefully read, show that what the man believed and what the "poet" saw are two quite different things.

But you have to be careful about literature, since critics are a busy tribe whose partisan intentions are usually to show that "poets" back the critic's dogmas. Take what some critics have done to *King Lear*. One critic, a man whom Alonzo admires immensely, but a partisan for all his intelligence and perceptiveness, has written: "That disaster follows from the hero's tragic flaw implies that the world is a moral organism in which events are morally meaningful." Prudently the man fails to let the reader know how Cordelia's death is a morally meaningful event. It is apparent, is it not, that what one can call the Leibnizian syndrome is not only endemic in men but almost universally pandemic.

There was literature, but not all of it was any longer of use to him. Some of it had never been for him; and much of it that had once sustained him had lost its nutritive power. All sorts of books considered great by great minds never had anything to offer him. The value of a book is a variable that contains a large number of factors relative to the reader, some of which are enduring and some transient. But there were a few poems (in the broadest sense of the term) that still helped him by guiding him so that through them he was able to perceive the nature of human experience and the constitution of the world. These, today, were much more useful than almost anything philosophers had to offer him: *The Oresteia, King Lear, The Brothers Karamazov, The Possessed*. There were a few others, but not many. Alas, neither Aeschylus nor Dostoevski could he read in the original, but what he got out of translations was immensely nutritive. There was the work of other writers, perhaps not as tall, but gigantic nevertheless. He never regretted the years he had spent with Rabelais in the twenties and early thirties. There was George Eliot. Some writers had once been useful but had lost for him the power to sustain—Henry James, for instance, and Kafka, and regretfully, Jane Austen, and many others.

XX

Was the Quest a Failure?

1

DOES IT NOT seem, I put it as a question, that all in all your quest was a failure? Not at all, he said with emphasis, leaning forward, I would assert categorically, if it were not so preposterous and asininely vain, assert with utter confidence, that when the account is balanced it will show that my life has been a great success in every respect in which I choose to live it. In one sense you can call me autistic, or more exactly, a radical idiot, for "I have always made my own," I have never measured the success of my activity by public standards but by what I set out to accomplish, how important I took it to be to me, and what talents, native and acquired, I could bring to bear on the task. My ancestors measured their stature by the height of the cane they were legally allowed to carry, and my neighbors today base their self-respect on the size of the automobile they drive. I base my self-respect on other things.

I remember Felipe Arroz, who went green and actually suffered physically in a very acute way every time a friend of his published a book or an article. The poor turd had a hard time because he was the associate editor of a well-known review and hated many of the contributors whom he was forced to publish. Well, I am as capable of envy as the next man, but fortunately I was never crippled by Felipe's illness. In my day others have accomplished much more than I have in the world's judgment, a judgment that usually is, I am satisfied, at the time and place, correct; but no one, no one, has accomplished more than I have, since I accomplished what I set out to accomplish and sometimes a little more than I had reason to expect—considering, of course, external and internal circumstances, the clubfoot of my ignorance, the limitations of my talent, and the many other handicaps I carried with me through life.

It is in this sense, but in this sense only, that I consider my life successful, especially as regards the philosophic quest that engaged me during almost all of my mature years. After all, to come *al fin de la jornada*, to the end of the march, upon the wisdom of Socrates, is no failure but a great success. For the knowledge I did not obtain led me to knowledge the value of which is greater than the knowledge most men have, even the greatest erudites, the incomparable polymaths. I am not a totally nescient man. I know great truths. First, I know what knowledge is and second that I cannot get answers to the ultimate questions I started asking when I began my quest. I know that the answers to these questions remain hidden forever in the ultimate mystery—for everyone. I also know about my finitude. To know this much is to know a great deal. It is to know much more than the self-deluded dogmatists know who believe that they have an uncontested corner on the truth.

Not at all, my quest has not been a failure; it has been a great triumph. I do not forget that I have suffered great anguish and that for a number of years I felt deep hatred and entertained seriously the thought of suicide. But on the whole my life has been good. I hope that at the last moment, if I am conscious, I remember that I did my best. When I allowed for the deep remorse that I have carried along all my days, often latent but always there since I became conscious, for acts I have committed that later, on reflection, I have condemned—the impulsive little brutalities and stupidities and the bigger ones—and when I allow for the nagging regret because of the opportunities I failed to snatch at, because, as Yeats (or was it Henry James?) put it, I did not dare enough (and not for women alone, as I believe he meant it), with proper diffidence, or rather, if you prefer, with a bit of smug complacency, I can assert that I have lived broadly, fairly generously, and as intensely as possible in the things I sought, especially love and knowledge—as it was possible, that is, given my condition and handicaps. Love—after my early twenties I never lacked it. As for knowledge, I began in search of answers to the ultimate questions and found out at long last that they can be asked meaningfully but that they cannot be answered.

This does not invalidate my success, for I found out quite some time ago that it is not the result that counts but the quest, not the conclusions but the effort to reach them. On the whole, in my terms, not in terms of what is called *the world*, let me repeat confidently, I have been singularly successful. I have never, never loafed. Let me say it once more even if it sounds unseemly, for it is the keystone of my claim: I have never, never loafed. Rich memories are available and ready at hand.

For me, the sun is setting, the sky is louring. But I hope (I wish I could pray for this grace as I used to be able to long ago for lesser ones) that when the storm begins to rage and the lightning begins to come closer and closer, I shall remember that there have been unutterably lovely days with the magnificent women I have loved and those among the others that I remember with gratitude; that there have been a few hours with true friends; that there have been a few students who have been grateful to me because I attended at the birth of their minds and was there when they tried to take their first steps; there have been a number of books I have read, verse that shook me profoundly when I first came upon it, and some that I still find radiant, a number of pictures I have seen, and great music I have listened to. And by no means least, a few bottles of that precious product the Germans call *Edelwein*.

If I had to do it again I would try to avoid the stupid mistakes I made and the gratuitous evil I inflicted. But on the whole, for me, life has been good. I am one of the lucky ones—there are not many of us— who say in retrospect, *Et in Arcadia, ego.*

Index

Index

Academics: Mencken on, 6, 42–43;
psychological myopia of, 65; their
minds, 111–12; and secularism, 142
Adams, Henry, 213
Adaptation: and human origins, 194; as
all-purpose word, 209
Aeschylus: *Agamemnon*, 145, 156–57;
Oresteia, 157; mentioned, 146, 152,
276
Aesthetic: primitive and honorific
meanings of, 274
Agassiz, Louis: opposition to evolution
of, 204
Albigenses, 285
Altruism: in Marxist theory, 125
Anthropology: its account of man's de-
velopment, 193–94
Anthropomorphism, 158, 161, 278–79
Anti-semitism, 15, 18–19
Aretino, Pietro, 138
Aristotle: *Poetics*, 269; *Posterior Analyt-
ics*, 275; mentioned, 164, 225
Arroz, Felipe, 290
Art: Apollonian, 52; Dionysian, 52; Af-
rican, 58; as biological adaptation,
209–10; Freud's account of, 219;
Alonzo's views on, 268–71, 277; res-
idential function, 269; ontological
element in, 269
Atheism: Alonzo's, 10–14
Augustine, Saint, 34
Augustinianism: contrasted with neo-
Pelagianism, 145
Austen, Jane, 289
Azorin, 44

Babbitt, Irving, 84
Barnes, Albert C., 58–60
Baroja, Pio, 44
Bécquer, Gustavo Adolfo, 44
Bergson, Henri, 38
Berkeley, Bishop George: on abstract
terms, 165; on primary and secondary
qualities, 239; not refuted by Samuel
Johnson, 241; mentioned, 34
Beyle, Henri. *See* Stendhal
Blackstone, Dick, 168
Boas, Franz: liquidates idea of progress,
53; redefines task of anthropology,
207; mentioned, 213
Body: Galileo's definition of, 238; of
physics, 239; physical, 239
Brickmaster, Phil, on teacher's unions,
111–13
Bryan, William Jennings: against theory
of evolution, 194; mentioned, 198,
210, 228
Buber, Martin, 15
Burtt, E. A.: *Metaphysical Foundations
of Modern Physical Science*, 241
Butler, Bishop Samuel: on conscience,
49

Caird, Edward, 204
Capone, Al, 176
Career, academic: Alonzo's objections
to, 42–43
Carlos (Alonzo's cousin), 11
Carnap, Rudolph, 121, 143, 282
Carter, G. S.: on human evolution,
194–95

Cassirer, Ernst: distinction between sign and symbol, 202–3; *The Philosophy of Symbolic Forms*, 203; mentioned, 197

Cathars, 285

Catholicism, Roman: *See* Roman Catholicism

Change: need to slow up, 261

Character, 103–4

Christian ethics, 251

Civilization: never static, 259

Class struggle, 124

Cohen, Morris Raphael: his learning, 32; influence on Alonzo, 32–36; on power, 33; as teacher, 34–36; contrasted with McGilvary, 45; "Vision and Technique in Philosophy," 69–70; mentioned, 38

Communists: doctrinaire attitudes of, 128; as utopians, 254. *See also* Stalinists

Conscience: naturalists on, 142; definition of, 249; mentioned, 222, 224–45

Conservatism: in universities of 1920s, 43, 56; of F. C. Sharp, 56–57; lacks positive base, 83–84; possible alternative for Alonzo, 253–54; varieties of, 256–60; formal goals of, 363; concrete goals of, 263–64; concept of man of, 264

Copernicus, Nicolaus: on celestial and sublunary worlds, 93; mentioned, 122

Cosmogony: astronomer's solution, 184–86; naturalist's solution, 186–88

Coulton, George Gordon: on character, 103

Coutourat, Louis: on Leibniz, 193

"Creative principle": in Nature, 96–97; for Leibniz, 97; as element of good life, 102; as religious object, 283–84, 285

Croce, Benedetto, 143

Cultural pluralism, 52, 55–56

Culture: necessity for human life, 100–1, 132; and dialectical materialism, 125, 132–33; evolution of, 204–8; institutions of, 208–9; as adaptation for survival, 211–16; burden of, 212–13, 214–16; its origin according to Freud, 217–18

Darwin, Charles: affect on twentieth-century attitudes of class structure, 53; and naturalism, 93; influence of on Marx, 121; Alonzo's acceptance of theory of evolution of, 194; and theory of natural selection, 206; social evolutionism subsequent to, 208–9, 228; mentioned, 82

Death, 147–48, 181

De Gaulle, Charles. *See* Gaulle, Charles de

Deism, 284, 287

Dell, Floyd: *Moon Calf*, 20, 21

Depression of 1929, 107–9, 137, 229

Descartes, René, 238, 274

Desire: and value, 164–67, 170–72; and the desirable, 174–77

Destiny: human, 264

Determinism: economic, 126

Dewey, John: influence on Albert C. Barnes, 59, 100; as liberal thinker, 84, 118; his appeal to Alonzo, 89–91, 150; *Experience and Nature*, 90; *Art As Experience*, 142–43, 202; ignores tragedy, 143, 144, 150; and the tragic sense of life, 152–53; on the good life, 167–68; his personal life, 167–68; abhorrence of rules, 246; against hedonism, 265; mentioned, 63, 87, 93, 103, 116, 134, 146, 147, 149, 152, 160, 273, 275, 282, 286

Dewey, John, and Tufts, James H.: *Ethics* (1st ed.), 153; individualism peak of evolution, 206; no group custom bound, 249

Dial, The, 37

Dialectic, 119–21

Dictatorship of workers, 235

Diffusion of culture, 258

Diogenes Laertius, 124

Disraeli, Benjamin, 204

Dostoevski, Feodor Mikhailovich: "The Grand Inquisitor," 27; *The Possessed*, 68, 289; not a philosopher, 269, 288; *The Brothers Karamazov*, 289

Dreiser, Theodore: *Sister Carrie*, 20;

mentioned, 277–78, 282
Dualism: Alonzo's assertion of, 82
Duce. *See* Mussolini, Benito

Economic factor: in history, 120–21; in Marxism, 124, 125; and the social process, 126–27
Eddington, Sir Arthur Stanley, 240
Eddy, Mary Baker, 152
Education: Alonzo's, 3–5, 41–57; objectives of, 80–81, 85; as tool of social reform, 119
El Greco. *See* Greco, El
Eliot, George, 260, 289
Eliot, T. S., 84, 156
Emergence: as explanation of beginning of life, 188–90; G. H. Mead on, 200–1
Empiricism: theory of mind, 92; contrasted with dialectical materialism, 119–20; and tragic vision, 158–60; and naturalistic moralist, 174–75; and uniformity of nature, 196, 211; a priori basis of its morality, 237
"Encounter": with God, 15
Energy: as cosmogenic factor, 186
Engels, Friedrich: on economic factor in history, 124; *The Communist Manifesto*, 125; beyond correction, 128; on origins of family, 217; doctrine in Russia, 308
England: factors of its demoralization, 231
Epimenides' paradox, 126
Epiphenomenalism: in Santayana, 39–40
Ethical life, 277
Ethics: of utilitarianism, 53–54; central problems for Alonzo, 54–55
Europe: Nietzsche on, 25, 27–28
Evil, 233, 254
Evolution: biological, 197, 204–6, 207, 209–10, 214–15, 228; of man, 197; social, 204–8, 227–28; and special creation, 227
Expanding universe. *See* Universe, expanding

"Fair Housing Committee," 114
Faith: epistemic, 15; acknowledged in

evolution, 197; lack of knowledge as result of, 198
Fascism, 110, 231, 255, 256
First Cause: problem not solved by naturalism, 182; God as, 188
France, fall of: Alonzo's responsibility for, 230–31; liberalism's responsibility for, 235
Franco, Francisco, 110, 116, 143, 144
Fraternities: anti-Semitism in, 18–19; need to abolish, 114–16
Freeman, The (A. J. Nock's), 23
Freud, Sigmund: on origin of man, 90, 216; *Civilization and Its Discontents*, 212, 222, 223; *The Failure of An Illusion*, 212; his theory philosophic, 217–18; human origins traced to Oedipus complex, 218; on art, 219; phylogenetic account of morality in error, 220–23; on origin of morality, 220–25; *Totem and Taboo*, 220, 222, 223; takes notion of primal herd from Darwin, 221; in error on *taboo*, 221; *The New Introductory Lectures on Psychoanalysis*, 222; confuses regret with remorse, 223; ontogenetic account of morality in error, 223–25; on God, 226; on satisfaction and pleasure, 265
Friedman, Milton, 259

Gale Scholarship, 20, 41
Galileo, Galilei: defines *body* in terms of primary qualities, 238; finds secondary qualities irrelevant, 238; confuses physical body with body of physics, 238–39; mentioned, 242
Gaulle, Charles de: *Vers l'armée de métier*, 231
"Generation of 1898" (Spanish), 44
Germany: causes of its triumph, 230
Gesture: becomes symbol, 199
Gibbon, Edward, 124
Gilson, Étienne, 274
Gladstone, William Ewart, 204
Gnostic theory, 185
God: Nietzsche on death of, 25–26; nonexistence of, 89; omnificent, 97; for naturalist, 97; on side of big battalions, 179; according to Freud, 226;

God (cont.)
  Alonzo's views on, 282–87; tran-
    scendent and immanent, 284–85
Gogarty, Oliver St. John, 32
Golden Age: in Spanish literature, 44
Goldenweiser, Alexander: redirects an-
    thropology, 207–8; mentioned, 213
Gomez, Juan Vicente, 3, 11, 171, 256
Good, 233
"Good life": as conceived by Santayana,
    36, 38–39; as conceived by Alonzo,
    98–104; essential components of,
    100–4; its criterion, 104; for
    naturalists, 164–67; for John Dewey,
    167–68
Gould, Joe, 42
Greco, El, 141
Greek tragedy, 143
Greenstone, Bill, 18, 55
Greenwich Village, 20, 42
Guderian, Heinz, 231
Guilt: source of for Freud, 221

Happiness. See Pleasure
Hartmann, Nicolai: tragic sense of life,
    152
Haten, Disney: on objectivity, 55; on
    New York philosophers, 106–7; an-
    nounces essay on tragedy, 149; ac-
    cuses Alonzo of defecting, 150;
    character of, 151; on Dewey on
    tragedy, 152–53; concept of tragedy
    of, 154–55; New York Times prefer-
    able to Herodotus, 154; use of lan-
    guage of, 155, 156; notion of tragedy
    and of Hegel, 156, 158; as a Pelagian,
    162; on betrayal of Dewey, 273
Hedonism, 264–65
Hegel, Georg Wilhelm Friedrich:
    meaning of philosophy for, 28; and
    Marxist theory, 119, 120; Lectures On
    History of Philosophy, 120; Lectures
    on Philosophy of History, 120; on
    Sophocles' Antigone, 156; on Aes-
    chylus' Agamemnon, 156; on evolu-
    tion of universe, 205; mentioned, 152
Heinrich, Karl: self-avowed Com-
    munist, 108; in Midland City, 109–
    10; on Lenin, 127; on Marxist theory,

128; breaks his word, 130; desires vic-
    tory of Hitler, 232
Hemingway, Ernest, 141
Heraclitus, 34
Heroism: ignored by utilitarianism, 50;
    ignored by naturalists, 145–46; rele-
    vant to philosophy, 181; more than
    survival value, 211
Herskovits, Melville J., 56
History: "laws" of, 121–23
Hitler: world pullulates with his sort,
    173; and Communists, 232; and fall
    of France, 235; mentioned, 109, 131,
    229
Hobbes, Thomas, 34
Holmes, Justice Oliver Wendell, 33
Holzkopf, Charles, 68, 73, 147
Homer, 146
Hook, Sidney, 187
Human values: in paintings, 59
Hume, David: An Enquiry Concerning
    the Principles of Morals, 50–51; on
    philosophers, 94–95, 276; rewrote A
    Treatise of Human Nature, 181; on
    nature, 186–87; mentioned, 29, 34, 191
Husserl, Edmund: and intuition, 15
Huxley, Julian: "Romanes Lecture,"
    225
Huxley, Thomas Henry, 82, 194, 209
Huygens, Christian: mathematics al-
    phabet of God, 187

Ideal: its basis in Santayana, 38
Idealists: Hegelian, 120–21; Marxists as,
    125
Indians, American, 257
Indoctrination of students, 76–87
Integrity, 103–4, 129
Intellectual life, 98–100
Intelligence: ground for naturalist's
    faith, 98; does not lead to "virtue,"
    103; its role in the moral life, 165. See
    also Empiricism; Naturalism
Instrumentalism: its philosophical ap-
    peal to Alonzo, 89–93. See also
    Naturalism; Dewey, John
James, Henry, 57, 289, 291
James, William: The Will to Believe,
    30–31; Varieties of Religious Experi-

ence, 52, 244; and Klotz, 63; tragic sense of life, 152; on moral life, 245
Jesus: his divinity, 12; his historicity, 14–15
Johnson, Samuel: refutes Bishop Berkeley, 77, 239; his false view of the world, 241
Joyce, James: *The Portrait of the Artist As A Young Man*, 20
Justice: negated by desire theory, 172–73, 178
Kafka, Franz, 289
Kant, Immanuel: obligation unaccounted for by Sharp, 49; Klotz ignores "Kingdom of Ends," 67–68; *The Critique of Pure Reason*, 71–73; on problem of cosmogony, 186; on evolution of heavens, 205; his distrust of happiness, 245; Kingdom of Ends, 251; mentioned, 203
Kierkegaard, Soren Aabye: aesthetic stage of, 166
King Lear (Shakespeare's): philosophy in, 54; critics on, 288; mentioned, 152, 289
Klotz, Maximilian: as teacher, 60, 70, 74; views of, 61; hatred of logic, 62; students' use of, 63; source of power of, 64; chairman of philosophy department, 66, 136; on Plato, 67; on Kant's ethics, 67; against technical philosophy, 69–70; approved reading of, 70; disapproval of G. H. Mead, 86; on tragedy, 146; effort of to fire Alonzo, 230; moral rigidity of, 247, 248; on Dewey and James, 248; mentioned, 229, 255, 261
Knowledge: and faith, 197–98; psychological obstacles to, 272–74; epistemological factor, 274; and dogmatism, 280–82
Krieger, Joan, 259–60
Krieger, Murray, 259
Krutch, Joseph Wood: influence on Alonzo, 3–5, 19–20, 23–24, 29: as no evangelist, 4; liberalism of, 4; as a teacher, 5; *The Modern Temper*, 143; mentioned, 19, 23, 41
Kuhn, Thomas, 272

La Mettrie, Julien Offrai de: *L'homme machine*, 94
Language: its genesis according to Mead, 198–202
Law: scientific contrasted with philosophic, 121; of historical logic, 122
Lawrence, David Herbert, 268
Lee, Vernon: on varieties of aesthetic experience, 52
Legan, Shimata, 281
Leibniz, Gottfried Wilhelm: God's power limited by, 97; monadic reflection of the universe, 101; political violation of principle of identity of indiscernibles, 110–11; on ideas, 202; mentioned, 193
Lenin, Nikolai: *The State and Revolution*, 127; his theory beyond correction, 128; his despotism, 256; mentioned, 122, 235
Leonard, William Ellery, 44
Lewisohn, Ludwig, 21–22, 43
Liberalism: of the twenties, 5, 7, 8; of Alonzo and his friends, 78–80, 129; future shaped by, 83; and World War II, 231–32, 234–35; and tolerance, 248; goals of, 253–54; cosmology of, 264; concept of man of, 264
Liberals: their character, 106; responsibility for Allies' defeat, 232; on evil, 233; on good, 233; faith in men of, 234; understanding of society of, 234; not all good men, 255; goal of, 263–64; on religion, 287
Life: beginning of, 182–84; 188–92
Lingle, Alfred "Jake," 177
Linton, Ralph: on debarbarizing students, 85
Lippmann, Walter, 287
Literacy, 260
Literature: and truth, 287–88
Littlemieck, Albert: as senior professor, 70; teaching of *The Critique of Pure Reason*, 71; as superficial teacher, 72; reason for reputation of, 73; mentioned, 147
Lovestonites, 131
Lucas, F. L., 28

Malinowski, Bronislaw: "instinct" for immortality, 210, 227; "A Theory of Human Needs," 226; A *Scientific Theory of Culture and Other Essays*, 226–27; fails to account for culture, 226–27; *Crime and Custom in Savage Society*, 249

Man: product of environment, 80; only animal, 84, 264; part of nature, 95; development from prehuman, 182, 193; evolution of, 197; as self-burdened animal, 214–15; of goodwill, 231; never acts ethically, 251; of the Right, 254, 255; professions of which do not define his quality, 255; as reactionary, 257; as standpatter, 258–59; condemnation to change of, 259; political, 263; liberal conception of, 264; conservative conception of, 264; destiny of, 264–65. *See also* Evolution

Manichaeism: and liberals, 8; and Left and Right, 255

Manrique, Jorge, 32

Marcuse, Herbert, 285

Marlowe, Christopher, 23

Marxism: its attraction for Alonzo, 105–6; and Darwinian hypothesis, 121; and economic factor in history, 122; *Communist Manifesto*, 125; and altruism, 125; philosophy of culture, 125; beyond correction, 128; and a better world, 132; mentioned, 118, 124

Master drive, 101–3

Materialism: in Santayana, 37, 39; Greek, 93; dialectical, 125–26; nineteenth-century, 210

Maxie Waxie. *See* Klotz, Maximilian

Mead, George Herbert: *Mind, Self and Society*, 86, 95, 198–203; on genesis of human mind, 189, 198–202

Medawar, Peter B., 274

Melos, Island of, 236

Melville, Herman: *Moby Dick*, 271

Mencken, H. L.: influence on liberals of 1920s, 6; on professors, 43

Meyer, Frank, 260

Midland City, 20, 41, 106

Might-makes-right theory of ethics,

54–55, 172–73, 236–37

Mill, John Stuart: his thought, 90; stupidity of conservatives, 261

Mind as constitutive, 143

Mises, Ludwig von, 259

Missing link, 90

Modern world: according to naturalism, 134–35

Moral actor, 247, 249

Moral decision: achievement of, 246

Moral experience. *See* Moral life

Morality: phylogenetic account, 220–23; ontogenetic account, 223–25; conditions of, 243–44; aim of, 246. *See also* Moral life; Value

Moral judgment: challengeable, 244

Moral life: and intelligence, 103; conditions of, 245; William James on, 245; and requiredness, 246; as acted, 249; and ethical life, 251

Moral perplexity: resolution of, 249, 250–51

Moral philosophy: and spontaneity, 170; fundamental task of, 170, 236–37, 242; Alonzo's need for, 236

Moral scheme: its nature, 246

More, Paul Elmer, 84

Morgan, L. H.: his doctrine in Russia, 208; and orthodox Marxists, 217

Moscab Hall: bronze plaque at, 85

Mumford, Lewis, 218

Music: responses to, 52

Mussolini, Benito, 79, 131

Mystery: obscurantist term, 139; and classical biologists, 139; and fundamental questions, 271–72; creative, 282

Myth: religious, 120; and symbols, 202–3; of Genesis, 220; Freud's use of, 220–21; basic to thought, 274

Nation, The: Alonzo's contributions to, 3, 41; influence on liberals, 8; the truth for Alonzo in, 23; danger of writing for, 43; Sharp's disdain for, 56; mentioned, 71, 73, 116

Naturalism: and John Dewey, 89; meaning of, 93–97; and life and consciousness, 94–95; its faith in intelligence, 98; limitations of, 133–

35; and piety, 137–42, 226; its positivistic ingredient, 140; and tragedy, 142–45, 158; its neo-Pelagian component, 145; and the good life, 164–65, 170–72; a Philistine theory, 168; as inadequate basis for moral theory, 169–72, 174, 177–78; lacks theory of life's beginning, 182; lacks theory of origin of culture, 182; lacks cosmogony, 184; and moral theories, 225–27, 236, 237; and mystery, 236; subjectivistic moral theory of, 236–37; a prioristic, 237; and primacy of science, 238; acceptance of by today's educated people, 264; category of *person* in, 266; its apathy to mystery, 286

Naturalists: seek pure knowledge, 140; are thin men, 141; need of to understand mystic experience, 184; and Hume's temper, 187; as fideists, 188; and emergence, 188–90; mortgage future of science, 190; criticism of theology, 286; incapable of religious response, 286

Natural law, 281

Nature: for Spinoza, 28–29, 93, 186; source of all that is, 93–97, 186, 211; piety toward, 96; "creative principle" in, 96–97; its uniformity assumed by empiricism, 196; for scientist, 240–41

Naturphilosophie, 120

Nazis: Alonzo's experience in Germany with, 108; a factor in Alonzo's change in views, 170, 232; mentioned, 139, 256

Nearing, Scott, 6

Neo-Pelagian doctrine: contrasted with Augustinian, 145

New England Puritans: restricted living of, 246

New Criticism, 270–71

New Republic, The: influence on liberals, 8; mentioned, 71, 73, 116

Nietzsche, Friedrich: influence of on Alonzo, 6–7, 25–29, 35, 37–38, 40; *Joyful Wisdom*, 26; Morris Cohen on, 33; dismissed by F. C. Sharp, 49; mentioned, 39, 89, 143, 145, 178, 180, 236, 248

Nock, Albert Jay: *The Freeman*, 23

Nominalism, 165, 270

Obligation, moral: not accounted for by Sharp, 49; as basis for naturalist, 100; not objective for naturalist, 177; as elicited by espoused and acknowledged values, 246–47

Oedipus complex, 218

Original sin, 145

Ortega y Gasset, José, 29

Otto, Rudolph: *The Idea of the Holy*, 283

Pacificism: of the liberals, 6; Alonzo's, 6, 16–18; Alonzo's destroyed by Spanish civil war, 110

Parker, De Witt, 269

Parsimony, principle of, 93

Pascal, Blaise, 138, 282

Pearl Harbor: marked end of an age, 229–30

Peirce, Charles Sanders, 38

Peking man, 90

Pelagians, 162–63

Perception: for Dewey, 202, for empiricists, 202, according to Kant, 203; and act of aesthesis, 274–75; art as categorical means of, 275–76

Pérez Galdós, Benito, 44

Perlman, Selig, 110, 111, 130

Perry, Charner: might establishes right, 172, 178; mentioned, 236

Person: primacy of, 250–51; an axiological category, 251; recognition of as supreme value, 260–61, 277; psychological vs. metaphysical category, 264; God as, 284

Philosophes: and the liberal's truth, 78

Philosophy: what it meant to Alonzo, 27–29, 88–89, 180, 182, 253, 254; for Hegel, 28; for Spinoza, 28–29; for Kant, 29; academic, 39; and science, 94, 140; Alonzo's conclusions about, 271, 279–82; and philosophers, 272–74; obstacles to, 272–77; rooted in act of aesthesis, 275; as indispensable activity, 276–77; inability to answer first and last questions, 277,

Philosophy (cont.)
291. *See also* Social philosophy
Philosophy of history: Santayana's, 36–37; Marxist, 122–23, 124; Hegelian, 158
Physics: does not explain nature of things, 94
Piety: of naturalist, 96–97; 137–42; meaning of, 138–39, 283, 284, 286; missing in Dewey's doctrine, 168
Piltdown man, 90
Plato: Alonzo's response to, 76; *Apology*, 124; *Laws*, 249; mentioned, 4, 34, 62, 67, 244
Pleasure: often denied by men, 215–16; higher and lower, 265–66; and happiness, 264, 266
Polanyi, Michael, 272
Political action: limits of Alonzo's, 262–63
Politics: or idiocy, 253
Positivism: and John Dewey's philosophy, 91; its intellectual crudeness, 91–92; its moral philosophy deductive, 91; its value to Alonzo, 92, 120, 279; and the meaning of life, 165
Positivists: as human beings, 91–92
Pound, president of State University, 41, 64, 70
Power: and philosophy, 97
Pragmatism: in Unamuno, 30; Alonzo's rejection of, 280; in Dewey's thought, 280
Prejudice: in academic world of 1920s, 43
Prohibition: as fountain of values, 175–77; mentioned, 179
Propaganda: defended in teaching, 76–80; and speculation, 126. *See also* Indoctrination of students
Protagorus: as source of liberal's truth, 78
Providence, God's, 11–13
Pulcheria, 246, 247

Quality: tertiary, Santayana's term, 232–39; secondary, defines mind, 238–39; primary, defines body, 238–39
Questions: fundamental, unanswerable, 271

Rabelais, François, 25, 33, 289
Rand School, 6
Ransom, John Crowe, 269
Raphael, D. D., 28
Rationalism: poverty of, 141–42
Reactionaries, 257–58, 259
Realists, epistemological, 274
Reality, 241
Reason: power of, 34, 35; and philosophical theory, 55; and radical moral problems, 172–73
Recognition, 202
Relativism: moral, 56; Klotz's, 62–63; and Marxism, 124; cognitive, 276
Religion: Alonzo's early, 3; Alonzo's break with, 10–15; criteria of truth in, 10; and revelation, 10. *See also* God: Roman Catholicism
Remorse: distinguished from regret, 221, 223
Respectability: appearance of often hypocritical, 179
Revelation: and religious truth, 10
Revolution: inevitability doubtful, 127; difficulties of, 132–33; its cost in Russia, 234–35
Rhav, Philip: knows nothing of piety, 138
Richards, Ivor A.: *Principles of Literary Criticism*, 143
Roman Catholicism: Alonzo's break with, 10–15; historical role of, 14
Roosevelt, Franklin D., 56, 108
Rosenfeld, Isaac, 130
Rostovzeff, Michael Ivanovich, 124
Rousseau, Jean Jacques, 84
Royce, Josiah, 38
Ruskin, John, 260
Russell, Bertrand: quarrel with Barnes, 59; mentioned, 90
Russo-German Nonaggression Pact, 129

Saint Augustine. *See* Augustine, Saint
Santayana, George: influence on Alonzo, 35–40; Cohen's course on *The Life of Reason*, 35–36; *Reason in Common Sense*, 36; his moral philosophy, 36, 38–39; his philosophy of history, 36–37; at Harvard, 37; as cosmopolitan, 37; fertility of his

thought, 38; on the ideal, 38–39; inconsistencies in *The Life of Reason*, 39; accounts for Nietzsche and Unamuno, 39; unsatisfactory philosophy of, 88–89; elegant thought of, 90; epigram on history, 121; *The Last Puritan*, 288; mentioned, 93, 98, 180

Sartori, Giovani, *Democratic Theory*, 160

Scheler, Max, 157

Schopenhauer, Arthur, 34

Science: its task, 94; and dialectical materialism, 119; Marxism as, 122–24; social, 240; world of, 240–41; metaphysical foundations of, 241; primacy of, 242

Scientific humanism, 264, 265

Sellars, Roy Wood, 93

Seneca, 51

Sermon on the Mount, 15

Shakespeare, William: *King Lear*, 145, 152, 289; mentioned, 23, 143, 146, 265–66

Sharp, Frank Chapman: as teacher, 45–47, 79; *Ethics*, 47, 48; moral philosophy, 47–52; method, 48; moral rectitude, 49, 155; chair anthropologist, 52; as conservative, 56, 255; Klotz's teacher, 68; course on Kant, 72–73; mentioned, 55, 68, 70, 79, 136

Shaw, Bernard: influence of, 6, 7, 24–25

Sidgwick, Henry: *Methods of Ethics*, 47

Signs, meaning of, 202

Sin, original. *See* Original sin

Skeat, Walter W.: *Concise Etymological Dictionary of the English Language*, 80

Smith, Al, 175

Social evolutionists: error of theories, 206

Socialism: Alonzo's flirtation with, 6–7; goals of, 253, 263–64

Socialists: known to Alonzo, 131; goals of, 263–64

Social philosophy: Alonzo's in the 1930s, 105; Alonzo's after World War II, 253–54, 277; Left and Right, 255

Social sciences: "laws" of, 121–22

Society: cost of destroying it, 234

Socrates: mentioned, 123–24, 125–26, 244, 291

Solalinde, Antonio, 42, 43, 44

Solon, 122

Sophists: allied to rising class, 126

Sophocles: *Oedipus Rex*, 145; *Antigone*, 156–57; mentioned, 152

Sororities: anti-Semitism of, 18–19; abolish them, 114–16

South America: Alonzo's attitude toward, 256

Spanish-American literature, 44

Spanish civil war: its beginning, 110; and anti-Fascism, 131; International Brigade, 146

Spanish Committee, 110, 113–14, 127, 129, 130

Spanish temperament, 31–32

Spearing, Herbert Green, 204

Spears, Allen, 123–24

Spencer, Herbert, 245

Spinoza, Baruch: *Ethics*, 137; mentioned, 28–29, 34, 90, 137–38, 284

Stalinists: Alonzo's cooperation with, 110, 128; mentioned, 113, 117, 130, 131

Stalin, Joseph: his opinions beyond correction, 128; mentioned, 129, 130

State University at Midland City: regents on freedom of inquiry, 85; no legal tenure, 230

Stendhal (Henri Beyle): *The Red and the Black*, 169

Subjectivism: denied by history of philosophy, 51; and value theory, 236

Substance: and philosophy, 97

Superego, 222, 224

Symbol, 199, 202–3

Szilard, Leo: on classical biologists, 139–40

Teacher's Union: its agitation, 113; members controlled by Stalinists, 129; mentioned, 110

Theism, 284

Thinker's role, 99

Thrasymachus: might establishes right, 172, 173; naturalism makes him right, 178; mentioned, 236

Thucydides: Hume on, 51

Tragedy: polysemic term, 153; term rel-

Tragedy (cont.)
     evant to philosophy, 181. *See also*
     Greek tragedy
Tragic vision: its scope, 145
Trinitarianism, 12, 14
Trotskyites: hated by Stalinists, 128
Trotsky, Leon: permanent revolution
     of, 132; mentioned, 119, 122, 132–33
Truth: demonstrated by action, 128;
     corrigible, 133; cumulative, 133
Tufts, James H.: Dewey and Tuft's
     Ethics, 1st ed., 153

Unamuno, Miguel de: *The Tragic Sense
     of Life*, 28, 29, 31; on immortality,
     29; his patron "The Knight of the
     Sorrowful Countenance," 29; and
     William James, 30, 165; his manli-
     ness, 30–31; mentioned, 44, 143, 181
Unity of the moral consciousness, 52
Universe, expanding, 185
Universe, intelligible: and science, 96;
     as value-free and classical mechan-
     ics, 238; as value-free, a challenge-
     able assumption, 241
University of Pennsylvania: teachers at,
     58–59
Utilitarianism: objections to, 48.

Valle Inclán, R. N. del, 44
Value: created by man, 98; springs from

natural sources, 126; and desire, 165;
     affirmation of by naturalistic theory,
     177–78; possesses the valuer, 236;
     and value-free universe based on
     classical mechanics, 238; and value-
     free universe challengeable assump-
     tion, 241; ontic, 243; knowledge of
     not apodictic, 244; espoused, 246;
     recognized, 247; acknowledged, 247;
     and pleasure, 265; men respond to its
     requiredness, 266
Venezuela, 256
Virtú dormitiva as explanation, 210

War of 1914, 231
Weiss, Paul, 32, 33
Westermark, Edward Alexander: applies
     evolution to ethical theory, 204
Wilberforce, Bishop Samuel: and T. H.
     Huxley, 82; opposed to evolution,
     204; mentioned, 198
Willemstad, Curaçao, 1
Women's Christian Temperance
     Union: and prohibition, 177, 178
Woodbridge, F. J. E., 93
Worker, false idea of, 105

Yeats, William Butler, 291
Young, Brigham, 152